SPACE LAW: VIEWS OF THE FUTURE

SPACE LAW: VIEWS OF THE FUTURE

A COMPILATION OF ARTICLES
BY A NEW GENERATION OF SPACE LAW SCHOLARS

TANJA L. ZWAAN
EDITOR - IN CHIEF

WALTER W.C. DE VRIES
PAUL HENRY TUINDER
ILIAS I. KUSKUVELIS
EDITORS

INTERNATIONAL INSTITUTE OF AIR AND SPACE LAW
LEIDEN UNIVERSITY

KLUWER LAW AND TAXATION PUBLISHERS
DEVENTER • ANTWERP
LONDON • FRANKFURT • BOSTON • NEW YORK

Distribution in U.S.A. and Canada
Kluwer Law and Taxation Publishers
101 Philip Drive
Norwell, Massachusetts 02061

D 1988/2664/69

ISBN 90 6544 374 6

"Young birds cry out for the truth,
while the old pine tree preaches wisdom"

CONTRIBUTORS

GENNADY M. DANILENKO
PHILLIP DANN
JIEFANG HUANG
ILIAS I. KUSKUVELIS
REINHARD MÜLLER
MILTON L. SMITH
IDA BAGUS RAHMADI SUPANCANA
PAUL HENRY TUINDER
WALTER W.C. DE VRIES
SIEGFRIED WIESSNER
TANJA L. ZWAAN

TABLE OF CONTENTS

ACRONYMS AND ABBREVIATIONS IX

PREFACE XIII

PROLOGUE
Karl-Heinz Böckstiegel 1

CHAPTER I
GENERAL PERSPECTIVES ON THE FUTURE OF SPACE LAW

Human Activities in Outer Space: A Framework for Decision-making
Siegfried Wiessner 7

The Creation of a Concept of the Law of Outer Space
Walter W.C. de Vries 21

The Influence of the Achievements and Failures of the Past on the Future of Outer Space Law
Tanja L. Zwaan 33

CHAPTER II
COMMERCIAL EXPLOITATION OF OUTER SPACE

The Commercial Exploitation of Mineral Resources in Outer Space
Milton L. Smith 45

Toward A Regulatory Regime for Competition in Space Transport
Huang Jiefang 57

CHAPTER III
POWER INTERESTS OF STATES CONDUCTING ACTIVITIES IN OUTER SPACE

Power and the Law-making Process Concerning Outer Space
Paul Henry Tuinder 69

The Method of Genetic Effectiveness and the Future of the Military Regime of Outer Space
Ilias I. Kuskuvelis 79

The Progressive Development of Space Law: New Opportunities and Restraints
Gennady M. Danilenko 99

CHAPTER IV
THE CHANGING ROLE OF STATES IN THE REGULATION OF SPACE ACTIVITIES

The Contribution of the Developing Countries to the Legal Formulation of Future Space Law
Ida Bagus Rahmadi Supancana 113

The Future Role of Municipal Law in Regulating Space-Related Activities
Phillip Dann 125

The Scope of Validity and Effectiveness of Environment-Related Norms in Outer Space Law
Reinhard Müller 135

EPILOGUE
Henri A. Wassenbergh 143

APPENDICES

I. Treaty on Principles Governing Activities of States in the Exploration and Use of Outer Space, including the Moon and Other Celestial Bodies of 27 January 1967 149

II. Agreement on the Rescue of Astronauts, the Return of Astronauts and the Return of Objects Launched into Outer Space of 22 April 1968 155

III. Convention on International Liability for Damage Caused by Space Objects of 29 March 1972 159

IV. Convention on Registration of Objects Launched into Outer Space of 14 January 1975 168

V. Agreement Governing the Activities of States on the Moon and Other Celestial Bodies of 18 December 1979 173

INDEX 184

LIST OF ACRONYMS AND ABBREVIATIONS

ABM	Anti-Ballistic Missile
Agrmt.	Agreement
ASAT	Anti-Satellite (system)
cf.	conform
CHM	Common Heritage of Mankind
Conv.	Convention
COPUOS	Committee on the Peaceful Uses of Outer Space (United Nations)
COSPAR	Committee on Space Research
DBS	Direct Broadcasting by Satellite
e.g.	exempli gratia (for example)
ECAC	European Civil Aviation Conference
ELV	Expendable Launch Vehicle
EOSAT	Earth Observation Satellite
ESA	European Space Agency
et al.	et alia (and others)
et seq.	et sequitur (and the following)
etc.	etcetera
ff.	and following
FOBS	Fractional Orbital Bombardment System
G.A.	General Assembly of the United Nations
GCL	General Concept of Law
Govts.	Governments
GSO	Geostationary Orbit
i.e.	id est (that is)
IAF	International Astronautical Federation
IATA	International Air Transport Association
ibid.	ibidem (at the same place)
ICAO	International Civil Aviation Organization
ICBM	Intercontinental Ballistic Missile
ICJ	International Court of Justice
id.	idem (the same)
IFRB	International Frequency Registration Board (ITU)
IISL	International Institute of Space Law

ILM	International Legal Materials
INMARSAT	International Maritime Satellite Organisation
int'l	international
INTELSAT	International Telecommunications Satellite Organization
INTERSPUTNIK	International Organization of Space Communications
ITU	International Telecommunication Union
LP	Legal Process
MAD	Mutual Assured Destruction (doctrine)
NASA	National Astronautics and Space Administration
NCL	Normative Concept of Law
NIEO	New International Economic Order
no.	number
para.	paragraph
PTBT	Partial Test Ban Treaty
Res.	Resolution
SALT	Strategic Arms Limitation Talks
SDI	Strategic Defense Initiative
Sess.	Session
SPOT	Système Probatoire pour l' Observation de la Terre
SLBM	Submarine Launched Ballistic Missile
STS	Space Transportation System
TCI	Transpace Carriers Incorporated
TIAS	Treaties and other International Acts Series (USA)
UK	United Kingdom
UN	United Nations
UN Doc.	United Nations Document
UNCOPUOS	United Nations Committee on the Peaceful Uses of Outer Space
UNCOPUOS/LSC	Legal Sub-Committee of the United Nations Committee on the Peaceful Uses of Outer Space
UNGA	United Nations General Assembly
UNISPACE	United Nations Conference on the Exploration and Peaceful Uses of Outer Space
UNTS	United Nations Treaty Series
US	United States
USA	United States of America
USSR	Union of Soviet Socialist Republics
UST	United States Treaty Series
viz.	namely
WMO	World Metereological Organization

PREFACE

Surrounded by the mountains at Innsbruck, during the 29th Colloquium of the International Institute of Space Law, Ilias Kuskuvelis launched the idea of publishing a book with contributions by young space lawyers from all over the world, containing their views on the future of space law.
The mountaineous scenery inspired Tanja L. Zwaan from the International Institute of Air and Space Law at Leiden University, and Walter W.C. de Vries and Paul Henry Tuinder, both from the Institute of Satellite Applications in Amsterdam, to join his prestigious project.

Once back home, the real work started. Some fifteen young academics were invited to join the project; in several countries well-known scholars helped in establishing the necessary contacts.
The book was to bring a new dimension to the existing academic collection; to fill a gap in past and present doctrines.
In order to achieve optimal results, a unique procedure was adopted. All the articles were first read and commented by all the authors mutually. After having been amended where necessary, the articles were submitted to a Screening Committee, consisting of Professor Dr. I.H.Ph. Diederiks-Verschoor, President of the International Institute of Space Law, Dr. N. Jasentuliyana, Deputy-Chief of the UN Outer Space Affairs Division, and Dr. V.S. Vereshchetin of the USSR Academy of Sciences. We wish to express our deep appreciation for the invaluable efforts of these outstanding scholars in ensuring the academic quality of the book.

This book is the first publication of the International Institute of Air and Space Law at Leiden University. The editors wish to thank the Institute for the trust it has placed in their project, and for the support they have enjoyed during the past year. Special thanks go to Professor Wassenbergh and Peter van Fenema of the Institute's Board of Directors, for their constantly challenging attitude, useful advice and moral support.
Another person whose contribution was vital to the book is Philip Mead, who corrected the English of the contributions so accurately.
Great admiration for Tanja's efforts in bringing this project to a successful end is shared by all the authors. That Innsbruck mountain, however, she still has to climb!

Finally, all the authors must be thanked for their cooperation and enthusiastic participation in this project. Without them this book would not have been before you. It is hoped that this contribution of a new generation of space lawyers will help to realise the worthy goal of a peaceful and beneficial exploration and exploitation of outer space, and that this book will bring forth new ideas and doctrines which will be useful for all those involved in space activities and their legal regulation.

The Editors
April 1988.

PROLOGUE

Karl-Heinz Böckstiegel*

Space law is coming of age. What started out as an exotic field of law and then continued with the discussion and codification of rules, following the development of exploratory space activities, is now confronted with the challenge of arriving at just and effective rules for the use of space serving many practical and conflicting economic, political and military interests. This does not mean that outer space has lost its special fascination for mankind or that space law has lost its special fascination as one of the last fields of international law still in the process of creation. But it does mean that space law, so to speak, has been brought back to Earth, confronted with many of the challenges and questions familiar to other fields of international law dealing with the consequences of technical development and the conflicting interests between individuals and between states.

In this context, this book comes at the right time from the right authors. Several young space lawyers, from different regions of the world and different social and legal systems, after careful research into the existing codification and literature, together have presented how they see the future of space law. This illustrates what I have always found to be one of the most encouraging aspects of working in space law: that here, more than in most other fields of international law, lawyers cooperate in a true spirit of mutual understanding in spite of differences of opinion that one may have with regard to specific questions. Such a good climate of cooperation between colleagues was to a certain extent of course favoured by two aspects: firstly, that space lawyers are a relatively small group of people meeting regularly within more or less the same circle, and secondly, that during the time of the mere exploration of outer space, different legal opinions did not lead to conflicting practical uses of outer space, one excluding the other. This favourable environment is now changing and in this context this new common effort of space lawyers from a younger generation is an even more encouraging step. The authors are, accordingly, leading the way for the undoubtedly growing number of lawyers who will have to deal with aspects of space law in the future. In addition, those of us who have been active in the field of space law for a longer period can profit from this publication for our own perspectives on the further development of space law. When I compare what I said in 1983 when invited to speak about "space law problems at the turn of the century" at the United Nations in New York with the contributions in this present publication, though I find some of my ideas confirmed, I am impressed by the wealth of new ideas in concept and detail.

But, of course, we should not allow ourselves to be carried away by creative legal thinking alone. First of all, as one should not overestimate the role of law, one should also not

* Prof. dr. jur; Director of the Institute for Air and Space Law and Professor of International Business Law, University of Cologne; Member of the Boards of Directors of the International Institute of Space Law of the International Astronautical Federation and of the International Institute of Air and Space Law of Leiden University; President of the Iran-United States Claims Tribunal, The Hague.

overestimate the role of space law in relation to the national and international environment in which it will have to develop. Also, in this field lawyers should realise that technical, economic and political demands will normally be of primary importance to society as a whole and to the individual, while the role of law is reduced rather to a service function enabling the most effective realisation of such demands. With the growing practical application of space activities, this environment will gain in importance for space law and conflicting interests in this sphere will make it more difficult than before to achieve accepted additional rules of international space law. This is especially so since one faces the dilemma of either continuing with the established consensus method in COPUOS, negotiating until a compromise between conflicting interests is found acceptable to all, or preferring to come to results at an earlier stage at the price of reaching legal solutions which are then not acceptable to the major states participating in space activities. There can be no doubt that, for the further development of space law, the patient working out of consensus is the preferable solution. But for practical space activities lawyers will have to find additional formulas for cooperation: All the indications from scientists, technicians and economists about the kinds and volumes of space activities in the future show that, on the one hand, many such activities may be of tremendous use for human society, but, on the other hand, for financial, organisational and political reasons, they will either only be feasible, or at least much more effective, if they are realised by means of international cooperation. One specific aspect of this growing need for cooperation in space activities is the need to involve the developing nations to a greater extent, which problem is addressed by the contribution of Supancana in this book. But as we know, *inter alia* from the discussions on the Law of the Sea Convention and on the Moon Agreement, the acceptance of the principal need for international cooperation does not mean agreement on the methods, forms, procedures and institutional framework of such cooperation. Here, space lawyers will have to develop additional legal frameworks. In doing so they might take into account the fact that agreement seems to have been easier in the past in two kinds of circumstances: firstly, where the states concerned have had a certain similarity in political and economic outlook and development, an example here being the successful work of the European Space Agency. And secondly, the results reached in specialised institutions such as the ITU and ICAO seem to indicate that agreement might also be easier, if all or the great majority of states concerned have a strong interest in performing activities which for technical reasons can only be achieved if they are internationally coordinated. The conclusion from this is that legal models for cooperation might be worked out "tailor made" for either specific areas of space activities or specific regions of the globe. It is therefore for good reason that the editor of this publication, in her own contribution, suggests that specific regimes should be established for specific space activities.

For more general and global solutions in future space law progress cannot expected to be rapid. Although, as my colleague Wassenbergh states in the epilogue to this book, present space law has a number of gaps and imperfections, it should also be realised that, nevertheless, within not much more than twenty years international space law has been codified to a greater degree than many other much older fields of international law. And such codification, though admittedly of often general and ambiguous principles, does present a number of basic norms on which present and future practical space activities can be based. In particular, one may refer to those rules regulating the freedom of outer space and the absolute liability for space activities. In the new environment for future space codification, since states and individuals are now more aware of their practical implications, major decisions will, much more than before, be under the influence of those basic conflicts that we find in other international efforts for cooperation: First of all, there is the conflict between nationalism and integration. States, intent on cooperation in space activities, will have to make up their minds whether they prefer a system in which every state remains entirely independent, or a system in which such a state accepts a certain integration with other states. Secondly, there is the conflict between market and planning found in so many variations both in national economies and in international economic relations. The long and difficult discussions on the economic aspects of the Law of the Sea Convention as well as on Article 11 of the Moon Agreement are only an illustration of what can be expected in future discussions on more concrete cooperative models in space law. Connected to this is the need to find models for an effective coordination between the North and South. This problem manifests itself with two qualifications regarding space law, because, firstly, space technology is, even more than most other kinds of technology, so sophisticated and so expensive that most developing nations will only achieve minimal progress by themselves, and, secondly, because certain practical space activities such as remote sensing and future solar energy from space would be economically extremely useful for most developing countries. As we all know, agreeing on this need in the abstract is much easier than agreeing on the methods and content of such involvement. One test will certainly be whether or not it proves possible to achieve the regime foreseen by Article 11 of the Moon Agreement. If my colleague Wassenbergh calls for a "regulated freedom", we may not be very far apart if I call for the following guidelines in future space law codification: for *state* activities in outer space as much regulation by international institutions as necessary, but as little as possible; and for *private* activities in outer space as much state regulation as necessary, but as little as possible. But I would want to add immediately that the real test for such abstract principles is their concrete application in practice.

For such concrete applications in the future, the contributions in this book will prove useful indeed. This is true both for those dealing with doctrine (de Vries, Tuinder, Danilenko, Supancana, Zwaan, and Dann) as well as those dealing with important fields of future space activities (Wiessner, Kuskuvelis, Müller, Huang, and Smith) to which I would add, as a further important field, dispute settlement on space activities.

The international legal community should be grateful to the editors and authors of this book and will no doubt make use of the information and suggestions presented therein. The publication will also undoubtedly contribute to building up an international reputation for the recently founded International Institute of Air and Space Law at Leiden University.

Chapter One

General Perspectives on the Future of Space Law

HUMAN ACTIVITIES IN OUTER SPACE: A FRAMEWORK FOR DECISION-MAKING

Siegfried Wiessner*

The times, they are a-changing. And, according to the Roman maxim, we are changing with them. *Nur wer sich wandelt, bleibt sich treu.*

Law, if viewed realistically, is not a static body of rules. Rather, it adapts to the myriad facets of life that develop every second before us. As flowers eventually break through concrete, even the most hardened legal prescriptions, "written in stone", have to give way to new configurations of social behaviour if new facts and new opinions so demand. These changes are sometimes delayed, branding the lawyer, and, especially, the judge, conservative elements in society. Ever so often, the adjustments do not come about without a fight.

The need for this systemic ability to change is most critical in arenas where today's feat in technology is only a stepping-stone for tomorrow's breakthrough. This is true for the awesome number of ethical and legal problems created by, say, genetic engineering and the broader field of biotechnology. Problems of that kind are faced, and solved, by and within the authoritative and effective decision-making processes of given territorial communities. We tread into more uncertain, but equally critical fields when we talk about the conquest of outer space as the last frontier the human race is overcoming.

For, then, we enter the realm of international law. First, activities of humans relating to outer space take place, or have effects, in an arena that is perceived to be beyond the reach of appropriation by any nation-state. Outer space is - still - regarded as "international", although that consensus may be shattered over time. Secondly, the uses made of and the activities performed in this common area may conflict and may lead to harmful consequences if not channelled into some form of coordinated behaviour.

Without a structure of vertical decision-making in the relations between nation-states, that channelling may either be done by treaty, bilateral or multilateral. Or it may arise out of a dialectic process of claim by one state, counter-claim by another, and judgment by the rest of the world as to which claim should prevail. That judgment, continually reconsidered in the world's constitutive process of decision-making, enunciates what we traditionally call the customary international law of any given time.

The ability of the contemporary inter-state system to reconsider its "normative" decisions is highest in the realm of customary law. It is lowest in the area of conventional law. Treaties have the advantage of conferring a certain sense of security about the scope and extent of

* Professor of Law, St. Thomas University, Miami, Florida, USA.

international legal obligations; a plethora of interpretation techniques (including, *inter alia*, the subsequent practice of the state parties) makes it possible to adapt the treaty language to the exigencies of a later time. These needs for adaptation, however, may meet an iron wall once they can no longer be satisfied within the plain meaning of a given treaty language.

The dawn of the Space Age has produced quite an assortment of multilateral treaties dealing with human activities in this newly-conquered arena. The most inclusive such document is the Treaty on Principles Governing the Activities of States in the Exploration and Use of Outer Space, Including the Moon and Other Celestial Bodies of 27 January, 1967.[1] Its broad and general nature and content made that agreement, for a long time, the "constitution" of outer space, boasting membership of 93 states including all the spacefaring nations.[2] Essentially non-controversial, it met the criteria for a document evidencing the content of customary international law, in fact, constituting the *fons et origo* of it.

This consensus about the Outer Space Treaty may be waning. It was the product of high-flying dreams of its time, but it was also limited to the then-present technology and the then-held expectations about future technology and human aspirations. Among other issues, the Treaty failed to foresee, and thus take into account, the scramble for scarce resources in the geostationary orbit, the problems of privacy and national security to be created by rampant remote sensing, and the filling of the near-Earth environment with "exotic" battle stations. Scholars had substantial input. The Treaty reflected a world in which globalism and the common interest of humankind were not yet unmasked by the ruling elites of dominant powers as ringing oratory, designed to disguise selfish claims by the have-nots to most generous transfers of wealth and technology.

This essay is (I) intended to raise consciousness about the limitations of the 1967 Treaty in describing current expectations about what is "right" or "wrong" with respect to particular human activities in outer space, and (II) geared towards providing a methodological framework best suited to capture the present expectations about the lawfulness of certain acts in that special arena, and to develop recommendations for legal regimes of particular areas, solutions for problems and conflicts of interest facing the international agenda at any given time. As concerns Part (II), the author owes his indelible gratitude for the guidance given by the lifetime work of Dres. Myres S. McDougal, Harold D. Lasswell, and W. Michael Reisman, and aligns himself in comparable perspectives.

---

[1] 18 U.S.T. 2410; T.I.A.S. 6347; 610 U.N.T.S. 205.

[2] U.S. Department of State, *Treaties in Force. A List of Treaties and Other International Agreements of the United States in Force on January 1, 1986*, 299-300 (1986).

I. PROBLEMS WITH THE 1967 TREATY

1. The first, unresolved problem revolves around the scope of application of this agreement: What do we mean when we refer to *outer space*? Wisely, the international community did not delve into the various demarcation lines suggested by the so-called "spatialist" school for the clearcut separation of airspace and outer space[3], the realm of state sovereignty, and the domain of international law, respectively. With the impending development of the aerospace plane[4], the "functionalists" advocating a flexible approach depending on the type of activity conducted seem to have gained a decisive upper hand.[5]

2. At the beginning of the Space Age, expectations flew high that outer space was *to be used exclusively for peaceful purposes*. In the late fifties, the General Assembly of the United Nations[6], as well as the top leaders of the spacefaring nations[7], expressed this as a common aspiration that would have outlawed any kind of military activities in outer space.[8] The United States and the Soviet Union, however, soon toned down the rhetoric. In the early sixties, they pressed for U.N. General Assembly resolutions adopting a more limited view of "peaceful purposes" and split up the legal regime of outer space into differently treated arenas.[9]

---

3 *Cf.* the recent proposals in the United Nations General Assembly by the USSR to establish a boundary between outer space and airspace "at an altitude not exceeding 110 km above sea level." U.S.S.R. Working Paper, submitted to UNCOPUOS, UN Doc. A/AC.105/C.2/L.139 (1983).

4 *See* President Reagan's announcement in his 1986 State of the Union Address: "We are going forward with research on a new Orient Express that could, by the end of the next decade, take off from Dulles Airport, accelerate up to 25 times the speed of sound attaining low Earth orbit, or fly to Tokyo within two hours."
It created what has come to be called the National Aero-Space Plane (NASP), or X-30, program. For details *see* Williams, *National Aero-Space Plane: Technology for America's Future*, 24 Aerospace America, 18-22 (November 1986). Other countries are targeting orbital planes as well; *cf.* the British HOTOL project, and the Japanese endeavors, described in Davis, *Japan Targets Aero-Space Plane*, 24 Aerospace America, 48 (November 1986).

5 *See* N. Matte, *Aerospace Law* 19 (1969); McDougal & Lipson, *Perspectives for a Law of Outer Space*, 52 Am.J.Int'l L. 407, 426 (1958). Kuskuvelis concludes that the spatialist approach is "inapplicable" in the context of an aerospace plane. Indeed, how could liability from the activities of an aerospace plane be reasonably determined under rules of spatial separation? *Cf.* Kuskuvelis, *The Aerospace Plane: In the Direction of an Aerospace Law*, Proceedings of 29th Colloquium on the Law of Outer Space 175, at 176 (1987).

6 UNGA Res. 1148 (XII) of Nov. 14, 1957; UNGA Res. 1348 (XIII) of December 13, 1958.

7 *Cf.* President Eisenhower's statement to Bulganin in his letter of 12 January, 1958:"I propose that we agree that outer space should be used only for peaceful purposes." 38 Dep't State Bull. 126 (1958).

8 C. Christol, *The Modern International Law of Outer Space* 22 (1982).

9 UNGA Res. 1884 (XVIII) of October 17, 1963; UNGA Res. 1962 (XVIII) of December 13, 1963. Interestingly, under section 102 (a) of the 1958 National Aeronautics and Space Act, "it is the policy of the United States that activities in outer space should be devoted to peaceful purposes for the benefit of all mankind." P.L. 85-568, 72 Stat. 426. This "holdover" from former, more inclusive days is still on the U.S. statute-books.

The 1967 Treaty follows this line.[10] The aspirations of humankind were relegated to the oratory of the preamble:

"The States Parties to this Treaty, ... Recognising the common interest of all mankind in the progress of the exploration and use of outer space for peaceful purposes, ...Have agreed on the following ..."

And these States, the major space powers, agreed, in Article III, that they

"shall carry on activities in the exploration and use of outer space ... in the interest of maintaining international peace and security and promoting international co-operation and understanding."

The only teeth that were put into this Treaty with respect to military uses of outer space were mild and enumerated in Article IV:

"(1) States Parties to the Treaty undertake not to place in orbit around the Earth any objects carrying nuclear weapons or any other kinds of weapons of mass destruction, install such weapons on celestial bodies, or station such weapons in outer space in any other manner.

(2) The moon and other celestial bodies shall be used by all States Parties to the Treaty exclusively for peaceful purposes. The establishment of military bases, installations and fortifications, the testing of any type of weapons and the conduct of military manoeuvres on celestial bodies shall be forbidden ..."

Thus, the only parts of outer space which were to be "demilitarised" were the moon and other celestial bodies. Nuclear weapons and other weapons of mass destruction were banned from being *stationed* in outer space. Thus, Articles III and IV did not prevent the buildup of ICBM's, SLBM's, and intermediate-range nuclear missiles that employ the medium of outer space merely to reach their targets.

Beyond that, the U.S. and the USSR have put into Earth orbit a barrage of "national technical means of verification" which are crucial for gathering intelligence about the military strengths and movements of the other side, for verification of arms control agreements, and for early warning of nuclear attacks.[11] In fact, such missiles and

---

[10] The superpowers brought about a cautious, minimalistic agreement carefully maintaining their broad freedom of action in outer space. *See* Walter McDougall's enlightening account ... *The Heavens and the Earth. A Political History of the Space Age* (1986).

[11] For a detailed account of military space activities, *see* SIPRI, *The Arms Race and Arms Control* (1982), especially chapter 5 at 97-114 and Table 5.1, at 110-11.

reconnaissance satellites have been considered essential for the maintaining of international peace and security, under the superpowers' "open skies" policy.[12]

The next step, beyond the passive reconnaissance function, was the stationing of anti-satellite systems (ASAT's) in outer space. Their presence was justified as defensive, perfectly legitimate "non-aggressive military use" of outer space.[13] Scientists soon pointed out that such devices could easily be used for offensive purposes.[14] Ultimately, however, any weapon may be perceived as contributing to the overall balance of deterrence designed to uphold the peace.

New military strategies go far beyond mere ASAT capability. The U.S. Strategic Defense Initiative, using several layers of defence against ICBM's, would employ weapons systems in outer space that can be used offensively as well as defensively. They include nuclear-driven devices such as particle beams, microwaves, hypervelocity pellets, X-ray lasers, and optical lasers.[15] In particular, the proposed X-ray laser would not only be powered by nuclear energy, but would set free a nuclear explosion if operated. It has thus been called a "third generation nuclear weapon".[16] As such, the X-ray laser would seem to violate the proscription against nuclear weapons in Earth orbit, laid down in Article IV (1) of the 1967 Treaty.[17]

Soviet proposals, in the United Nations, to completely "deweaponise" outer space[18] have proven unsuccessful.

---

[12] *Cf.* President Eisenhower's *Statement Proposing Reciprocal Aerial Inspection* of July 21, 1955, Documents on American Foreign Relations 1955, 215-216, reprinted in M. McDougal & W. Reisman, *International Law in Contemporary Perspective: The Public Order of the World Community* 508 (1981).

[13] *Cf.* Christol, *supra* note 8, at 30-37.

[14] *Id.*, at 30.

[15] Science 232, 152 (11 April 1986).

[16] von Kries, *International Space Law Implications of the U.S. SDI and ASAT Programs: The Current Legal Debate*, 30 Zeitschrift für Luft- und Weltraumrecht 309, 313-314 (1986).

[17] *Id.* This analysis does not touch on the compatibility of SDI, and, in particular, its "exotic" technologies part, with the 1972 ABM Treaty.

[18] *Cf.* the Draft Treaty on the Prohibition of the Use of Force in Outer Space and from Space against the Earth submitted by Foreign Minister Gromyko on 22 Aug., 1983, UN Doc. A/38/194, the Draft Resolution entitled "Use of Outer Space Exclusively for Peaceful Purposes for the Benefit of Mankind", submitted on 27 Sept., 1984, UN Doc. A/39/243, and the Draft Resolution of 16 Aug., 1985 on "International Co-operation in the Peaceful Exploitation of Outer Space under Conditions of Its Non-Militarisation", UN Doc. A/40/192. For further background, *see* Müller, *The Prevention of an Arms Race in Outer Space - The Present International Law and Aspects of Its Necessary Improvement*, Proceedings of the 29th Colloquium on the Law of Outer Space 62 *et seq.* (1987).

We have to realise that the competition of contending value systems on Earth cannot be prevented from entering the arena of outer space. Security is a nation's vital need, the *conditio sine qua non* of a territorial community. Without a world government and a consensus on the basic social values, this competition between contending value systems, by its own dynamics, will not spare the critical arena of outer space. How can outer space be preserved as the fairy place of peace if, on Earth, the consensus on the most basic restriction on the use of force, Article 2(4) of the United Nations Charter, is breaking down? We might end up settling for agreed-upon astronautical rules of the road that govern, as a sort of a regulation on the lowest common denominator, the use of the ever-shrinking voids of outer space.[19]

3. The universalistic spirit of the 1967 Treaty also found its expression in Article I (1):

"The exploration and use of outer space ... shall be carried out for the benefit and in the interests of all countries, irrespective of their degree of economic or scientific development, and shall be the *province of all mankind.*"[20]

What does this clause mean? In the U.S. Senate hearings on advice and consent to the Treaty, it was made clear that this prescription would not translate into obligations by the haves of space technology to the have-nots.[21] At best, the term "province of all mankind" was "embryonic".[22] It did not carry with it the distinctive connotations of equitable sharing and common inclusive management which are packed in the standard of a "common heritage of mankind".[23] The latter term, used in the 1979 Moon Agreement[24], was decisively rejected by the space superpowers, together with the Moon Agreement itself. Outer space thus remains a free-for-all; the benefits clause of Article I (1) vanishes into legal nirvana before the freedoms of use, exploration and exploitation of outer space as

---

19 Wiessner, *The Public Order of the Geostationary Orbit: Blueprints for the Future*, 9 Yale J. World Pub. Order 217, 252 (1985); DalBello, *'Rules of the Road': Legal Measures to Strengthen the Peaceful Uses of Outer Space*, Proceedings of the 28th Colloquium on the Law of Outer Space 8 (1986); von Kries, *supra* note 16, at 317-318.

20 This idea of international cooperation also underlies Articles IX and XI.

21 The U.S. Department of State expressed the view that the provision did "not create legal obligations with respect to the terms of international cooperation on any existing or future space projects." Treaty on Outer Space: Hearings Before the Committee on Foreign Relations, U.S. Senate, 90th Cong., 1st Sess. 70 (1967). According to an "understanding" the U.S. Senate Committee on Foreign Relations attached to its advice and consent to ratification, "nothing in Article I, paragraph 1 of the treaty diminishes or alters the right of the United States to determine how it shares the benefits and results of its space activities." S. Exec. Rep. No. 8, 90th Cong., 1st Sess. 4 (1967).

22 Wiessner, *supra* note 19, at 252.

23 *Id.*, at 264.

24 Agreement Governing the Activities of States on the Moon and Other Celestial Bodies, Dec. 5, 1979, Article 11, UNGA Res. 34/68.

enumerated in Article I (2) and (3).[25] This is another example of the inadequacies of the 1967 text.

4. A fundamental presumption of the 1967 Treaty is that outer space and the celestial bodies *cannot be appropriated.*[26] In the context of SDI, it has been contended that the array of objects to be placed in Earth orbit and the necessity to create "keep-out" zones around them[27] would constitute an appropriation of outer space, contrary to Article II of the Treaty.[28] I confess to having some problems with this proposition: Would the declaration and enforcement of any keep-out zone constitute an appropriation? If so, what about the semi-permanent satellite positions on the geostationary orbit and their assigned latitudes? Is that not also an appropriation of outer space? If not, how large must the zones be to be considered "appropriations"? Should the difference between these security zones be one of quality rather than quantity, depending on the intent of the parties?

Another issue concerning appropriation arises in the context of possible future space mining. It may lead not only to the exploitation of valuable parts of the moon, but to the virtual consumption of entire asteroids. By what twist of the language can this still be called mere "use", and not "appropriation", of the celestial body?[29]

5. The 1967 Treaty fails to take into account, to the extent needed, the numerous activities of *private enterprise* which enter into the use of outer space.[30] Soviet scholars have asserted that the emergence of international private space law under the 1967 Treaty is not likely.[31]

---

25 This does not mean that the *res communis* standard of unrestricted use governs each and every area and resource situated in outer space. A case in point is the geostationary satellite orbit. Its heavy, and growing, inclusive regulation makes it a prime example of a *res publica internationalis. Cf.* Wiessner, *Access to a Res Publica Internationalis: The Case of the Geostationary Orbit*, Proceedings of the 29th Colloquium on the Law of Outer Space 147 (1987); *id., supra* note 19, at 263-266.

26 Article II proclaims: "Outer space, including the moon and other celestial bodies, is not subject to national appropriation by claim of sovereignty, by means of use or occupation, or by any other means."

27 *Cf.* 23 Aerospace America 80 (September 1985).

28 D. Waller, J. Bruce & D. Cook, *SDI: Progress and Challenges.* Staff Report Submitted to Senator William Proxmire, Senator J. Bennett Johnston and Senator Lawton Chiles, 38 (March 17, 1986): "Keep-out zones, however, create countless headaches for military planners and diplomats. First, the 1967 Outer Space Treaty, which declares that no nation can claim sovereignty over outer space, would have to be changed. ..." Same result: von Kries, *supra* note 16, at 315.

29 *Cf.* Goldman, *Space Activities: Transforming Space Law*, Proceedings of the 28th Colloquium on the Law of Outer Space 227, 230 (1986).

30 For an excellent overview, *see* E. Finch & A. Moore, *Astrobusiness* (1984).

31 *See, e.g.*, Kolossov, *On the Problem of Private Commercial Activities in Outer Space*, Proceedings of the 27th Colloquium on the Law of Outer Space 66, 67 (1985). The author also expresses his view that direct participation of private industry in space activities "cannot but create problems for international cooperation". *Ibid.*

The 1967 Treaty is largely State-oriented: Article VI provides that a State has to "authorise and supervise" the activities of its non-governmental entities in outer space. Article VII establishes liability by the launching state, and Article VIII requires retention of jurisdiction and control over space objects by the States "on whose registry" such objects are launched.

One does notice private parties operating in the first commercial arena: communications satellites. Important business needs are satisfied by these space stations. They provide for telephone, telex, and record traffic, but also tv, radio, data transmissions, videoconferencing, weather forecasting, and navigation. Remote sensing is being privatised: the Land Remote-Sensing Commercialisation Act of 1984 moved control over civilian remote sensing to private EOSAT, which now has to compete with SPOT-Image, a private French company with some Dutch and Swedish participation. The media are considering operating their own satellite, raising grave concerns of national security and foreign policy (will the media be able to independently verify the Government's accounts of interventions?) and individual privacy.[32] The future aerospace plane will be a most appreciated means of intercontinental transportation, beyond its initial, predominantly military, use. Even launching may be taken over by private parties.[33] Materials processing[34] will take place on the space station envisaged by President Reagan.

All these activities presuppose some kind of supervision and control of the participant private parties' activities by nation-states. Whereas the attribution of space objects to individual states was dealt with by the 1975 Registration Convention[35], the issue of the minimum degree of control of a nation-state over its private "national" space object remains as it was - barely touched on by the 1967 Treaty.

6. The problem of *liability* is addressed only most generally in the 1967 Treaty. Article VII provides that the launching State is internationally liable for the damage caused by its space object. The 1971 Liability Convention[36] provides more detail. New issues, however, will arise with the advent of the aerospace plane. Should liability for its operation and its

---

32 *US Unhappy: Media Using Satellite Photos*, 10 Transnational Data Report, 8, (February 1987).

33 The U.S., after the Challenger tragedy and its increasing focus on military payloads for the rest of its shuttle flights, will face increasing challenges on the commercial launch market from Europe (Ariane), Japan, and even China and the USSR. Under the 1984 Commercial Space Launch Act, P.L. 98-575, 98 Stat. 3055, however, private citizens or corporations may, under government license, perform launches from U.S. soil.

34 Dula, *Materials Processing As a Subject of Space Law*, Proceedings of the 28th Colloquium on the Law of Outer Space 224 (1986).

35 Convention on Registration of Objects Launched into Outer Space, Nov. 12, 1974, UNGA Res. 3235 (XXIX).

36 Convention on International Liability for Damage Caused by Space Objects, 29 Nov., 1971, 24 U.S.T. 2389, T.I.A.S. 7762, 10 I.L.M. 965 (1971).

registration be determined by the established rules of air law or space law, or should we strive to tailor a special regime for that particular object?[37]

7. *Space debris* has become a major threat to human activities in outer space.[38] Current regimes of liability, based as they are on negligence theories of negative obligations, duties *not* to commit certain acts, even the 1967 Treaty's strict liability for the harmful effects emanating from one's own space object, might no longer be enough - in view of both the increasing "contamination" of the area, and the increasing difficulties in identifying whose country's space object has caused the damage.[39] It seems to be advisable to contemplate *positive* duties to remove dangerous debris, similar to the duty to perform necessary repairs in domestic property law. This duty might be incumbent upon a country that is predominantly active in one particular area of outer space, or on the international community as a whole who might commission such mine-sweeping missions from the leading space powers.[40]

8. This, by necessity, incomplete list of problems may be concluded for now by reference to the novel legal issues created by the establishment of an international space station.[41] Looming large are the *jurisdictional and substantive law conflicts* on such a complex, "international" space structure. Who owns the station? Who decides which disputes where? On board the station? According to which law?

9. One may conclude that the 1967 Treaty fails to address major novel issues of space law, and that some of its fundamental policies are honoured today only in their breach. This state of things will worsen in the future with increasing military and commercial use. Thus, beyond the 1967 Treaty, it is up to scholars to ascertain what are the expectations about

---

[37] *Cf.* the good discussion by Kuskuvelis, *supra* note 5.

[38] Kessler & Cour-Palais, *Collision Frequency of Artifical satellites: The Creation of a Debris Belt*, 83 J. Geophysical Research 2637 (1978); more recently, Temple, *The Impact of Space Debris on Manned Space Operations*, Paper No. IAA-86-420, submitted to the 37th IAF Congress in Innsbruck, 1986.

[39] Space objects, especially after the end of their useful lifetime, may disintegrate into little pieces, such as nuts and bolts, which escape radar detection. In collision with satellites, they may inflict major damage: a collision at 10 km/s, *e.g.*, would eject from a satellite 115 times the mass of the impacting debris. Kessler & Cour-Palais, *supra* note 38.

[40] For a way to finance such endeavours, *see* the proposal to auction unused options to use geostationary satellite slots to the highest bidder. The revenues from these auctions might finance a world space technology centre. Wiessner, *supra* note 19, at 269-273.

[41] McDougal, Lasswell and Vlasic already referred to this host of problems arising with the operation of "international spacecraft" in their 1963 seminal book: M. McDougal, H. Lasswell & I. Vlasic, *Law and Public Order in Space* 674, 690, 695, 703, (1963). -- As to the present space station project, *cf.* the Special Section in 24 Aerospace America, September 1986, at 24 *et seq.*; Galloway, *The Space Station: United States Proposal and Implementation*, 14 J. Space L. 14 (1986). The legal issues are addressed quite comprehensively in: Congress of the United States, Office of Technology Assessment, *Space Stations and the Law: Selected Legal Issues*, Doc. No. OTA-BT-ISC-47 (August 1986).

lawfulness or unlawfulness of specific human activities in outer space. Where evidence on the outcome of the world's constitutive process of decision-making in relation to a particular problem is lacking or inconclusive, it is the critical task of scholars to advance solutions in the global common interest. Such recommendations should ideally promote the abundant and economic use of great sharable resources for the benefit of the whole of humankind. To complete this task successfully, scholars must employ an adequate methodological framework.

II. TOWARDS AN ADEQUATE FRAMEWORK FOR DECISION-MAKING

To determine what the present expectations of the world community are on which human activities in outer space are "right" or "wrong" and what the law is or should be, one has to be clear about one's conception of "the law".

1. The first premise I suggest is that law is essentially designed to govern the activities of and the interaction between human beings. In short, it governs human conduct, wherever such acts or omissions or the effects thereof take place. Just as property law is not properly viewed as the law of things, but as the law relating to interests of persons in things, space law is not properly seen as the law *of* outer space, but as the *law relating to human activities in or with respect to outer space*. This characterisation encompasses not only direct human actions beyond the Earth's atmosphere, but covers any chain of events set in motion by human beings and having effects on the medium, such as the journey of *Voyager* through the Solar System. The characterisation would have to be revised once the human race enters into some kind of interaction with extraterrestrial intelligence.

Starting from this premise, we have to realise that law relating to outer space is, at present, *created on Earth*.[42] This might change with the establishment of permanent space habitats for humans.[43] But now, and for the foreseeable future, space law is created in the same processes and within the same structures of decision-making as other compounds of legal prescription. What, then, is the "law" created on this planet?

2. Law, in particular the coarchic realm of international law, is the ever-changing outcome of collaboration and of a particular process of communication. It involves a message that is

---

[42] *Cf.* Christol, *supra* note 8, at 48: "It would have been inconceivable for the space environment and its exploration, use, and exploitation to be immune from an Earth-based rule of law."

[43] The U.S. National Commission on Space, in its May 1986 Report, recommends establishing a permanent space station, a spaceport in low Earth orbit, an initial lunar outpost, a spaceport in lunar orbit, astronaut outposts on Phobos, Deimos, and Mars, and the start-up of a Martian resource development base to provide oxygen, water, food, construction materials, and rocket propellants, within the next fifty years. These stations would constitute a "Bridge Between Worlds" that would open up the Solar System. Pioneering the Space Frontier 13-18 (1986).

intended to be both authoritative and controlling[44], a decision about the lawfulness of conduct.[45] This decision may be an abstract and general one, usually contained in a convention, or it may be one focusing on the concrete and special circumstances of a particular problem. In the international arena, this message is the world community's response to conflicting claims raised by human beings in their interaction with each other in the world social process. In order to comprehend this process, a problem-oriented, contextual, and multidisciplinary approach is indispensable.[46]

Law arises from this process of claim and counterclaim, from von Jhering's "battle for law", in which we all have a moral duty, a vocation to fight for the interests and values we want to see preserved. This dynamic nature of the law is most pronounced in the area of international law where little or no vertical structure of decision-making is in place. Instead, we face a highly imbalanced array of actors, with greatly varying bases of power, perspectives and strategies, in often complex situations. They interact to create the fragmented set of rules that we term "international law".

3. To investigate this process of decision-making with the utmost degree of professional veracity, one has to leave von Jhering's "heaven" of legal concepts. One has to delve into the real world and analyse how the international community's decision-making processes resolve the issues confronting them.

Methodologically, one has to complete five intellectual tasks:

(1) delimit the problem in terms of the values at stake and investigate the facts;
(2) identify claims, claimants, their perspectives, their versions of the relevant facts, policies, and remedies;
(3) identify past trends in decision about comparable problems in the light of the factors conditioning those decisions;

---

44 Reisman, *International Lawmaking: A Process of Communication*, 75 Proceedings of the Am. Soc'y Int'l L. 101-120 (1981). The presence of both authority and control is essential to the concept of law. Authority has been defined as the "structure of expectation concerning who, with what qualifications and mode of selection, is competent to make which decisions by what criteria and what procedures." Control has been defined as effective power. McDougal & Lasswell, *The Identification and Appraisal of Diverse Systems of Public Order*, 53 Am. J. Int'l L. 1, 9 (1959). *See also* Reisman, *A Theory About Law from the Policy Perspective*, Law and Policy 75, 88-89 (Weisstub, editor, 1976).

45 The process of authoritative and controlling decision-making may be further broken down into the following sequence: (1) the gathering, processing and disseminating of *intelligence* relevant to the making of choices, (2) the *promotion* or recommendation of policy, (3) the *prescription* of one of the competing policies as "law", (4) the *invocation* of an authoritative response to an alleged violation of the prescription, (5) the *application* of policy to an alleged deviation and specification of a particular sanction, (6) the *termination* of pre-existing prescriptions, and (7) the ongoing *appraisal* of the general performance of the community's decision-making functions. Reisman, *supra* note 44.

46 McDougal, Lasswell & Reisman, *Theories About International Law: Prologue to a Configurative Jurisprudence*, 8 Va. J. Int'l L. 189, 196 (1968).

(4) project future trends in decision in the light of conditioning factors as they have changed or will change;
(5) recommend solutions, or make decisions that in the context most closely approximate postulated policies in the global common interest.

In detail, these tasks include the following:

(1) Lawyers, as experts in decision-making, have to demarcate the particular *problem* society is facing and investigate the factual parameters, using the methods favoured by the sciences most apt to deal with the issue. To understand a particular problem, for example the scarcity of the twin resource of the geostationary satellite orbit (orbital locations and frequencies), one has to grasp the *facts* by employing the assistance of the universe of knowledge with its own competent methodologies (in this instance of scientists and engineers) to determine the activities involved, the nature and type of the resource concerned, *etc*.. In this example, facts calling for analysis would include the present and future use of the geostationary orbit, the physical constraints on its utilisation, and the degree of regulation necessitated by these conditions.

(2) A necessary second step is the identification of claimants and their *claims* in the struggle for law in any given set of problems. In the case of the geostationary orbit, one would have to state the demands to the unrestricted use of this resource, on a first-come-first-served basis, by the major spacefaring nations; the claims of most equatorial countries to exclusive control over that valuable band in outer space; and the rising demands of the Third World to equitable sharing via planning the use of the orbit.

(3) The outcomes of the continuing battles have to be addressed in the display and analysis of *past trends in decision*. How did the world community as a whole react to the competing claims? In the case of the geostationary orbit, we would have to mention the 1967 Treaty with its less-than-clear reference to the "province of all mankind", and the longstanding, up-to-the- present-day inconclusive, discussions within UNCOPUOS on this issue. We would also have to address the decisions reached within the ITU: the general obligation of "equitable sharing" in Article 33 (2) of the International Telecommunication Convention[47], and the sprinkled areas of *a priori* planning within the traditional first-come-first-served framework of coordination of the use of the radio spectrum by the IFRB.

This part of the inquiry comes closest to the traditional analysis of international law, in any given set of problems. It is, however, more comprehensive than the exclusive, normativist focus on the behaviour of nation-states. To obtain a full picture of the decision-making process, one has to understand its dynamics, its *conditioning factors*. The analysis of these

47 International Telecommunication Convention, November 6, 1982, Bundesgesetzblatt 1985 II, at 426.

factors makes one better equipped to not only understand, but also predict the outcomes of particular conflicts of interest in particular historical situations.

Factors to be analysed are both environmental and predispositional:

- the situation of decision (geographical, historical, cultural and technological ramifications);
- the participants in the decision-making process (international officials, governments, private groups and individuals);
- their perspectives (value demands, identifications, expectations);
- their bases of power (armies, wealth, resources, technology, loyalties, *etc.*);
- their range of available strategies; and
- the short-range outcomes of options in decision and longer-term effects of each decision.

(4) To *predict future decisions*, their constraints and consequences, one does not only have to look to decisions of the past and their conditioning factors, but also to the changes within these parameters of decision, including new conditioning factors, that may have occurred. In an impending litigation before the International Court of Justice, for example, the litigants would be well advised to find out about the particular jurisprudential or ideological background of the members of the bench, the changes in fact and law that occurred since their last decision on a similar subject, and so forth. In a scholarly context, we might want to anticipate future societal and technological developments.[48] In the context of the geostationary orbit, for example, it would behoove us to take into account alternatives of conflict resolution based on technological innovation, the relative bases of power of states and private citizens/corporations involved, as well as their interest or need to reach an agreement.

(5) The preceding intellectual tasks have been largely descriptive, scientific, analytical. The fifth step in the framework of decision-making is *prescriptive*. It culminates in the choice among options in decision. Through it one endeavours to work out, on the basis of the information accumulated, a solution to the problem that is in the global common interest. In order to gain the most widespread acceptance of the prescriptive proposal, the policies on which it is based have to be clarified and related to the particular instance. To be aware of the often underlying value judgments, the author, in particular one writing in scholarly function[49], should use a process of introspection to identify his or her preconceptions,

---

48 They can only be based about our vision at this point of time, our "future constructs". *Cf.* Reisman, *Private Armies in a Global War System: Prologue to Decision*, 14 Va. J. Int'l L. 1, 31-33 (1973). These constructs may turn out to be wrong or imprecise.

49 A lawyer may act in many roles, the most important being an advocate, a counsellor, a judge, and a scholar. Of these, the scholar has the greatest latitude, and the greatest obligation to promote the *common* interest.

predilections, and particular views engrained by upbringing and environment, which might influence his or her judgment.

Ideally, the proposals advanced reflect both the aspirations of the individual who advances them, and the aspirations of humankind as a whole. This outcome is most probable when the aspirations of humankind are formulated in a broad and general fashion. As an example, again we might turn to the policies of equitable sharing, flexibility, efficient and economic use on which the world community agrees concerning the use of the geostationary satellite orbit.

III. CONCLUSION

This inclusive analysis of facts, claims, and trends in decision enables one to reach a comprehensive picture from which to draw conclusions and to make recommendations suited to gain community consensus. This framework helps to complete the most critical task of a scholar in the field of law: to contribute to the minimisation of the use of force and the preservation of human dignity by advancing practical solutions to pressing social problems in the global common interest - to be a warrior in the strife, sometimes quixotic, for legal order in a violent world.

THE CREATION OF A CONCEPT OF THE LAW OF OUTER SPACE

Walter W.C. de Vries*

"The principles of Declaration 1962 of 'Legal Principles Governing the Activities of States in the Exploration and Use of Outer Space' and the 1967 Treaty on 'Principles Governing the Activities of States in the Exploration and Use of Outer Space, including the Moon and other Celestial Bodies', although raised to the level of law, basically belong to method, and for the further development of the law of outer space, these principles have to be seen in their proper context."

1. INTRODUCTION

Within a few decades, the law of outer space could evolve into a new branch of international law. Like every branch of international law, the law of outer space needs its own specific principles and rules governing man's activities related to outer space.
In each field of law, when new human endeavours ask for new rules, there is always a tendency to resort to existing law. The problem and challenge in the early days of the space age was the complete lack of a set of rules with respect to outer space. Moreover, the words of Professor Bos that "the international lawyer finds himself in the not too enviable position of having himself to frame his own concept of law", hold even more truth for the international space lawyer.[1]
The theory of *analytical conceptualism*, introduced by Professor Bos[2] as a methodology of international law, is considered to be so unique for the framing of a concept of the law of outer space that the present writer has taken the freedom to adapt several of his thoughts and views in an attempt to unfold the first steps towards a methodology of the law of outer space.

In this article, law is seen as a projection of the human mind.[3] That is to say that law manifests itself as a product of legal thinking. And as legal thinking is a universal phenomenon inherent in man, its scope is not strictly limited to more 'earthly' matters. However, legal thinking in relation to outer space only became of practical importance when man actively started to explore and make use of outer space. Prior to this, legal thinking on outer space had been more of an academic inquiry.

---

* Institute of Satellite Applications, Amsterdam, The Netherlands.

1 With these words Professor Bos introduces his theory of analytical conceptualism as a methodology of international law. Maarten Bos, *Methodology of International Law* 28 (1984).

2 *Ibid.*

3 *Id.*, at 2.

Today, we are witnessing a great variety of space activities, and ever increasing developments. In dealing with the legal problems arising from these activities, a major task of the space lawyer and scholar is to provide a legal framework in which to place conduct in regard to outer space. In this respect, he has himself to frame a concept of the law of outer space enabling him to find the applicable law.
In this task, he has to take into account the specific features inherent in outer space activities as well as the problems which find their origins in more down-to-earth fields like international relations.

2. A FRAMEWORK FOR THE CONCEPT OF THE LAW OF OUTER SPACE

At the very centre of our analysis of outer space activities, three dominant notions should be distinguished: the *General Concept of Law* (GCL), the *Normative Concept of Law* (NCL) and the *Legal Process* (LP).[4] Together, these notions will serve as a framework to create a concept of the law of outer space.

The general concept of law is above all supposed to delimit law as such from other cultural and historical phenomena. When we deal with legal matters, we have, in the first place, to distinguish *law's empire* from other disciplines. For this, the general concept of law is introduced, containing a set of principles[5] which are thought to be of a nature so basic and general that they belong to every legal order, national as well as international and independent from any culture or time. As a consequence, the GCL is of a rather static nature and applies *eo ipso* to all fields of law, the law of outer space included.

This is in contrast to the normative concept of law, which contains another set of principles, reflecting the feelings and ideas of what we now, within this specific legal order of outer space, think of as being normative and which needs to be applied to regulate outer space activities. These principles are a result of a process of normative legal thinking on outer space.
In determining these principles, our normative thinking has been heavily influenced by the potentialities of the medium of outer space as well as by the more political surroundings in which they are generated.
Looking back to the early days of the space age, when the first steps were made to lay down principles which should govern our activities in outer space, the international

---

[4] *Id.*, at 3.

[5] *Id.*, at 5; Professor Bos has identified four principles illustrating the outer limits of law so understood, *viz.*:

- the principle that everyone is born into a general legal order or, in other words, that no legal order of a general nature is optional to its subjects;
- the principle that no subject can be allowed to frustrate the law through an act of his own volition;
- the principle *pacta sunt servanda*; and
- the principle *nemo plus iuris transferre potest quam ipse habet*.

community had to face several problems, which have, in turn, influenced our normative concept of law.

Only two states, the USSR and the USA, possessed the technology and the means to reach outer space. Since the political environment was mostly determined by their consent, much depended on their willingness to participate in the regulation of future space activities. Moreover, during those days, the world was divided into two blocs with mainly divergent views and political ideas, headed by the USSR and the USA.
Furthermore, since space technology was still in its infancy, one difficulty was 'what and how' to regulate. For, nobody could foresee future developments and, naturally, the USSR and the USA felt little inclined to bind themselves by regulations which would trouble them in the exploration and use of outer space. No matter how big these problems might have appeared, the willingness to regulate outer space activities was thought to be more urgent.

The most appropriate way was through an agreement drafted within the United Nations. The United Nations as the world's foremost political forum with essentially universal membership became the focal point for the development of the law of outer space. At its 13th session in 1958, the UNGA established the *Ad Hoc* Committee on the Peaceful Uses of Outer Space (COPUOS) which was replaced one year later by a permanent body.[6] Its work resulted in the adoption of resolution 1962 containing a Declaration on Legal Principles[7] which should govern outer space activities. This Declaration formed the basis for the 1967 Outer Space Treaty[8], which may be seen as the greatest achievement so far and a major step in the creation of an international legal order of outer space.

As normative thinking is always under pressure to adapt to new inventions and changes, the normative concept of law is of a highly dynamic nature. It is the task of the lawyer to be ever vigilant in order to keep pace with developments within this particular legal order. Indeed, it is the space lawyer and scholar who translates, through his legal thinking, normative feelings and ideas into legal terms.

Thirdly, there exists the legal process in the course of which the law of outer space manifests itself. Here, the results of legal thinking come into being as the combined projection of the general concept of law and the normative concept of law. The latter, in particular, has to take into consideration factual elements such as power and history as well

---

6 UNGA Res.1348 (XII) of 13 December 1958 & UNGA Res.1472 (XIV) of 12 December 1959.

7 UNGA Res.1962 (XVIII) of 13 December 1963.

8 Treaty on Principles Governing the Activities of States in the Exploration and Use of Outer Space, including the Moon and other Celestial Bodies, 27 January 1967, 18 UST 2410, TIAS 6347, 610 UNTS 205 (hereinafter the Outer Space Treaty).

as moral elements.[9] Within the legal process, the law of outer space crystallises into one of the 'recognised manifestations of law', such as treaties or custom.

As already mentioned above, the most important 'recognised manifestation' of the law of outer space is the 1967 Outer Space Treaty which was followed by four more agreements.[10] Taken together, they form the hard core of the law of outer space. In the meantime, both in other fields of law and within several international organisations, regulations have been drawn up concerning outer space activities.

While the GCL, NCL and LP supply us with a structural framework for the development of the law of outer space, analytical conceptualism also provides us with a means to measure the intrinsic value of the law so developed.

Method *lato sensu* will enable us to get a clearer picture of how we should proceed with our work and provide a context within which the Outer Space Treaties should be seen.

3. PRINCIPLES OF METHOD OF THE LAW OF OUTER SPACE

In addressing himself to the need for the creation of a concept of the law of outer space, the space lawyer carries in his armoury a wide range of principles and assumptions. In determining which to apply, the space lawyer has to distinguish method from law.

In restating the fact that law is a product of legal thinking, method is here understood as a closed, autonomous and self-contained way of thought, enabling the lawyer to unveil the law as such.[11]

Having defined method as such, it should immediately be noted that method is not limited to the art of interpretation which may be called method *stricto sensu*, but also comprises a set of principles originating from the GCL and NCL.

Method *stricto sensu* and these principles, taken together, may be called method *lato sensu*.[12] While law has 'binding force', method *lato sensu* is 'clad with authority'.[13] However, both are part of the working tools used by the lawyer in framing a concept of law of outer space and it is here that the lawyer's ability and insight come to the fore in distinguishing those principles of method from those of law.

---

9 Bos, *supra* note 1 at 15-27.

10 Agreement on the Rescue of Astronauts, the Return of Astronauts and the Return of Objects Launched into Outer Space, 22 April 1968, 19 UST 7570, TIAS 6599, (hereinafter the Rescue Agreement); Convention on International Liability for Damage Caused by Space Objects, 29 March 1972, 24 UST 2389, TIAS 7762 (hereinafter the Liability Convention); Convention on Registration of Objects Launched into Outer Space, 14 January 1975, 28 UST 695, TIAS 8480 (hereinafter the Registration Convention); Agreement Governing the Activities of States on the Moon and other Celestial Bodies, 5 December 1975, UN Doc.A/34/99 of 12 December 1979.

11 Bos, *supra* note 1, at 2.

12 Bos, *supra* note 1, at 10.

13 *Id.*

Analytical conceptualism identifies three categories of principle belonging to method *lato sensu*, namely:

. principles of structure
. principles of conduct
. method *stricto sensu*[14]

In most legal orders some fundamental principles have been codified and have no external distinction from other rules of law. Raised to the level of law, they have formally become binding as law, but basically they have no 'binding force'. Rather, they are 'clad with authority' and have to be identified as such. It is in this light that the 1967 Outer Space Treaty should be seen.

With the conclusion of the Outer Space Treaty many principles have been raised to the level of law. However, it is our assertion that originally these principles belonged to method *lato sensu* and that they still tacitly reveal their function as being 'clad with authority' rather than having 'binding force'.
To support this assertion we will examine how method *lato sensu* stands at the base of the construction of a legal framework of outer space activities and how these principles have come under pressure from the rapidly changing normative concept of law.
We will leave the examination of method *stricto sensu* for another occasion and will limit ourselves to the 'principles of structure' and the 'principles of conduct'.

a. Principles of Structure of Outer Space

As with all new fields of law, one main question is to define this new dimension in our legal thinking. Here, we have to find answers to questions of a more structural nature, such as the delimitation of outer space and which kind of principles and rules we are to apply to this new environment.
As to the latter, Article II of the Outer Space Treaty states that outer space, including the Moon and other celestial bodies, is not subject to national appropriation by claim of sovereignty, by means of use or occupation, or by any other means.
The principle of non-appropriation, now so fixed in our legal thinking, was but one alternative at the time of drafting. At the end of the fifties, several other theories were proposed.[15] Looking at today's use of outer space, questions arise as to what extent this principle should be applied.

---

14 *Id.* The principles of structure and the principles of conduct are in turn divided into those originating from the GCL and those originating from the NCL. In this article we will not discuss this distinction because of lack of space.

15 E.R.C. van Bogaert, *Aspects of Space Law* (1986) at 25-35 gives an overview of the several theories which were proposed.

For, at the same time it was agreed in Article I that outer space shall be free for exploration and use by all states without discrimination of any kind, on a basis of equality and that there shall be free access to all areas of celestial bodies.
As the particular examples of the use of the geostationary orbit have shown, these two principles turn out in practice to be in conflict with each other. The terms free for exploration and non-appropriation were seen by the lesser developed countries as an infringement on their rights of future access to this special orbit.

The problem becomes clearer when we realise that up until now no agreement exists on the delimitation of outer space. Although several proposals have been made and the topic has been on the agenda of the COPUOS ever since the beginning in 1958, an agreement has not been found. Using or abusing this lack of a legal norm, seven equatorial countries brought the topic of non-appropriation and free access into the political arena with their Bogotà Declaration in which they tried to extend their sovereignty to the geostationary orbit.[16]
How factually absurd this declaration may seem, from a strictly legal point of view it was very hard to find counter-arguments. However, as a political statement, the position of the lesser developed states has come to the fore and confronts us with but one of the shifts in normative thinking on outer space. It demonstrates that the structure, once so accepted in the 1960's, has since then come under attack.

Apart from the freedom of exploration of outer space, a more fundamental principle was laid down. The international community agreed that the exploration and use of outer space should be governed by international law and the Charter of the United Nations.[17]
This, however, is not a simple question of applying existing rules to this new environment: very many rules require adaptation and in many situations new ones, destined purely for outer space, have to be created. However, as Judge Lachs pointed out, none of this implies the extension to outer space and celestial bodies of "international law, including the Charter of the United Nations" *in toto.*[18]
Many articles of the Charter are destined for specific environments and thus do not lend themselves for application in other areas such as outer space. However tempting it would be to draw analogies, we should keep in mind that outer space has some specific features not comparable with other environments.

---

16 *Declaration of Bogotà* (3 December 1976) in Jasentuliyana/Lee, Manual on Space Law III, 383-387. Signatories are *Brasil, Colombia, Equador, Indonesia, Kenya, Uganda* and *Zaire* .

17 Outer Space Treaty, *supra* note 8, Article III.

18 Manfred Lachs, *The Law of Outer Space* 15 (1972).

The extension of international law has been limited, however, in so far as the jurisdiction and control over a space object is retained by the State on whose registry an object launched into outer space is carried.[19] This principle determines the legal status of objects launched into outer space and registration is accordingly meant as proof of the exercise of sovereign rights over such objects.

In the extending of general international law to outer space another feature linked to the present state of international law has been transferred, namely, that the subjects to which these principles are being directed are limited to States. However, the 1967 Outer Space Treaty leaves open the possibility that private entities could participate in different space activities but that States are to be held internationally responsible for their activities.[20]
A last question on the structure of the legal regime of outer space is whether the validity of the principles governing the activities of States extends *erga omnes*. Most scholars agree that this is correct.[21] The most important reason to support this, is that up until now, the majority of states have adhered to the 1967 Outer Space Treaty, hereby including all the big nations.

b. General Principles of Conduct Governing Outer Space Activities

Having set out the structure of outer space, we now come to another set of principles, namely those which regulate conduct in outer space. These principles of conduct, like the above mentioned principles of structure, are derived from the normative concept of law for outer space activities.
It should also be kept in mind, however, that these principles have been heavily influenced by our normative thinking on how behaviour and conduct in outer space should be regulated.

When, in 1957, the USSR first reached outer space, this event formed a summit in the arms race between the USSR and the USA. Despite the fact that the launching took place as a non-military event within the activities performed in the Geophysical Year, nevertheless, outer space could eventually be used for military purposes. Aware of this possibility, the UNGA immediately adopted a resolution[22] in which it was laid down that outer space

---

19 Outer Space Treaty, *supra* note 8, Article VIII.

20 Outer Space Treaty, *supra* note 8, Articles VI, VII & XIII. *See further* Diederiks-Verschoor & Gormly, *The Future Legal Status of Non-governmental Entities: Private Individuals and Companies as Subjects and Beneficiaries of International Space Law*, J.S.L. 145 (1977); *see also* Zwaan & de Vries, *Regulating Remote Sensing of the Earth from Outer Space, Taking into Account the Present Trend of Privatisation of this Activity*, Proceedings of the 30th Colloquium on the Law of Outer Space (1988).

21 Lachs, *supra* note 18, at 17.

22 *See supra* note 6.

should be used exclusively for peaceful purposes. But as developments and technology rapidly advanced, outer space has become an attractive medium for military purposes. It is now estimated that 70 % of all activities in outer space is conducted, in one way or another, for military purposes. Legitimation has been found in Article IV which provides for a partial demilitarisation of outer space and a complete demilitarisation of the Moon and other celestial bodies. However, the recent plans of the USA to eventually deploy their SDI programme have created uproar within the international (legal) community as to whether or not these developments are in conformity with the wording of Article IV. For an extensive overview of this topic, I would like to refer to other articles in this book.

Notwithstanding strained international relations, the UNCOPUOS succeeded in agreeing that outer space activities should be carried out for the benefit and in the interests of all new nations, irrespective of their degree of economic or scientific development and that outer space should be the province of all mankind.[23] This gives meaning to the principle to contribute to the development of mutual understanding and to the strengthening of friendly relations between states and peoples, which is one of the major goals of the United Nations.

One provision which is directly derived from the United Nations Charter, is that, in the exploration and use of outer space, States shall be guided by the principle of co-operation.[24] A notable first result was the conclusion of the Outer Space Treaty itself.

The preamble firmly declares that this Treaty aims to contribute to broad international co-operation in the scientific as well as the legal aspects of the exploration and use of outer space for peaceful purposes. Due to the enormous costs inherent in outer space activities and the unequal division of technical know-how, international co-operation will be the only means by which everybody can benefit from the profitable uses of outer space.

In the exploration and use of outer space, the risks of harm or loss can be very great and the question arose whether the basic general principles of international law would prove to be adequate for this purpose. Dangerous experiments or the use of nuclear energy may, in the case of an accident, affect the whole of mankind.

Therefore, as a first step, states shall bear international responsibility for national activities in outer space, irrespective of whether such activities are carried out by government agencies or by non-governmental entities. Consequently, launching states are held internationally liable for damage suffered by another state. The same rule is to be applied to the component parts of a space object.[25]

As we have seen, this principle has already been worked out in a more elaborate treaty, the 1972 Liability Convention.

---

[23] Outer Space Treaty, *supra* note 8, Article I.

[24] *Id.*, Articles I, III & IX.

[25] *Id.*, Article VII.

In an effort to make the lives of the astronauts more secure, they shall be regarded as envoys of mankind and, in the event of accident, distress or emergency landing, all possible assistance shall be rendered to them.[26] Due to humanitarian reasons, it was possible for this principle to be specified in an agreement, within one year of the conclusion of the Outer Space Treaty, in which the rights and obligations of States have been laid down in order to safeguard the lives of astronauts.[27]
Under this same Rescue Agreement, the problem of an object launched into outer space which has returned to earth and has been found on territory under the jurisdiction of another State, on the high seas, or in any other place not under the jurisdiction of any State, has also been regulated. States are accordingly bound by the principle that on gaining knowledge of such an occurence or discovery, they shall inmediately notify the launching authority and the Secretary-General of the United Nations.[28]

Although this principle is more limited than in the case of astronauts, it has been enacted to regulate state conduct in case such events should occur.

4. EVALUATING THE 1967 OUTER SPACE TREATY AS THE 'MAGNA CHARTA' OF OUTER SPACE

The fact that most of the above-mentioned principles found their way into the several outer space treaties meant that many scholars came to the conclusion that the 1967 Outer Space Treaty has become the 'Magna Charta' of outer space and consequently has 'binding force' as positive law.
We have seen that the wording of the Treaty has been laid down in a very general and broad way. This was not only done to anticipate future developments, but more for the reason that these principles could serve as a basic instrument to be worked out in more elaborate agreements. However, facing today's problems one is inclined to say that too many words have been spent on discussions which undermine the basic tenets of these principles, instead of working on their refinement. That is not to say that a rethinking or reinterpretation of some of these principles would destroy the foundations of the law of outer space, but that this process should be seen in the light of further developments in the law of outer space and not as an end in itself.

The inability to assess the growing number of nations participating in the legal process of the law of outer space, the commercialisation of outer space and the influence of technological innovation may be seen as reasons for such a development.

---

26 *Id.*, Article V.

27 Rescue Agreement, *supra* note 10.

28 *Id.*, Article 5.

After an over-enthusiastic reaction following the relatively quick drafting of the Outer Space Treaty and its four agreements on specialised subject areas, very quickly some major problems began to arise from beyond the horizon. The growing number of new states with a completely different cultural, economic and political background were confronted with a set of principles and rules of international law and the law of outer space, often unknown to them. International law finds its roots in Western Europe where principles and rules have been evolved in a more or less coherent society.

On this basis, the drafting of the Outer Space Treaty took place on the international level, while most of the participants could hardly imagine the possibilities presented in outer space. With the entry of these new nations and having accepted them as full members under international law, one cannot possibly demand the same approach towards the principles laid down in the Outer Space Treaty.

On the other hand, these new nations cannot claim rights, in order to protect their future access to space activities, from principles which are not meant to be interpreted in such a way.

Whilst the Outer Space Treaty is directed above all at States, there is a recognisable trend towards commercial entities becoming more and more engaged in space activities. One cannot expect that these actors will have the same attitude as their governments towards principles which have been set up in a most general form. As private enterprises come under the jurisdiction and control of their own State, their municipal law will be applicable. On the other hand, the State stays internationally responsible for them. And it will not be the first time in the history of international law that in cases of conflict, existing rules will not be sufficient.[29]

Technological progress may be considered to be an autonomous process which does not deal with law in the first place.[30] More than in other fields of law, technological innovations are immediately felt in the law of outer space. In the development of military activities in outer space, who could have foreseen the eventual deployment of SDI. In an attempt to define exactly what will be prohibited or allowed[31], such definitions can soon become obsolete through new technological developments.

And as we have seen in the discussions concerning the principles of free-flow of information versus prior consent as regards DBS transmissions, technological developments have made it possible to receive signals from fixed satellite services with the same equipment as is necessary for receiving DBS signals.

---

[29] Lachs, *supra* note 15, at 284-285.

[30] Johan K. de Vree, *Foundations of Social and Political Processes* 253 (1982).

[31] Galloway, *Expanding Article IV of the 1967 Space Treaty: A Proposal*, Proceedings of the 25th Colloquium on the Law of Outer Space 89 (1983) and Gorove, *The 1967 Outer Space Treaty and some Alternatives for further Arms Control*, in Maintaining Outer Space for Peaceful Uses , Proceedings of a Symposium held by the United Nations University (Jasentuliyana, editor, 1984, GLDB-1/UNUP-537).

A final but important remark may be made. Due to the above influences and changes, our normative concept of the law of outer space has changed greatly. It is very unlikely that such developments have yet come to an end. Moreover, such changes will unquestionably play a role in framing a concept of the law of outer space. We cannot but repeat that the 1967 Outer Space Treaty is 'clad with authority' rather than having 'binding force' as positive law.

5. CONCLUSION

We should bear in mind that the 1967 Outer Space Treaty, although raised to the level of a 'Magna Charta', may not suffice for the future. As our normative thinking is continually changing and gradually emerging within the legal process, new principles may arise which might even be contrary to those enumerated in the 1967 Outer Space Treaty.

However, it is our task to build upon the principles of the Outer Space Treaty, not by tampering with the normative concepts laying behind these principles and by replacing such concepts with current normative thoughts, but by working out these principles in separate treaties in which new principles and more concrete rules are defined. In this work we should keep in mind that the basic principles as laid down in the Outer Space Treaty belong to method *lato sensu* and have to be identified as such. In this way the 1967 Outer Space Treaty can truly fulfill a role as the 'Magna Charta' of outer space.

But at the end it is us, the new generation of space lawyers, who should continue the work of those who set out the first steps towards creating the law of outer space. Hereby the distinction proposed above, between method and law may be of help.

THE INFLUENCE OF THE ACHIEVEMENTS AND FAILURES OF THE PAST ON THE FUTURE OF OUTER SPACE LAW

Tanja L. Zwaan*

1. INTRODUCTION

Too many publications dealing with outer space law start with the words: "After the launching of the first Sputnik in 1957...".

This one will not, for I will try to adopt an original approach - a *new* approach - to this fascinating field of international law. Let me be clear: I do not mean that contributions starting with those words are not original. Many of them are, and many of us have learned substantially from such contributions. Nor do I imply that all contributions starting with these words contain one and the same approach to space law. It is true, however, that I was surprised to see that so many authors use the "Sputnik event" as a starting phrase for their academic writings. Perhaps this is inevitable, for it was, after all, this very event that "gave birth" to a new challenge: the creation of a law of outer space.

As the title of this chapter suggests, I shall try to "speculate" on the future of outer space law on the basis of past achievements and shortcomings. This retrospective starting point is, I believe, the best reference to fully appreciate and analyse the requirements of a sound further development of space law. For we can learn from the past, both from successes and from failures.

It must be kept in mind that today's situation differs from the one existing at the time when the first principles and rules of space law were created. The future law of outer space must be adjusted to such new circumstances.
I shall try to summarise the changes which have taken place, and which, in my view, necessitate a changed approach in the future. I shall then try to propose the elements of such a changed approach. It should be stressed that this article will merely indicate some broad principles; it is not my intention to deal with specific, detailed space activities.

2. THE PAST

Looking back to the beginning of space law, I believe that the following features and characteristics have influenced the results that were achieved at the time. First of all, most states were not aware of the effects - and benefits - of space activities. For many of them,

* Co-Director, International Institute of Air and Space Law, Leiden University, The Netherlands; Member, IISL.

discussing outer space amounted to curiosity and "science fiction". Also, the "space-powers", those who were actually active in this field, were very few; thus, agreement on the rules which should apply was not that hard to reach (no real competition existed). Most authors agree that the results of the early space law negotiations are quite startling, especially when compared with other fields of law, such as air law or the law of the sea. Indeed, it must be admitted that as much as five international UN treaties have entered into force in less than two decades.[1] Moreover, it is striking that the treaties concluded contained provisions about certain topics that were not then "real"; they referred to subjects that might arise in the future. One can take as an example the Liability Convention, where the case of a collision between two space objects "elsewhere than on the surface of the earth" is regulated; it can hardly be said that this was relevant at the time of the conclusion of the treaty.[2] There are many more examples. This anticipatory treaty-drafting is a quite unique feature of space law. In most other fields, law merely confirms and codifies actual practice and relates to current events in that specific field.

The existing universal space law instruments were drafted by the UN COPUOS.[3] This body works by consensus (no voting takes place), which has caused lengthy debates, but which has, on the other hand, usually resulted in widely accepted treaties.[4] At the beginning of its existence, COPUOS counted many experts among the delegates representing the different states. They dealt with the problems in a most competent way. This certainly contributed to the rapid drafting and ratification of the abovementioned treaties. Another advantage of COPUOS is that it assembled legal and technical experts as well as politicians. This interdisciplinary approach permitted an overall view of what was desirable politically and legally, and what was possible in terms of technology. After all, "law" is not an objective in itself. Law merely fulfils a service, or mediatory function, to efficiently and effectively meet the demands of society.[5] Thus, space law would not have been so widely accepted if it were concluded within a framework other than the United Nations (*e.g.* the International Law Commission mainly considers issues of a general, abstract nature).

---

1 The Outer Space Treaty of 1967, The Rescue Agreement of 1968, The Liability Convention of 1972, The Registration Convention of 1976 and The Moon Agreement of 1979.

2 Article III of the Liability Convention.

3 The United Nations Committee on the Peaceful Uses of Outer Space, established in 1958.

4 *See* Carl Q. Christol, *The Modern International Law of Outer Space* 17-18 (1984).

5 Böckstiegel, *Prospects of Future Development in the Law of Outer Space*, VIII Annals of Air and Space Law 306 (1983); *See also* on the need for an interdisciplinary approach: Christol, *supra* note 4, at 1.

The past success within the UN in formulating space law demonstrates the advantage of, and the need for, an interdisciplinary approach.[6]

Nevertheless, it must be realised that the five UN space treaties are rather general in content. Many terms are not defined, and numerous provisions have given rise to varied interpretations and theories (*e.g.*, "peaceful purposes" in Article IV (2) of the Outer Space Treaty; "space object" in the Liability Convention; "the province of all mankind" and "use" in Article IV (1) of the Moon Agreement). This may be seen as the major shortcoming in this "first stage" of the space law age.

3. THE PRESENT

Let us now turn to the present. We can already see that many of the features and characteristics mentioned above no longer apply. The most striking difference is that the number of states interested and active in space activities has substantially increased. The United States and the Soviet Union are no longer the only "space powers"; Japan, China, Europe, India and others have entered onto the playing field and have their own interests. The developing nations have discovered the advantages and benefits of space activities.[7] Even if they do not yet have the technological and financial means to devise their own satellites or to build their own launching sites, they want to share in the results of the activities undertaken by states which do have these means (*e.g.* access to data obtained by remote sensing, to satellite communication, *etc.*).

As a result of this "discovery of own interests", a certain tendency towards nationalism has become apparent.[8] Most states (except, perhaps, third world states, who prefer international management of, for example, the geostationary orbit) seek nowadays to protect their "national" interests, whereas in the past "global" ("mankind") interests prevailed (and thus global treaties were concluded). On the other hand, it must be noted that an "integration tendency" will probably continue to balance the abovementioned "nationalistic tendency". The financial burdens of space activities are so heavy that few states can carry them individually. Moreover, technology has become so specialised that

---

[6] *See Space Activities and Emerging International Law* 6 (N.M. Matte, editor, 1984):"(...) in order to gain a clear understanding of space law, it is necessary to analyse space activities from the perspective of other disciplines - specifically engineering, political science and economics"; *see* for a detailed discussion of these interrelationships, *ibid.*, at 110-127.

[7] "Man's initial scepticism towards the Space adventure has nearly vanished, as tangible and intangible benefits of space technology, for the poorest of nations, become evident"; D. Wadegaonkar, *The Orbit of Space Law* 1 (1984). But, on the other hand, *see* Christol, *supra* note 4, at 844: "However, on the whole, the influences of the superpowers, and of certain European and Latin American states, have been much greater than those states which have not engaged in space activities and are lacking in space capabilities".

[8] *E.g.* Export controls on transfer of space technology in the United States and the Bogotà Declaration of the equatorial states of 3 December 1976.

many space ventures will require co-operation between several states.[9] The international space station of the US exemplifies these two factors. Nevertheless, in many areas this balance has shifted, at the expense of the integration and co-operation tendencies, towards a more nationalistic attitude of states.[10]

Furthermore, the "actors" in the space arena have changed. In the past, states were the only entities active in outer space. Nowadays we see an ever increasing interest of private enterprise in the commercialisation of outer space activities. Twenty years ago, space commerce did not exist, but it is now becoming a pressing reality.[11]
Commercial enterprises will want to know precisely what their legal position is when engaging in - expensive and risky - space activities. We urgently need clear and explicit laws to govern the activities of commercial enterprises. Unfortunately, the law-making process has slowed, and has become bogged down in lengthy discussions on general principles.

It seems that the solutions and methods of the past are no longer effective. The COPUOS has turned into a sort of international debating society where states engage in eternal discussions on minor issues. Agreement is extremely hard to reach. Its membership continues to increase and thus, because of the rule of consensus, the risk of one state blocking progress has also increased. It has even been proposed to abandon the rule of consensus and to replace it by a "qualified majority rule", *i.e.* to turn to voting as a last resort in cases where dissenters constitute an unreasonable and isolated or unimportant minority.[12] This would definitely change the character of COPUOS. Moreover, it seems rather difficult to me to determine how one is to decide whether a minority is "unreasonable and unimportant".
It is clear, however, that the working method of COPUOS is not as effective and efficient as it was in the past. The drafting of the principles on Remote Sensing, which has been

---

[9] *Cf.* Diederiks-Verschoor, *Global Use and Regulation of Space Activities,* in: Space Activities and Implications: Where From and Where To at the Treshold of the 80's, 152 (Proceedings, Mc Gill University 1980): "When we speak about global use, there are some limitations. The use is hampered by three main areas: (a) Consent, or a political limitation; (b) Finance, or an economical limitation; (c) Technology, or a scientific limitation".

[10] Böckstiegel, *op. cit.*, at 309.

[11] Jericho & McCracken, *Space Law: is it the Last Legal Frontier?* 51 Journal of Air Law and Commerce 800 (1986).

[12] Jasentuliyana, *Treaty Law and Outer Space: can the United Nations play an Effective Role?* XI Annals of Air and Space Law 224 (1986). *See also* Christol, *supra* note 4, at 848: "Past success with the consensus process does not necessarily mean that acceptable agreements may not result from other procedures. Yet, departures from tested processes (...) would necessarily have to be carefully considered". *Also,* Matte, *supra* note 6, at 200: "(...) the only possible result of consensus can be the lowest possible denominator of unanimous agreement between participating states. (...) A generally acceptable compromise often seems preferable to a majority decision which is unacceptable to a minority of states, especially where those states are space powers".

extremely time-consuming, may serve as an illustration. Representatives are no longer as specialised and as devoted as they were at the beginning of COPUOS' existence. This is due mainly to the fact that they often have to perform several functions at the same time and cannot be completely up-to-date on the latest developments in the field of space law. Legal progress on the whole has thus slowed down, whereas technological developments seem to keep accelerating at an amazing speed. The law can hardly keep pace with the requirements imposed upon it by space technology. The anticipatory treaty-making process seems to belong to the past.

4. THE FUTURE

First and foremost, the anticipatory character of space law making has to be recovered, or at least the lawmaking must keep up with technological developments and not run behind it. If this cannot be realised, technological progress will definitely be hampered. After all, as was mentioned above, commercial enterprise will be reluctant to engage in space technology if the legal consequences of such activity cannot be calculated in advance. The financial risks are simply too large. It is therefore necessary to reassume the "science fiction" attitude of some thirty years ago. Imagination combined with practicality must be the starting point. The law has to be anticipated, but it must also be more specific to correspond with the complex situations and interrelations of today (and tomorrow). The generalities of the past do not respond to the realities of today. Thus, two elements have to be ensured: (a) anticipation and (b) specification.

a. Anticipation

(i) Actors

With regard to the anticipatory character of law-making, it has to be kept in mind that the commercialisation of space activities will certainly increase. Thus, the law has to recognise and to distinguish between public and private *actors*. This involves a reconsideration of questions of liability and responsibility, and of registration (and thus nationality/ ownership).

(ii) Form

Due regard must also be given to the fact that the "realisation of the benefits process" will become more and more important. Thus, increasing numbers of states will seek to be involved in the law-making process to ensure their "national" interests. This will involve ever longer debates and less specialised representatives.

Even if the present author fully recognises the right of all states to have their say, the risk of the predominance of political considerations and relations is apparent. It might therefore be necessary to reconsider the *form* of law-making. Up till now, space agreements have been concluded in the form of international UN Treaties. Although the value of a multilateral treaty is recognised, other possibilities exist, such as recommendations, resolutions and other multilateral, regional, or even bilateral instruments. These involve less complex politics, and agreement may be easier to reach. Moreover, such instruments can always be transformed into treaties at a later date.[13]

(iii) Forum

Connected to the question of the form of the law, is the question in which *forum* that law should be framed. As an alternative to the United Nations, which has been used up till now, it might be advisable to try and reach agreement within specialised universal organisations (*e.g.* the ITU), smaller, regional or bilateral bodies, or groups consisting only of the two actors themselves, whether states or multilateral corporations.[14] These fora would, like COPUOS, have to involve legal and technological experts as well as politicians to ensure that the agreements reached can be implemented at all levels. One can, of course, argue that the value of regional and bilateral agreements is limited because they do not bind the whole community of states, while the subject is of universal interest. Nevertheless, I believe that it might set an example, and as such serve as a model and create precedents. Naturally, this does not mean that, in addition, there is no need at all to have certain multilateral or universal instruments and rules.

(iv) Topics

Finally, it is important to anticipate the *topics* that have to be dealt with by future space law. It is already possible to name certain areas which will be explored and exploited in the future. These include: nuclear power sources, manned space stations, solar power satellites and material processing in outer space. These topics all involve specific features which have to be regulated by law. One can, for instance, think of protection from radiation, of the legal status of international spacecraft and crew, of the effect of microwave exposures on human life and the environment, of property rights and of the disposal of materials in outer space.

b. Specification

When "anticipation" has been ensured, the *content* of future law has to be considered. The law must become far more specific in its content. Not only because space activities are

[13] "One cannot help but remarking that the bilateral agreement promises to be the potentially major vehicle for international cooperation in space activities. Bilateral agreements have invariably led to the development of principles of international law relating to space, which have later become embodied in multilateral treaties", Wadegaonkar, *op. cit.*, at 9.

[14] For an extensive discussion of regional and bilateral cooperation in space acitivities, *see* E.R.C. van Bogaert, *Aspects of Space Law* 264-81 (1986).

becoming more and more varied, but also because the "players" are growing in number. Broad principles no longer suffice, and if they have to be incorporated in the law, their meaning has to be clarified. I believe that this cannot be left to the entities that have to *apply* the law.

Specificity will be promoted by the establishment of *different legal regimes* for each of the diverse activities concerning outer space. Thus, a separate legal regime should be established for each of the following activities:

(i) activities on earth which are aimed from earth at outer space, such as the launching of "space objects";

(ii) activities which take place solely within outer space, such as the operation of manned space stations (space-oriented activities);

(iii) activities in outer space which are aimed from outer space at the earth, such as remote sensing, telecommunications, or DBS (earth-oriented activities); and

(iv) activities taking place in the air-space which are necessary to deploy the activities mentioned under (i), (ii) and (iii).

Of course, in practice, interrelations between these regimes exist. For example, the operation of a space station (ii) cannot become effective before the component parts of the station have been transported to their location by a space object (i) through the air-space (iv). Likewise, a space object may be launched (i) with the objective of putting a telecommunications satellite into orbit (iii), again by means of the air-space (iv).

Nevertheless, it will be beneficial to apply different legal rules to different activities. Each has its own specific characteristics and implications. The following examples demonstrate the different problems that may arise:

The launching of a space vehicle may create important risks for the territory of the launching state, or even for that of other states if the launching fails and the vehicle causes damage on the earth's surface.

The operation of a manned space station provides a different example. The legal status of international spacecraft and crews has to be determined. Thus, questions of private international law have to be solved; the order and terms of personnel selection, training and formation of international crews have to be determined; jurisdiction and control matters need to be settled and the legal protection of astronauts' lives and health must be ensured. Although Article 8 of the Outer Space Treaty establishes that the state of registry shall retain jurisdiction and control over the object and its personnel, it applies only to the situation where the object is in outer space; further regulation is needed for the situation where the object passes through the air space of foreign states and for the situation where the object has to make an emergency landing on foreign territory.[15]

If a telecommunications satellite of another state is to be put into orbit, it seems reasonable to transfer liability to that state once the satellite successfully reaches its orbit. For, the launching state has nothing to do with, nor can it exercise any influence whatsoever over, the operation of the satellite in orbit. It might even be used for non-peaceful activities. Under present law, the launching state will nonetheless be held responsible (and liable) for such activities. This is why it seems to me that after the putting into orbit of a space object, regime (i) should be replaced by regime (iii). Likewise, remote sensing has its own specific implications for sensed states; a specific regime should be created to govern these consequences, taking into consideration such questions as sovereignty over natural resources, intervention in domestic affairs, as well as the fundamental freedom to seek, receive and impart information.

It is submitted that all *earth-oriented* space-activities (*e.g.* DBS or remote sensing) should *also* be governed by general international law (*lex generalis*), instead of *just* international space law (*lex specialis*).[16] This does not, of course, exclude the need to establish certain new rules, in order to keep pace with technology.

Finally, the right to free transit through foreign air-space should be codified, for example, in cooperation with ICAO. One might argue that such "right of overflight" has never been contested since numerous satellites have been put into orbit without opposition by the "overflown states", and that this "tacit consent" has resulted in acquiescence by the community of states.[17] On the other hand, the relatively short period of time involved here may be an obstacle to the possible existence of a rule of customary international law.[18] It is therefore still necessary to codify this rule in a legal instrument.

---

[15] *Cf.* Vereshchetin, *The Legal Status of International Space Crews*, III Annals of Air and Space Law 544 (1978); *see also* Gorove, *Legal Aspects of International Space Flight*, *ibid*., at 409.

[16] *Cf.* Wassenbergh, *Speculations on the Law governing Space Resources*, V Annals of Air and Space Law 613 (1980); *see also ibid*., at 617: "Near-earth orbit activities, for instance, although governed by space law, may have a direct relevance for environmental laws on earth"; *and* similarly, Vereshchetin, *On the Principle of State Sovereignty in International Space Law*, II Annals of Air and Space Law 433 (1977): "When space activities directly concern foreign states' territories, the principle of respect for state sovereignty requires added significance. Consequently, those uses of outer space which make themselves felt on the Earth are the most important in terms of legal regulation."

[17] Wadegaonkar, *op. cit*., at 4.

[18] *See* van Bogaert, *op. cit*., at 19-21; "As the law of outer space is, however, closely bound to the rapidity of technological development, the use of custom will be more limited than in other branches of international law". However, Prof. B. Cheng does not think that a short lapse of time precludes the formulation of customary space law; he speaks of "instant customary law", *see* V Indian Journal of International Law (1965).

5. CONCLUSION

Space activities are growing in complexity. Many legal issues are involved, and definition and regulation are needed. It is no longer feasible to regulate these new issues under one single legal regime. It is therefore proposed that:

(1) specific regimes should be established for specific activities;

(2) the need for these regimes must be anticipated; and finally

(3) their formulation must be specific.

It is hoped that such a structure may be of use for space law experts as a guide in the future development of the law of outer space.

Chapter Two

Commercial Exploitation of Outer Space

THE COMMERCIAL EXPLOITATION OF MINERAL RESOURCES IN OUTER SPACE

Milton L. Smith *

1. INTRODUCTION

The return of mankind to the Moon is inevitable. Moreover, our exploration of the solar system is also sure to follow the dreams of many. As we venture into these regions, we will need to use the mineral resources that we find on celestial bodies. We already know that many of the minerals used on earth are available on the Moon.[1] As the title indicates, this article concentrates on one particular use for outer space mineral resources, their exploitation on a *commercial* basis.

Commercial activities may take various forms. Space-related commercial activities generally involve private industry, government, or both together. Regardless of their form, commercial ventures are always motivated by a quest for profit.
In addressing commercial exploitation, this article ignores the actor(s) and concentrates on the motivation -- to make a reasonable profit on the investment placed at risk. Many believe it will be possible to make such a profit from mineral resources in outer space if a suitable legal regime is established.

For a legal regime to be suitable for commercial exploitation of mineral resources in outer space, it must protect investments and permit orderly exploration and recovery. On earth, nations routinely have legal regimes granting such protection through deeds, registration systems, leases and other contracts. The regime must protect *exclusive* rights to a specified area, for a particular purpose (extraction of a mineral), for a certain period of time. Although the regime must protect against harmful interference by others, it does not have to grant title. Very often, a mining venture will not have title to the area being mined. What the venture must have is a "miner's right" of use or usufruct.[2] This is a right to use the property of another and take the fruits. Furthermore, for a legal regime to be considered suitable for commercial exploitation in outer space, it must be expected to remain stable during the course of the venture.

---

* Director of Space and International Law, Air Force Space Command, Colorado Springs, CO. B.S., USAF Academy; J.D., George Washington Univ.; LL.M., Mc Gill Univ., Institute of Air and Space Law (D.C.L. Candidate).
The opinions expressed in this article are solely those of the author and do not necessarily represent the official views or policies of any agency of the US Government.

[1] *See* Staff of Senate Comm. on Commerce, Science, and Transportation, 96th Cong., 2d Sess., Agreement Governing the Activities of States on the Moon and Other Celestial Bodies, 281 (Committee Print 1980) [hereinafter Committee Print].

[2] *See* Goldie, *Title and Use (and Usufruct) -- an Ancient Distinction Too Oft Forgot*, 79 AJIL 689 (1985).

This article examines the suitability of the two legal regimes applicable to the commercial exploitation of mineral resources in outer space: the Outer Space Treaty[3] and the Moon Agreement.[4] It then draws conclusions and makes recommendations. Although this article occasionally focuses on the Moon, its reasoning and substance is generally applicable to any celestial body in our solar system, since the same legal principles govern all these areas.

2. THE OUTER SPACE TREATY

The Outer Space Treaty is the "Magna Charta" of space law. It establishes broad, general principles for the use and exploration of outer space. Because it uses very general terms, it is subject to varying interpretations. In spite of its somewhat ambiguous nature, it has over ninety Parties, including all of the space powers. Consequently, its importance cannot be overlooked.

In general, the Outer Space Treaty establishes a legal regime that is favourable to commercial activities in space. It implicitly recognises the legitimacy of activities by private enterprise in outer space, although nations bear responsibility and liability for the space activities of their non-governmental agencies.[5] Furthermore, space activities must be conducted with due regard to the corresponding interests of other Parties, and if an activity may cause harmful interference with the outer space activities of other Parties, consultation must occur before the activity may proceed.[6]

While natural resources are not specifically addressed in the Outer Space Treaty, several of its provisions are relevant to the exploitation of resources in outer space. Article I establishes that the exploration and use of outer space shall be conducted "for the benefit and in the interests of all countries . . . and shall be the province of all mankind".[7] This "common interests" clause must not be confused with the "common heritage of mankind" concept discussed *infra*.[8] It imposes no requirement for direct sharing of benefits in any specific manner, but requires only that space activities be beneficial in a very general

---

[3] Treaty on Principles Governing the Activities of States in the Exploration and Use of Outer Space Including the Moon and Other Celestial Bodies, January 27, 1967, 18 U.S.T. 2410, T.I.A.S. No. 6347, 610 U.N.T.S. 205 (entered into force October 10, 1967) (hereinafter the Outer Space Treaty).

[4] Agreement Governing the Activities of States on the Moon and Other Celestial Bodies, December 5, 1979, U.N. Doc. A/RES/34/68, 18 ILM 1434 (hereinafter the Moon Agreement).

[5] Outer Space Treaty, *supra* note 3, Articles 6 & 7.

[6] *Id.*, Article 9.

[7] *Id.*, Article 1.

[8] *See infra* notes 30 - 33 and accompanying text.

sense.[9] History has shown that practically every nation has benefited in some manner from the exploration and use of space. These benefits include the availability of weather and other remote sensing information from satellites, access to international and domestic telecommunication satellites, and increased knowledge about our universe.[10] All of these benefits have been realised by developing countries without their risk of investment capital.

Article I also establishes the principle of the freedom of exploration and use of outer space. Some commentators question whether the term "use" includes all activities, particularly the exploitation of natural resources. The weight of authority, however, considers the terms exploration and use to be general terms covering all activities in outer space. The negotiating history of Article I establishes that it "encompasses the exploration, use, and exploitation of both the space environment and the resources located in that spatial area".[11] Additionally, the issue of whether the Moon Agreement placed a moratorium on the exploitation of lunar resources would have never surfaced unless that exploitation was permitted by the Outer Space Treaty.[12]

Article II of the treaty establishes that outer space is "not subject to national appropriation by claim of sovereignty, by means of use or occupation, or by any other means".[13] The purpose of the non-appropriation clause was to implement the freedom of use principle. Appropriation is inconsistent with freedom of use. This clause also furthers the common interests provision since appropriation of an area might only benefit the appropriator.

A few authorities consider that the non-appropriation clause applies only to nations. They assert that an individual, private association or international organisation may lawfully appropriate any part of outer space.[14] This literal interpretation of the non-appropriation clause goes too far. The Outer Space Treaty recognises the legal personality of international organisations.[15] It also provides that each nation is responsible for the space activities of its

---

[9] Gorove, *Implications of International Space Law for Private Enterprise*, 7 Annals Air & Space L. 319, 321 (1982). But *see* N. Matte, *Aerospace Law: Telecommunications Satellites* 78 (1982) ("there is a basic obligation that falls upon States carrying out space activities to be responsive to the interests of developing countries and to provide for some method of distributing the benefits derived from such activities.").

[10] For example, to further world knowledge about the Moon, NASA has provided lunar sample materials to scientists in over twenty nations with a requirement that results of their analysis be published. Committee Print, *supra* note 1, at 338.

[11] *See* C. Christol, *The Modern International Law of Outer Space* 39 (1982).

[12] For discussion of the moratorium issue, *see infra* notes 36 - 37 and accompanying text.

[13] Outer Space Treaty, *supra* note 3, Article 2.

[14] *See* Gorove, *Interpreting Article II of the Outer Space Treaty*, 37 Fordham L. R. 349, 351 (1969).

[15] *See* Outer Space Treaty, *supra* note 3, Articles 6 & 13.

non-governmental entities (*i.e.* individuals and corporations).[16] The only interpretation consistent with the treaty's purposes of assuring freedom of use, and use in the common interest, is that the prohibition on appropriation applies to all entities, and not solely to nations.[17]

Even given this broad applicability, the issue of what activities (other than an outright claim of sovereignty) would constitute an appropriation, raises difficult questions. The mere act of mining resources, in itself, is not an appropriation of the area actively being mined. It is an exercise of freedom of use. It also seems clear, however, that a claim to *title* over an area would amount to appropriation. Titles are granted by sovereign entities. A usufructuary claim of exclusive rights to exploit certain mineral resources in a specified area amounts to more than simply mining one area, but it is less than a claim of title. The crucial issue regarding commercial exploitation of outer space minerals is whether this type of a usufructuary claim would constitute an appropriation of the area claimed.

One author has concluded that the non-appropriation clause prevents the assertion of exclusive claims over both outer space areas and outer space resources.[18] If this conclusion applies only to resources *in place*, then it would not rule out a usufructuary claim to the fruits of mining. It appears that the author's conclusion, however, was meant to apply to resources in general; it would rule out any exclusive claim "by all prospective explorers, exploiters, and users".[19] This position is based upon a rule of inclusivity of use as opposed to exclusivity of use. The author argues that only inclusive uses are permitted -- "the present rule is to share and not to monopolise no matter by whom or by what means such claims may be asserted".[20] Use of the word "present" belies a weakness in this argument. The Outer Space Treaty is being interpreted in the light of subsequent events. Indeed, several statements in the article demonstrate that this interpretation of the non-appropriation clause comes not from the Outer Space Treaty, but rather from the subsequent Moon Agreement, the United Nations Convention on the Law of the Sea[21], and the common heritage of mankind concept.[22] Those subsequent developments, which are

---

16 *Id.*, Article 6.

17 Christol asserts that the negotiating history of Article 2 indicates that the "by any other means" limitation of the non-appropriation clause extends the prohibition against national appropriation to other entities. Christol, *Article 2 of the Principles Treaty Revisited*, 9 Annals of Air & Space L. 217, 263 (1984).

18 *Id.*, at 241.

19 *Id.*

20 *Id.*, at 263.

21 United Nations Convention on the Law of the Sea, U.N. Doc.A/Conf. 62/122 (October 7, 1982).

22 For example, the author states that: "In seeking to understand the spirit of the [Outer Space] Treaty, ...it is proper to inquire if the terminology of Article 2 is compatible with the thesis - increasingly in

not subscribed to by any of the space powers, should not influence the interpretation of the Outer Space Treaty.

A strong argument can be made that a usufructuary claim of exclusive rights to exploit certain minerals within a reasonably limited area of outer space would not constitute appropriation. The Outer Space Treaty permits commercial ventures in outer space, and mining activities in outer space are a valid exercise of freedom of use. Since commercial mining requires exclusive claims to reasonably limited areas, it can be argued that such claims are also a valid exercise of freedom of use. Without such claims there could be no such use. Furthermore, appropriation generally requires the taking of property for exclusive use with a sense of permanence and with an intent to appropriate.[23] Claims which were limited in time to only that period reasonably necessary for efficient and effective commercial mining, and which expressly disavowed any intent to appropriate, would not constitute such appropriation.

The freedom of use clause also provides some hurdles to the establishment of exclusive mining claims in outer space. All states have freedom of use, but some uses, by their nature, must be exclusive. For example, if France were to construct a lunar scientific base consisting of buildings covering two acres, those two acres would be unavailable for use by other nations. Although other nations would be able to visit the base on a basis of reciprocity, they would be obliged to avoid interference with the normal operations of the facility.[24] The legitimacy of such uses should depend upon their reasonableness.

As with the freedoms of the high seas[25], the freedoms of use of outer space must be exercised with regard to the interests of other states so that their exercise of such freedoms is not unreasonably denied. Otherwise, there would be no meaning to the freedom of use provision. The reasonableness of an exclusive claim for mining an area of outer space would depend upon the particular facts. Pertinent questions would include the geographical

---

vogue in recent years - calling for inclusive access to the free and equal use of common areas and the resources of such areas".

* * *

The policy judgments of the members of the world community in general, while supportive of the *res communis* principle, have been augmented by the Common Heritage of Mankind principle as set out in the Moon Agreement and the 1982 Law of the Sea Convention. These new conditions will necessarily have an impact on the interpretation to be accorded to the [Outer Space] Treaty, including Article 2. Christol, *supra* note 17, at 244 V (emphasis supplied).

23 *See* Gorove, *supra* note 14, at 352; Christol, *The Geostationary Orbital Position as a Natural Resource of the Space Environment*, 26 Netherlands International L.R. 5, 10 (1979).

24 Outer Space Treaty, *supra* note 3, Article 12.

25 *See* generally I. Brownlie, *Principles of Public International Law* 238-240 (1979).

extent of the claim, its duration, and whether the minerals being mined were available at other locations.

Given the disenchantment of developing countries with the principle of "first come, first served", it is likely that objections to any exclusive claims in outer space would be raised. Objections by developing countries could cause political problems, but it is objections by developed nations with a foreseeable capability to infringe upon claimed areas that would be of more practical importance to commercial mining ventures. The potential for such objections must be resolved before commercial ventures will entertain the possibility of mining in outer space.

In summary, mining is a permissible exercise of the freedom of use guaranteed by the Outer Space Treaty. Both the non-appropriation and the freedom of use provisions, however, raise potential problems for exclusive claims in outer space. The language of the Outer Space Treaty is so broad and general that these provisions are susceptible to varying interpretations. Since disagreement on these issues exists, the Outer Space Treaty, of itself, cannot provide a satisfactory legal regime for the commercial exploitation of minerals.

3. THE MOON AGREEMENT

The Moon Agreement emerged from the United Nations in 1979, after eight years of discussion. Five nations, none of which are space powers, have ratified the Agreement and it became effective between those five in 1984. This Agreement applies to the Moon and all other celestial bodies in our solar system except for Earth. Many of its provisions are taken almost directly from the Outer Space Treaty. Aside from provisions relating to the exploitation of natural resources, the Agreement mainly reaffirms or slightly expands existing space law in a manner that is irrelevant to this inquiry. The provisions regarding natural resources, however, are quite significant and far reaching.

The Moon Agreement acknowledges that exploitation of natural resources is, in general, a legitimate use of outer space. During scientific investigation, natural resources may be collected and removed from the Moon, or used locally for mission support.[26] Exploitation of resources on a commercial basis is also envisaged.

The key section of the Moon Agreement with regard to commercial exploitation of natural resources is Article XI. This Article reiterates the principle that the Moon is not subject to national appropriation, and it addresses the issue of property rights.
Equipment, installations, *etc.*, may be placed on the Moon and moved freely, but their location does not create any rights of ownership to the area at which they are located.[27]

[26] Moon Agreement, *supra* note 4, Article 6.

[27] *Id.*, Article 11 (3).

Additionally, property rights cannot be established over the surface or subsurface of the Moon, nor over natural resources "in place".[28] Use of the phrase "in place" is critical. It permits the establishment of property rights over natural resources that have been extracted.[29] This coincides with the usufructuary nature of mining. By far the most important aspect of Article XI, however, is its declaration that the Moon and its natural resources are the common heritage of mankind (CHM). The concept of the CHM has been the subject of a great deal of literature.[30] Developing countries have frequently asserted that the CHM applies to all international common resources including those of the deep seabed, Antarctica, the Geostationary Satellite Orbit and the radio frequency spectrum (the orbit/spectrum resource), as well as to celestial bodies. Nevertheless, both the definition of the CHM and its status in international law are debatable.

Two primary theories regarding the CHM have been advocated. One theory holds that the CHM establishes common ownership, and that all countries are entitled to substantive property rights over the natural resources of an area that is the CHM.[31] In essence, this type of CHM regime would secure economic benefits for developing countries which may have cost them nothing. It is not surprising that many of the proponents of this theory are from developing nations. The other theory regarding the CHM is quite different. It considers that the above theory of the CHM is "foreign to existing international law and may even come into conflict with existing rules of international law".[32]

---

28 *Id.*

29 This interpretation is verified by the negotiating history of the phrase. *See* Menter, *Commercial Space Activities Under The Moon Treaty*, Proceedings of the 23rd Colloquium on the Law of Outer Space 35, 39 (1981).

30 *See, e.g.*, Dupuy, *The Notion of the Common Heritage of Mankind Applied to the Seabed*, 8 Annals of Air & Space L. 347 (1983); Matte, *Limited Aerospace Natural Resources and their Regulation*, 7 Annals of Air & Space L. 379 (1982); Williams, *The Exploitation and Use of Natural Resources in the New Law of the Sea and the Law of Outer Space*, Proceedings of the 29th Colloquium on the Law of Outer Space 198 (1987).

31 One oft quoted proponent of the CHM as it relates to the law of the sea has stated that: "The common heritage of mankind is the common property of mankind. The commonness of the "common heritage" is a commonness of ownership and benefit. The minerals are owned in common by your country and mine, and by all the rest as well. . . If you touch the nodules at the bottom of the sea, you touch my property. If you take them away, you take away my property". Pinto, statement, in *Alternatives in Deepsea Mining* 13 (S. Allen & J. Craven, editors, 1979).
Proponents of this school of thought have enumerated certain elements which they contend establish a CHM legal regime. These elements typically include prohibiting appropriation of any part of the area; establishing an international regime which will exert control over the area; and providing an "equitable sharing" of the benefits derived from the area, as determined by the controlling regime. *See* Christol, *supra* note 11, at 286; Fleming, DuCharme, Jakhu & Longman, *State Sovereignty and the Effective Management of a Shared Universal Resource: Observations Drawn From Examining Developments in the International Regulation of Radiocommunication*, 10 Annals of Air & Space L. 327, 330 (1985).

32 Wassenbergh, *Speculations on the Law governing Space Resources*, 5 Annals of Air & Space L. 611, 621 (1980).

Instead, it holds that the CHM is simply a continuation of the general concepts of *res communis* and the common interests clause of the1967 Outer Space Treaty.[33]

The Moon Agreement is worded broadly enough to permit varying definitions of its CHM concept. The CHM concept of the Moon Agreement ultimately is to find its expression from within the provisions of the Agreement itself when an international regime is established. The Agreement calls for Parties to "undertake to establish" this international regime when exploitation "is about to become feasible".[34] The Agreement does not define the details and procedures of the regime, but it does set out the main purposes. Those purposes include the orderly and safe development of natural resources, their rational management, and expansion of opportunities for their use. The regime is also to provide for an "equitable sharing" by all Parties in the benefits derived from the natural resources. In this sharing, two groups are to be given special consideration: developing countries, and countries that contributed in some fashion to the exploration of the Moon.[35] Apart from these main purposes, little is known about the particular CHM concept of the Moon Agreement.

The present uncertainty surrounding the Moon Agreement's CHM provisions raises serious doubts about the suitability of this Agreement as a legal regime for the commercial exploitation of outer space resources. Some have even questioned whether commercial exploitation may legally commence under the Moon Agreement before the international regime that it calls for is established. One of the first issues raised after the Agreement was opened for signature was whether its call for establishment of an international regime when exploitation "is about to become feasible"[36] created a moratorium on commercial exploitation of natural resources pending establishment of the regime. The moratorium issue has been thoroughly examined in the literature. Most agree that the Agreement was not intended to create a moratorium. That conclusion is based primarily on the Agreement's negotiating history.[37] Notwithstanding this conclusion, the language of the Agreement itself does not clearly rule out a moratorium, and this produces another degree of uncertainty.

---

[33] *See* Finch & Moore, *The 1979 Moon Treaty Encourages Space Development*, Proceedings of the 23rd Colloquium on the Law of Outer Space 13, 14 (1981).

[34] Moon Agreement, *supra* note 4, Article 11 (5).

[35] *Id.*, Article 11 (7).

[36] *Id.*, Article 11 (5).

[37] The negotiating history of the Treaty within COPUOS and the UN General Assembly "confirm that no moratorium is intended. Specific proposals for a moratorium in the course of the negotiations failed to obtain the required consensus". Menter, *Commercial Space Activities Under the Moon Treaty*, Proceedings of the 23rd Colloquium on the Law of Outer Space 35, 40 (1981); *see also* Finch & Moore, *supra* note 33, at 15; Committee Print *supra* note 1, at 318-324.

Apart from the moratorium issue, the Agreement presents several other problems for commercial enterprise. As discussed previously, the general meaning of the CHM is a matter of debate, and within the Moon Agreement it is undefined and subject to varying interpretations. Nevertheless, the Moon Agreement clearly declares that the Moon and its natural resources are the CHM. If the CHM amounts to common property, as developing countries assert, there may be legal ramifications to the taking of CHM mineral resources without permission of other "owners", and quite possibly over their objection. Additionally, exploitation of natural resources must provide the "equitable sharing" called for in Article XI even if that exploitation occurs before an international regime is established.[38] Opinions are likely to differ regarding what is "equitable". Another problem is that if commercial exploitation commenced and then an international regime was established, it is unclear how existing operations would be affected by the regime. Finally, nothing in the Moon Agreement specifically legitimises exclusive claims over areas to be explored or exploited.[39]

Commercial exploitation of the Moon's natural resources cannot be undertaken until uncertainty is resolved regarding the above issues. Commercial operations require a stable legal environment. Some authorities believe that these uncertainties can be adequately resolved by ratifying the Moon Agreement with specific understandings.[40] They also assert that nations ratifying the Moon Agreement are not bound to accept the international regime that might later be established to manage the Moon's resources. Notwithstanding these points, the Moon Agreement as it currently stands does not provide sufficient stability for commercial exploitation to commence. "[L]arge capital investments cannot be made by free enterprise without clear legal guidelines that allow commercial operations to exploit space resources for a profit."[41] Significantly, the Report of the National Commission on Space concluded that "the Treaty's provisions for the use of natural resources on other celestial bodies suggest a collectivised international regime analogous to the seabed mining regime in the Law of the Sea Treaty. Such a regime could seriously inhibit American enterprise in space".[42] Thus, although nothing in the Moon Agreement is incompatible with the

---

38 The Treaty provides that "all the activities with respect to the natural resources of the moon shall be carried out in a manner compatible with the purposes specified in paragraph 7 . . . ". Moon Agreement, *supra* note 4, Article 11 (8). Paragraph 7 includes the "equitable sharing" requirement. *Id.*, Article 11 (7).

39 One article could be interpreted to prohibit exclusive claims. Article 9 provides that lunar stations "shall use only that area which is required for the needs of the station . . ." and that stations shall not "impede the free access to all areas of the moon . . . .". *Id.*, Article 9 (1) & (2). It could be argued, however, that since exclusive claims are necessary to commercial exploitation, therefore, such claims are "required" for the needs of a station undertaking commercial exploitation.

40 The American Bar Association, after much debate, concluded that the Moon Agreement could be ratified with certain understandings.

41 Dula, *Free Enterprise and the Proposed Moon Treaty*, Hous. J.Int'l L. 3, 24 (1979).

42 The Report of the National Commission on Space 166 (1986).

commercial exploitation of mineral resources, it does not provide a satisfactory legal regime for such exploitation.

4. CONCLUSIONS AND RECOMMENDATIONS

Neither the Outer Space Treaty nor the Moon Agreement provides a stable legal environment clearly recognising the validity of exclusive claims to exploit mineral resources. Therefore, neither treaty establishes a suitable legal regime for commercial exploitation. However, two paths to a suitable legal regime are available.

One path is to work through the United Nations for agreement on establishing an international regime to govern the exploitation of mineral resources in outer space. This new agreement could be in the form of a supplement, or protocol, to the Moon Agreement; perhaps the agreement it envisages in establishing an international regime.[43] If associated with the Moon Agreement, this agreement would have to resolve the numerous issues raised by the Agreement in a manner that would accommodate commercial enterprise. The CHM concept would have to be defined in an acceptable manner. "Equitable sharing" would need to be defined to permit recovery of investment and protect a reasonable profit before any sharing of benefits would be required. Exclusive claims would have to be legitimised by the regime. Finally, a commercially suitable international regime would have to be established; many models, such as INTELSAT and INMARSAT, have been suggested for such a regime.[44] On the other hand, this new agreement could be approached as another of the various international agreements supplementing the Outer Space Treaty. The Moon Agreement would be ignored, and probably relegated to an arcane position in the history of space law.

The other path to a commercially suitable legal regime is for the space powers potentially capable of exploiting outer space mineral resources to work outside of the United Nations and secure an agreement among themselves. In this agreement, each Party would have to recognise the validity of exclusive claims filed by any other Party. Such an agreement already exists among eight developed nations regarding the mining of the deep seabed under the high seas.[45] It could serve as a model for an agreement on exploiting mineral resources in outer space.

---

[43] *See supra* notes 34 - 35 and accompanying text.

[44] *See* Galloway, *Issues in Implementing the Agreement Governing the Activities of States on the Moon and Other Celestial Bodies*, Proceedings of the 23rd Colloquium on the Law of Outer Space 19, 22 (1981); Note, *Extraterrestrial Law on the Final Frontier: A Regime to Govern the Development of Celestial Body Resources*, 71 Geo. L.J. 1427 (1983).

[45] *See* Provisional Understanding Regarding Deep Seabed Mining, done at Geneva, August 3, 1984, reprinted in 23 ILM 1354 (1984). All Parties to this agreement have compatible domestic legislation modeled after the United States' Deep Seabed Hard Mineral Resources Act, 30 USC 1401 *et seq.* (1980).

Such a regime would be fully compatible with the Outer Space Treaty. In essence, Parties to such an agreement would simply be limiting, on a reciprocal basis, an aspect of their freedom to use outer space. They would limit their freedom, for a certain period of time, to exploit outer space mineral resources in areas already claimed by other Parties to the agreement. The principle that states may surrender certain aspects of their freedom to use outer space is well established. The International Telecommunication Union Convention and Radio Regulations place significant limits on the freedom of states to use the orbit/spectrum resource.

If the Parties to such an agreement included the key space powers, the protection provided for exclusive claims should be sufficient for commercial exploitation. Whether such agreements will be possible for outer space activities is a matter of conjecture. Successful initiation and operation of the international space station may shed light on this issue, as will the future of deep seabed mining.

Unless one of these paths is followed, commercial exploitation of outer space mineral resources is very unlikely to occur. Exploitation may be undertaken by governments, perhaps even in conjunction with private industry, but it would not be on a commercial basis. Of the two paths, the first is preferable because it would further international harmony and community. Unfortunately, there is little potential for a suitable international agreement to emerge from the United Nations given the current political climate. Developing countries seem intent on pursuing the New International Economic Order and the common heritage of mankind, as defined by them. If such a CHM regime had been applicable during the exploration of Earth, this author doubts that Columbus would have ever received financial backing.

This is not to say that we should revert back to the days of discovery, occupation, and claims of sovereignty. It is to say that one of the prime motivations behind costly exploration has always been the potential of commercial exploitation, and that exploitation of outer space should be permitted on a commercial basis. Nor is it to say that developed nations who may be able to engage in such commercial exploitation have no obligation to share the benefits with developing countries. One of the gravest problems facing our world is the large disparity between the rich and the poor, the haves and the have nots. This disparity must be overcome. Nevertheless, if the common heritage of mankind is viewed as *a sine qua non* for resolving this disparity, it may serve only to slow the exploration and exploitation that, over time, may benefit the entire world.

Nations undertaking the large investment to exploit resources of outer space should share the benefits with the remainder of the world. Those nations, however, should be the ones to determine when and how those benefits are shared.

TOWARD A REGULATORY REGIME FOR COMPETITION IN SPACE TRANSPORT

Huang Jiefang*

1. INTRODUCTION

Commercial space transport - the carriage of goods and/or persons for remuneration between one point on the earth and a point, an orbit or a trajectory in outer space - has undergone both qualitative improvement and quantitative expansion. Notwithstanding tragic accidents such as the explosion of the "Challenger" space shuttle and the failures of some expendable launch vehicles (ELV's), the technical performance of space transport, either by reusable or expendable launch vehicles, has improved both in terms of payload capability and the precision of propulsion and orbit control systems. Corresponding to these technological developments, there has also been a noticeable increase in the number of entities participating in commercial space transport. The previous monopoly for launching services held by the United States was brought to an end when Arianespace of the European Space Agency (ESA) emerged as a second commercial launching power. This duopoly was turned into an oligopoly when China became a third competitor in commercial space transport by commercialising its Long March 2 and Long March 3 launch vehicles. The continuing increase of competitors in the space transport market will add more complexity to the legal relationships between carriers and their customers and between the carriers themselves.

This is reminiscent of the development of maritime transport in the 19th century and air transport in this century. These developments illustrate an important point. When a mode of transportation moves from its experimental period to a mature, multi-carriers stage, apart from the legal framework regulating the carrier - customer relationship, it is necessary to formulate a set of rules of conduct to regulate the inter-carrier relationship. In the late 19th century, when trans-oceanic shipping services became widespread after the introduction of the steamship, the *laissez faire* approach to the inter-carrier relationship turned out to be inadequate for the growing shipping industry. In order to prevent "ruinous competition", major shipping companies started to organise liner conferences. This trade association has the major function of regulating the entry and exit of shipping lines on the route, allocating the share of trade and determining the rates of shipping service.[1] The rapid expansion of international aviation and the heated competition among airlines in the post-Second World War period also had a similar result. It gave rise to numerous worldwide, regional and

---

* LL.B. (Wuhan University, China), LL.M. (Institute of Air and Space Law, McGill University, Canada), D.C.L. Candidate (McGill University). Member of the International Institute of Space Law. The view expressed in this article is that of the author and does not necessarily represent the view of the organisation to which he is associated.

[1] Bennathan & Walters, *Shipping Conference: An Economic Analysis*, 4 Journal of Maritime Law and Commerce 93 (1972).

bilateral agreements, as well as to international organisations which were designed, and continue today to regulate the grant of the freedom of flight, the determination of capacity and the setting of tariffs.[2]

The development of space transport in many ways resembles that of civil aviation and, to a smaller extent, that of the shipping industry. At the first stage, many prefer to regard space transport capability as a source of national pride and political prestige. In the long run, however, economic considerations will also come into play and competition for economic benefit will occur. When space travel becomes a routine and popular practice and when competition among carriers is intensified in future, one may wonder whether an international regime should be established in order to resolve legal issues concerning transit and traffic rights, capacity control and price determination. The present inquiry attempts to give a preliminary analysis of this question.

2. POSSIBLE ISSUES OF TRANSIT AND TRAFFIC RIGHTS IN SPACE TRANSPORT

Unlike international maritime and air transport, space transport may be operated within the jurisdiction of one State and does not necessarily involve the territory or jurisdiction of another. In most circumstances, the destination or intended stopover of payloads and/or passengers is outer space, which is "free for exploration and use by all States without discrimination of any kind, on a basis of equality and in accordance with international law".[3] Accordingly, space transport usually does not require the prior permission of another State.

This situation is likely to change when manned space stations come into existence. Such stations will function as laboratories for scientific research and workshops for assembly or manufacturing. They will also serve as staging bases for more ambitious missions or transport "terminals" in outer space, to and from which the space vehicles will travel.[4] According to the forecast of some specialists, space stations will eventually develop into a populated Orbital Space City and generate enormous space traffic.[5] Therefore, out of

---

[2] For a comprehensive survey of these agreements and organisations, *see* B. Cheng, *The Law of International Air Transport* (1962) *and* P.P.C. Haanappel, *Pricing and Capacity Determination in International Air Transport* (1984).

[3] Article I of the Treaty on Principles Governing the Activities of States in the Exploration and Use of Outer Space, Including the Moon and Other Celestial Bodies, 1967 (hereinafter the Outer Space Treaty.)

[4] H. Mark, *The Space Station: Mankind's Permanent Presence in Space,* in People in Space 67, at 71 (J. Katz, editor, 1985). *See also,* K.S. Pedersen, *American Experiences and Perspectives: International Cooperation on a Permanently Manned Space Station,* in Space Stations 27 (K. Böckstiegel, editor, 1985).

[5] Yamanaka and Nagatomo, *Spaceports and new industrialised areas in the Pacific Basin,* Space Policy 342 (November 1986). According to these writers, the population of 2005 - 10 Orbital Space City will

technical or commercial considerations, space carriers of certain countries will find it attractive to have access to the space stations which are under the jurisdiction of other countries. Depending on the purposes of "landing", access to the space stations of other countries may be classified into the following two types:

1. Access for transit purposes: a space vehicle of State A takes off from the territory of State A and "lands" at the space station registered by State B for technical reasons only, *i.e.* for such purposes as refuelling, resupply, repairs or maintenance, but not to pick up or set down passengers or cargo;
2. Access for traffic purposes: a space vehicle of State A takes off from the territory of State A and "lands" at a space station registered by State B to set down or pick up passengers or cargo.

Both types of landing mentioned above will involve the jurisdiction of at least two States because the space station in question is under the jurisdiction and control of State B, the State of registry.[6] It may be asked, therefore, whether such jurisdiction and control will restrict the access of space carriers of other States. To put it differently, can the State of registry exclusively reserve the transit and traffic rights at the space station to its national carriers in order to protect them from international competition? Theoretically, the jurisdiction over the space stations should not be regarded as being tantamount to the "complete and exclusive sovereignty"[7] that every State enjoys over the airspace above its territory. Nevertheless, for practical purposes, by exercising its jurisdiction and its right of ownership over the space station, the State of registry may be able to restrict or even ban the "landing" of vehicles of other States. Examining the Outer Space Treaty and the other four major space agreements, we do not find any provisions specifically prohibiting States from doing so. Article XII of the Outer Space Treaty does require all stations on the moon and other celestial bodies to be open to representatives of other States Parties to the Treaty "on a basis of reciprocity". But it is questionable whether this provision will by analogy be applicable to stations in outer space *stricto sensu*. Even if the analogy is admitted, the principle of reciprocity will still impose restrictions upon the freedom of "landing" of other States.

On the basis of these considerations, it seems safe to say that the freedom of outer space does not automatically and unconditionally guarantee the freedom of access to space stations under the jurisdiction of other States. Such access, either for transit or traffic purposes, will have to be secured by new international agreements. In this connection, it

---

be about 1000, including scientists, engineers, visitors and sightseers. Thus, the traffic volume to and from the City will be: passengers: 120 persons per day; cargo: 120 tons per day, *See, id.*, at 350.

[6] *See* Article VIII of the Outer Space Treaty. *See also*, S. Gorove, *Legal Aspects of Stations in Space*, in Space Stations 143, at 144 (K. Böckstiegel, editor, 1985).

[7] Article I, Convention on International Civil Aviation, Chicago, 1944.

should be mentioned that in the Memorandum of Understanding on the Detailed Definition Studies (Phase B) Concerning a Space Station, NASA (U.S.) and ESA have agreed to incorporate into the future space station agreement "principles regarding access to and use of all elements of the Space Station system, including through European space transportation systems as they become available, on a basis which provides for equitable and non-discriminatory treatment for all partners".[8] The Contracting Parties appear to have recognised the need to establish a legal framework governing the access of the Parties to the space station. The space station envisaged by this agreement is basically an international cooperative project. Nevertheless, ESA is still sensitive to potential issues regarding access of European space carriers to the space station and wishes to seek an "equitable and non-discriminatory" solution in advance through international agreements.

In formulating international agreements regulating access to space stations, the legal frameworks offered by maritime and air transport may be taken into account. One framework is the restrictive practice of reciprocity as illustrated by numerous air transport agreements.[9] The other is the more liberal approach of maritime transport which is often termed "open port" policy. According to this policy, the carriers of country C are allowed to carry a significant part of traffic volume between country A and B in the absence of reciprocal rights of the national carriers of the latter two countries.[10]

3. CAPACITY CONTROL IN SPACE TRANSPORT

Capacity in space transport means the total traffic volume or payload which a space carrier may transport between earth and outer space over a given period. This volume may be expressed in terms of the capacity of the space vehicles used for transport, multiplied by the operational frequency of such vehicles over a given period and route. In maritime transport, traffic volume on particular routes is allocated through a liner conference by means of quotas on sailings and cargo, employed singly or in combination. Failure to carry out the allotted sailings, except with conference permission, often results in the loss of those rights, while carriage in excess of a carrier's quota entails payment of excess revenue for distribution among the other carriers.[11] In the field of air transport, capacity is either predetermined or subject to *ex post facto* review by the States Parties to a particular air service agreement.[12] In recent years, the free determination method has also been

[8] *See* Space Policy 434 (November 1985).

[9] *See* Cheng, *supra* note 2, at 289 *et seq.*

[10] *See* Article 2, Convention on a Code of Conduct for Liner Conferences; *see also*, Haanappel, *supra* note 2, at 25.

[11] Bennathan & Walter, *supra* note 1, at 106.

[12] *See* Cheng, *supra* note 2, at 424-433.

introduced in a number of air transport agreements, giving maximum freedom to designated airlines to determine capacity with little or no government involvement or control.[13]

In space transport, no system of capacity control, except in the case of launching to the geostationary orbit[14], has yet occured. At this moment, a *laissez-faire* approach to capacity determination still prevails, which allows any space carrier to operate its services with unrestricted capacity. Nevertheless, there are some indications that future space transport will probably require a certain degree of capacity control.

For certain categories of transport services, unrestricted capacity is simply a physical impossibility because there is a natural ceiling on the traffic volume imposed by the maximum capacity of the "terminals" in outer space. The geostationary orbit is a well-known example of such terminals. The maximum capacity of the orbit has imposed a limit on the number of satellites carried or to be carried to the orbit and has triggered international regulation of the allocation of the orbital positions and frequencies used. Similarly, traffic volume to be carried to the future space stations must also be subject to the practical constraint of the capacity of the space stations. As a result, capacity regulation for space stations seems to be inevitable. Such regulation should include, *inter alia,* the following subject matters:

1. The frequency for each space carrier to visit or "land" at a space station within a given period;
2. The timetable for each carrier to "land" at the space station and the maximum length of stay.

Capacity control in space transport is also one of the means to prevent the problem of over-capacity and destructive competition. According to an analyst, despite the present shortage of space transport vehicles, worldwide oversupply of such vehicles will occur in the future due to the fact that more and more states are actively developing their own transportation systems and attempting to enter the lucrative but competitive market.[15] In the absence of international regulation, oversupply, or overcapacity, of space transport vehicles, coupled with an unregulated pricing system may lead to a price war among space carriers.

---

[13] For details, *see* Haanappel, *supra* note 2, at 144-145, 189.

[14] The use of the geostationary orbit is regulated by the International Telecommunication Union. For relevant information, *see* N.M. Matte, *Aerospace Law: Telecommunications Satellites* 103-105 (1982); R. Jakhu, *Legal Regime of the Geostationary Orbit* (unpublished D.C.L. thesis, Institute of Air and Space Law, McGill University, 1983).

[15] Hertzfeld, *Launch Vehicles and the Commercial Use of Outer Space: The Underlying Economic Issues*, Space Policy 379 (November 1985).

Therefore, it is desirable to equitably allocate the capacity among space carriers. This will help to maintain a broad equilibrium between the world's space transport capacity and the traffic offered, and to optimise the use of limited resources devoted to space ventures.
In connection with the possible physical and economic constraints mentioned above, there will also be political or even psychological motivation for imposing capacity control. States having jurisdiction over space terminals may be inclined to limit the capacity of foreign space carriers in order to protect their national security, to support their national carriers or to serve other purposes.

For the reasons stated above, it is likely that in future space transport, the present system of unrestricted capacity will be replaced by an equitable capacity allocation system, taking into account the interests of all concerned. In the formulation of capacity regulations, space lawyers may draw useful experience from the precedents of maritime and air transport[16], but special attention should be given to the uniqueness of this mode of transportation. For instance, some payloads may be launched either by shuttles or ELV's, whilst some can only be delivered by shuttles.[17] This fact has to be taken into account in the allocation of capacity, so that various service requirements of customers can be satisfied.

4. PRICING OF SPACE TRANSPORT

If the legal issues concerning space transit and traffic rights, and capacity control may still be regarded as purely doctrinal speculation without immediate or practical significance at this stage, price competition among space carriers has indicated the necessity for international regulation. On 25 May, 1984, Transpace Carriers Inc. (TCI), a U.S. private expendable launch vehicle operator, filed a petition before the U.S. Trade Representative, charging Arianespace with "predatory pricing", that is, charging U.S. customers 25 to 30 percent below the price charged to customers in the member nations of the ESA.[18] TCI asked for a halt to the two-tier pricing schedule, a prohibition on Arianespace advertising and marketing in the U.S., and sanctions on the goods and services of France and other ESA member States. In turn, Arianespace stated that the TCI complaint was "inappropriate" and missed "the real target" which was shuttle subsidisation.[19]

---

[16] *See supra* note 11 and 12.

[17] Foley, *Reagan Rejects NASA Bid to Honor 31 Shuttle Contract,* Aviation Week and Space Technology 23 (October 13, 1986).

[18] *See* E. Finch & A. Moore, *Astrobusiness, A Guide to the Commerce and Law of Outer Space* 105 (1985).

[19] *See* A. Young, *Space Transportation Systems* 116 (unpublished LL.M. Thesis, Institute of Air and Space Law, McGill University, 1984).

The petition of TCI was dismissed by a presidential decision of 17 July 1985, which states that the practices with respect to the commercial satellite launching services of Arianespace "are not unreasonable and a burden or restriction on U.S. commerce".[20] But the petition has signalled a message to space lawyers that this kind of dispute is likely to arise in the future. The continuing increase in the number of commercial space carriers can only intensify such claims or counter-claims.

As is well known to all, many space transportation systems are not operated for purely commercial reasons. Accordingly, States or groups of States establishing those systems will regard the revenue from commercial transport as sideline income rather than the single source of cost recovery or investment return. Accordingly, many states will not always decline to adopt a below-cost pricing policy in order to compete with foreign space carriers and to reap the marginal revenue which is otherwise unavailable. Consequently, the possibility of a price war cannot be totally ruled out.

To prevent such a destructive price war, it seems desirable for the relevant States to jointly establish a regime, including appropriate procedures, to regulate pricing in space transport. In this respect, it may be useful to make references to the three pricing formulas used in air transport agreements.

The first is the liberal pricing system set forth in the United States Model liberal bilateral air transport agreement. Under this liberal system, a designated air carrier is allowed to establish a price on the basis of "commercial considerations in the market place"; governmental tariff intervention is limited to the prevention of predatory or discriminatory prices or practices, and to the protection of airlines from government subsidy or support.[21]

The second formula is the pricing system established under the U.S.-U.K. 1946 Air Transport Agreement (Bermuda I). This formula delegates the tariff setting function to an international ratemaking body, such as the International Air Transport Association (IATA), subject to the final approval of the relevant governments.[22]

The third formula is the pricing system initiated by the China-U.S. Air Transport Service Agreement and further developed by the U.S.-ECAC Memoranda of Understanding. These agreements establish a price band (zone of reasonableness) around a reference fare level within which carriers are free to set tariffs in the absence of governmental intervention.[23]

---

20 *Investigation of ESA halted*, Space Policy 430 (November 1985).

21 *See* Haanappel, *supra* note 2, at 146.

22 *Id.*, at 28-29.

23 Treaties and Other International Acts Series 10326, Article 13 and Annex IV. *See also* Haanappel, *supra* note 2, at 178.

The first formula, the liberal pricing system, is conducive to free competition among space carriers, but it does not seem readily adoptable at this stage to space transport, because the environment for free competition on the basis of market forces does not yet exist. In addition to the common practice of two-tier pricing, governmental subsidisation and intervention, there are also overwhelming political considerations which would weaken, if not invalidate, the market forces. All these factors render the liberal pricing system mentioned above untenable in the field of space transport until a more favourable environment for free competition has taken shape.

The second formula, the IATA ratemaking system, has long been accepted as workable, but it is also subject to the criticism that its cartelistic practice severely limits price competition and pays little or no attention to the interests of customers.

The third formula, the price band system, seems to be recommendable for future space transport because it favours a certain degree of price competition while at the same time it may prevent destructive price wars. It would also be desirable to combine the second and the third formulas, that is, to delegate the price determination function to an international organisation, which in turn prescribes price band systems. In this way, space transport will not only gain advantages from a multilateral forum, but will also retain the strength of price competition.

5. PROPOSED INSTITUTIONAL MECHANISM FOR COOPERATION AMONG SPACE CARRIERS

Access to transit and traffic rights, the control of capacity, and the determination of prices represent three major aspects of inter-carrier relationships in future space transport. As a matter of fact, the three are often intertwined with one another. States desiring to protect their national space carriers may take measures in all three areas to influence the competition among carriers. To attain an orderly and harmonious legal relationship among space carriers, it is necessary to adopt a comprehensive approach at the international level to the issues relating to transit and traffic rights, capacity and pricing.

As a first step, consultation should be held among nations having the capability to undertake commercial space transport; their aim should be to conclude an international agreement or to work out *interim* arrangements replacing the present *laissez-faire* approach to competition among space carriers. Consultation should first focus on pricing. Then, depending on the future development of space transportation systems, it may also include the matters of transit and traffic rights as well as capacity control.

Consultation among States could also go one step further by forming a trade association of space carriers similar to IATA or a liner conference, with the participation of commercial space carriers. In view of the direct involvement of governments in space activities and their supervisory responsibilities for private space enterprises, the prospective trade association should take the form of a governmental or quasi-governmental organisation.The mandates for this organisation would be various. In addition to discussing matters of transit and traffic rights, capacity and tariffs, it could also perform other functions of a trade association, including the coordination of transport time-tables and the formulation of the general conditions of contract for space carriage.

Once space transport has become large-scale business, consideration may also be given to the establishment of a multifunctional, inter-governmental space agency with wide-ranging responsibilities and concerns. This agency would be able to comprehensively regulate space transport, and possibly other space activities, just as the International Civil Aviation Organisation regulates air transport, with the objective of facilitating the development of regular and efficient space transport services adequate to the requirements of space exploration and exploitation.

6. CONCLUSION

The foregoing analysis does not pretend to cover all potential legal issues arising from the future competition in space transport. Nor does it intend to provide a detailed prescription for the resolution of these issues. It merely attempts to indicate, through several actual or speculative examples, that competition among space carriers may call for a certain degree of international regulation. It is also submitted that in view of the history of maritime and air transport and the present trends in space transport, a carefully designed legal regime governing inter-carrier relationships is preferable to a *laissez-faire* approach. In considering such a legal regime, the existing regulations for the other modes of transportation may be used as a reference and a point of departure, but the unique features of space transport should not be ignored.

CHAPTER THREE

POWER INTERESTS OF STATES CONDUCTING ACTIVITIES IN OUTER SPACE

POWER AND THE LAW-MAKING PROCESS CONCERNING OUTER SPACE

Paul Henry Tuinder*

PREFACE

The aim of this chapter is to indicate how, as a consequence of doctrinal developments concerning the law of outer space in general, and in particular the peaceful uses of outer space, the legal structure has become clearer. The increasing use of outer space indicates more congruent interests among the space powers and will affect the possibilities to effectively regulate the use of outer space. It is submitted that lawyers can offer a better framework for solving existing problems by utilising the following analytical scheme.

1. INTRODUCTION

"The purpose of the 1967 Principles Treaty[1] was to create conditions in which states would not have to invoke practical defensive measures flowing from the self defense principle. International law allows states to exercise only those lawful measures necessary to maintain a security position essential to the protection of their vital interests and to guarantee their continual survival".[2]

It is the task of the lawyer to provide a regulatory framework in order to prevent an unrestricted assertion of such rights and it is in this perspective that the writer seeks to present another method to meet this task, by combining the political science theory propounded by Professor De Vree[3] with the theory of the law of outer space. This combined approach will be applied to the problem of the extension of the arms race to outer space.

The present situation is of great concern to international fora dealing with security issues judging from the number of times the militarisation of outer space is placed on their agendas.[4] Despite the efforts within the United Nations to solve this problem[5], it has

---

* Institute of Satellite Applications, Amsterdam, The Netherlands.

1 Treaty on Principles Governing the Activities of States in the Eploration and Use of Outer Space, Including the Moon and Other Celestial Bodies, 610 UNTS 205.

2 Carl Q. Christol, *The Modern International Law of Outer Space* 37 (1982).

3 Johan K. De Vree, *Foundations of Social and Political Processess: The dynamics of human behaviour, politics and society, Volume 1: Theory* (1982).

4 Colloquia of the International Institute of Space Law; Bilateral negotiations between the USSR and the USA, Helsinki (1978), Berne (1979) and Geneva (1985).

5 Treaties which have been signed and are relevant for the control of military uses of outer space are the Partial Test Ban Treaty, 480 UNTS 430 (1963), the Agreement Governing the Activities of States on the

proved impossible to prevent the extension of the arms race to outer space. Outer space has become an important area for the military forces of the space powers because of its possibilities to function as a force multiplier.[6] It offers opportunities for operating verification, communication, and surveillance systems. At the same time civil opportunities are growing rapidly and the commercial uses of outer space such as remote sensing, satellite broadcasting, and weather-forecasting require cooperation to ensure that the use of outer space is as beneficial as possible for all mankind.

Developments since 1983 were dramatically accelerated by the Strategic Defense Initiative of the Reagan administration as formulated in the "Star Wars" speech of 23 March, 1983. Both the USA and the USSR have developed ASAT-capable systems.[7] The Reagan administration considers a "broad interpretation" of the ABM Treaty as justified, which leaves it the opportunity to develop and test a space-based anti-ballistic missile defence system. This could violate Article V of the ABM Treaty which prohibits "the development, testing, or deployment of ABM systems".[8] The USSR has constructed near Krasnayorsk a ballistic missile detection and tracking radar that seems to violate Article VI(b) of the ABM Treaty.[9]

These military uses and especially SDI have had a destructive influence on the legal structure which was created to establish a stable security order concerning the strategic nuclear forces of the space powers. Five years after the first SDI announcement it has become clear that SDI is merely the old ABM concept using new technologies[10], but international law and especially space law cannot react adequately to this threat. As a consequence, the concepts of parity and equal security (ABM Treaty) and of peaceful uses

---

Moon and Other Celestial Bodies, December 5, 1979, UN Doc. A/34/20 (1979), and the Treaty on the Limitation of Anti-Ballistic Missile Systems, May 26,1972, 23 UST 3435.

[6] D. Engels, J. Scheffran, E. Sicher, *Die Front im All: Weltraumrustung und atomarer Erstschlag* 23 (1984).

[7] Paul B. Stares, *Space Weapons and US Strategy: origins and development* (1985).

[8] The text of Article V(I) of the ABM Treaty is: "Each Party undertakes not to develop, test, or deploy ABM systems or components which are sea-based. air based, space-based, or mobile-land based".
The 'broad interpretation" is based on Agreed Statement D which states: "In order to insure fulfillment of the obligation not to deploy ABM systems and their components except as provided in Article III of the Treaty, the Parties agree that in the event ABM systems based on other physical principals and including components capable of substituting for ABM interceptor missiles, ABM launchers, or ABM radars are created in the future, specific limitations on such systems and their components would be subject to discussion in accordance with Article XII and agreement in accordance with Article XIV of the Treaty".

[9] Department of Defense and Department of State of the USA, *Soviet Strategic Defense Programs*, Washington, 10 (1985).

[10] Union of Concerned Scientists, *The Fallacy of Star Wars* 162 (1984).

of outer space (Outer Space Treaty) have disappeared from discussion. As we will see below juridical discussion is now reduced to the level of semantic argumentation.

2. THE MEANING OF "PEACEFUL PURPOSES"

Controversy concerning the meaning of "peaceful purposes" resulted from the term peaceful purposes being included in the preamble of the Outer Space Treaty and the text of Article IV of the Treaty.

This Article states that:

"1. States Parties to the Treaty undertake not to place in orbit around the earth any objects carrying nuclear weapons or any other kind of weapons of mass destruction, install such weapons in outer space in any other matter.
2. The Moon and other celestial bodies shall be used by all States Parties to the Treaty exclusively for peaceful purposes. The establishment of military bases, installations and fortifications, the testing of any type of weapons and the conduct of military manoeuvres shall be forbidden. The use of military personnel for scientific purposes shall not be prohibited. The use of any equipment or facility necessary for peaceful exploration of the Moon and other celestial bodies shall also not be prohibited".

The expression "exclusively for peaceful purposes" as provided by Article IV(2) relates only to the Moon and other celestial bodies, whereas the use of outer space is restricted by the expression "peaceful purposes" as provided in the Preamble of the Treaty. Thus the term "exclusively" was omitted, which was one of the reasons for extensive discussions among space lawyers.[11]

Two schools of thought on the meaning of "peaceful purposes" may be recognised: one that equated peaceful with "non-military" and one that equated peaceful with "non-aggressive".[12] State practice has made it obvious that "peaceful" has to be interpreted as "non-aggressive", for both the USA and the USSR use satellites for military purposes. This result, although it does not help to solve the present problems, is important for doctrinal reasons because we can say that space lawyers have reached a common agreement as to which direction a more specific treaty should develop.

As stated before, this result can be seen as a big advantage for developing a more specific legal regime. But since it took so long to come to this understanding on the Outer Space

---

[11] *See* for the political aspects: Walter A. McDougal, ... *the Heavens and the Earth: a political History of the Space Age*, (1986); *see* for the discussion concerning "non-agressive" versus "non-military": E.R.C. van Bogaert, *Aspects of Space Law* (1986).

[12] S. Gorove, *Studies in Space Law: its Challenges and Prospects* 10 (1977).

Treaty, state practice has developed too quickly to be controlled and regulated according to the existing rules.

It is not a question of amending the Outer Space Treaty in order to create a more effective legal system. Rather one has to return to the old assumption that the Outer Space Treaty is merely a foundation on which more precise norms regulating the use of outer space have to be built.[13] Without such an extension to new areas of activity, regulations will become obsolete because of their inability to give answers to questions arising from the practical uses of outer space. We are faced with a situation in which the Outer Space Treaty has to regain its funtion of providing a basis for further regulation and in this way offering a tool for solving future problems concerning the use of outer space. In other words, the inability of legal specialists to create extra regulations meeting the needs of the space powers has created a vacuum.

In order to close this gap and create an effective regulatory system, one has to take into account the actual interests of the space powers and existing body of rules into which this regulatory system has to be fitted.

3. THE EXISTING LEGAL BODY

The law of outer space started to take form in the early sixties. Principles were formulated in the United Nations Resolutions 1962 (xviii), 1884 (xviii) and 222 (xxi) which culminated in the Outer Space Treaty. This Treaty establishes broad legal principles covering the most important aspects of state activities in exploring outer space. The Treaty must be considered an important phase in the creation of space law and it became the foundation for further regulation of activities. The general principles required a more detailed implementation in order to form a basis for solving problems created by advancing space technology. Apart from the Principles Treaty, several other regulatory norms have been established and included in the Rescue Agreement[14], the Liability Convention[15], the Registration Convention[16], the Moon Agreement[17], the ITU Convention and the Radio Regulations.[18]

---

[13] Manfred Lachs, *The Law of Outer Space* 162 (1977).

[14] Agreement on the Rescue of Astronauts, the Return of Astronauts and the Return of Objects Launched into Outer Space, April 22, 1986, 672 UNTS 119.

[15] Convention on International Liability for Damage Caused by Space Objects, March 29, 1972, 24 UST 2389, TIAS 7762.

[16] Convention on Registration of Objects Launched into Outer Space, January 14, 1975, 28 UST 695, TIAS 8480.

[17] Agreement Governing the Activities of States on the Moon and Other Celestial Bodies, December 5, 1979, UN Doc. A/34/20 (1979).

[18] World Administrative Radio Conferences of the International Telecommunications Union of 1959, 1963, 1971, 1977, 1979, and 1985.

As foreseen, problems were raised by technological advancements which could not be solved by the Outer Space Treaty. With regard to the term peaceful purposes, the signatory states did not succeed in implementing this principle. This inability can be explained by the broad character of the Outer Space Treaty. Important is the fact that the Treaty was almost universally accepted and ratified, which implies that most of the states committed themselves to using outer space according to its principles, without having access to the space technology required for actually using it!
This means that the coordination was not only highly effective but it also implied the existence of a consensus about the direction in which outer space had to be explored. This consensus revolved around the belief that the most beneficial way for exploring outer space was to gain access to space technology and utilisation through cooperation.
Whereas the broad character of the Treaty implied only vague regulation, the consensus about cooperation implied the need for further elaboration of these principles. The function of these principles was to provide criteria of legality for the later development of specific regulations. Emphasis must be placed on this fact since the Outer Space Treaty is often used for deriving practical solutions which could deprive the Treaty of its essential function as a basis for the law-making process concerning outer space.

What is the environment in which the principle of "peaceful purposes" must be implemented ? To answer this question, legal and political factors have to be analysed and fitted into a framework showing their interdependence and how they effect each other. As stated before, the Outer Space Treaty forms the legal framework for further regulation. Treaty interpretation has to be implied in accordance with the Vienna Convention on the Law of Treaties[19] and the Charter of the United Nations (Article 1, Outer Space Treaty).

It is clear that the Outer Space Treaty, which has been ratified by the major part of the international community[20], is the basis for regulation of the peaceful uses of outer space.
As mentioned above, discussions indicate that peaceful has to be interpreted as "non-agressive". To come to a better understanding of the meaning of "non-agressive" it is necessary to analyse Article 51 of the Charter of the United Nations which provides for the right of self-defence, and the ABM Treaty which limits the way this principle of self-defence may be effected with regard to ballistic missile defence. This paper will not deal with the Moon Agreement, which provides for total demilitarisation, since this was already stated in Article IV(2) of the Outer Space Treaty when using the expression "exclusively for peaceful purposes".

---

19 International Legal Materials 679 (1969).

20 *Supra* note 2 at 909, 910.

It is not only a question of legal sources but also a question of the power interests of the states which determine what kind of regime will be feasible. Therefore we need to see international relations in the context of international law and we have to analyse what its influences are and by what it is influenced.

To answer this question the writer will use the theory of Professor De Vree, analysing the factors which form the elements of the international system.[21]

4. THE SYSTEM THEORETICAL APPROACH OF DE VREE

The theory of Professor De Vree describes the mechanisms according to which interaction and action are rendered. Thus, the theory does not seek to describe actual behaviour because common distinctions between domestic and international affairs, for example, have little theoretical meaning.

Whatever limited process one wants to study, it it necessary to include all major aspects, phases, and forms of human action and interaction in general.

The theory is a tool enabling us to order, explain, and orient ourselves in the highly irregular world and thus precedes actual experience and empirical research.

This system theoretical approach to human behaviour and social life is based upon a decision-theoretical model.[22] This means that human behaviour is looked upon as a matter of choosing between behavioural options that are ordered in terms of their expected attractiveness or utility.[23]

The social and behavioural system is seen as an energy- and information- processing system and its power is its capacity to use the energy at its disposal.[24]

The central function which rules or standards of behaviour are to serve is to render interaction and action predictable.[25] But this predictability is dependent on the precision and formulation of the rules. These are always a matter of application to a larger or smaller set of different situations.[26] They appear to be strongly influenced by the shifting and evolving relations of power and affinity in a system and are bound to be respectively imprecise and ambiguous.[27]

---

21 *Supra* note 3.

22 *Id.*, at 23.

23 *Id.*, at 26.

24 *Id.*, at 437.

25 *Id.*, at 284.

26 *Idem.*

27 *Id.*, at 286.

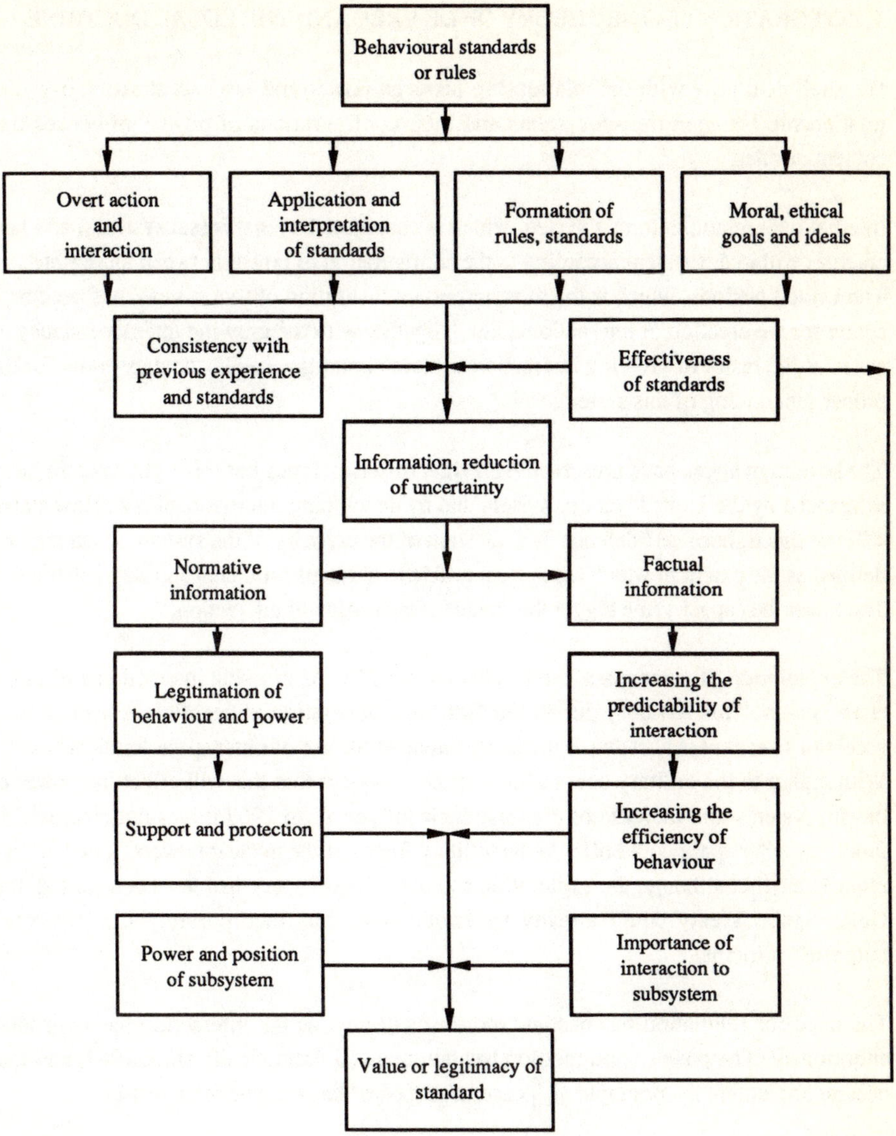

Function of rules and standards[28]

28 *Id.*, at 287.

5. INTEGRATION OF THE THEORY OF DE VREE AND THE LEGAL DOCTRINE

We shall deal now with the relationship between power and law. As stated above, the relationship between the subsystems and their configurations of power influences the content of rules.

International relations form a system which is constituted by states (subsystems) and law emerges within the system according to the configuration of power between these states. The United Nations, which is the most important institution of this system, has become a centre for the creation of international law. Together with the growing interdependency of states as the result of growing interactions, international law has become essential for the proper functioning of this system.

The sovereign states have preserved their right of self-defence but this right has also been influenced by the United Nations system and by developing international law. How states will use this right of self-defence is a question of the capacity of the system which may be defined as the extent to which the system is able to solve its problems and stay coherent.[29] The lower the capacity, the bigger the chance of escalation of interaction.

The exploration of outer space can be characterised by the growing interaction within the state-system. This not only due to the fact that cooperation is beneficial for obtaining access to space but is also due to the implications of the use of outer space for all states. With regard to the military uses of outer space it is clear that this will affect the power of the subsystems and increase or diminish their influence. In 1967 it was not clear which functions outer space could offer to the military forces of the nuclear powers. It is therefore remarkable that although the exploration and use of outer space had just been started, the Outer Space Treaty could already be established, thus incorporating the "peaceful purposes" principle.

The need for regulation has become more urgent now as the interaction has expanded enormously. The power configuration has not changed dramatically since 1967, and the need to implement the principle of "peaceful purposes" has become more urgent.

6. CONCLUSION

The principle of self-defence and the military forces of the states that have to assure this principle characterise the capacity of the states-system. This capacity was never at such a level that interaction would imply the exclusive operation of peaceful purposes only. Law has an important function in the growth of the capacity of the states-system; it is at the same time influenced by it.

---

[29] *Supra* note 23.

States were able to achieve regulated interaction at a certain level, meaning that we can speak of an institution, or system, functioning according to certain standards. It also implies the limitation of such regulation.

The question of the function of international law and how it can be established is dependent on the structure of the states-system. With the evolution of the states-system, law has become more important and has established its own system.

Without regulation, interaction would not have grown so fast, as predictability of interaction could not be assessed. Increasing regulation implies the functioning of law according to certain standards. Otherwise there can be no "consistency with previous experience and standards".[30]

Evolution of space law shows that regulation concerning the use of outer space has to be consistent with the principles of the Outer Space Treaty. For example, all legal discussions refer to this Treaty. Also the practical uses of outer space are defined in terms of the Treaty. This means that although the Treaty was influenced by the conflicting interests of the space powers which resulted in the exclusion of the term "exclusively" in the Treaty, the configuration of power between the states has not substantially changed.

The military uses could be assessed better by the space-powers; we have been able to observe the situation in which both powers limited their military uses only to strengthen the Mutual Assured Destruction doctrine.[31] The legal environment has now become clearer. Thus, a new treaty implementing the "peaceful purposes" principle must be feasible.

---

[30] *Supra* note 27.

[31] The idea behind SDI, "..to render nuclear weapons impotent and obsolete", requires a 100 % secure defence system which is, according to experts, impossible. In case of a leak of 5 % in the situation of an "all out" nuclear war between the USA and the USSR, it would cause more than 30 million deaths in the USA. The present writer believes that the "Assured Destruction" doctrine will prevail and lead us to a new "MAD-monumentum", only at a different level.

THE METHOD OF GENETIC EFFECTIVENESS AND THE FUTURE OF THE MILITARY REGIME OF OUTER SPACE.

Ilias I. Kuskuvelis*

1. INTRODUCTION[1]

Thinking about the future of the Military Regime of Outer Space (hereinafter the Military Regime), or about the future in general, cannot be a matter of guesswork, nor should it consist of mere speculations. A theoretical framework and a method are indispensable.

The theoretical framework for this study is provided by the Modified Structural Realist Paradigm[2] and the assumption-clarification that in the origin of any legal or technological evolution is politics or political decisions. The variables of technology and law are consequences of, or depend on politics.

This rationale suggests that the Military Regime and the International Regime of Outer Space (hereinafter the Space Regime) in general are created and shaped by politics. Yet, this is not enough if we are to make some projections about their future. Postulating that the Military Regime is very likely to be changed or maintained in the future according to the same processes and under the same conditions as its creation and its present maintenance requires that we discover and identify these processes and conditions.

Consequently, a quantitative and qualitative method accounting for the creation and the maintenance of the regime could also account for its future (maintenance or change). Towards this end, the Method of Genetic Effectiveness will be utilised. *Genetic* encompasses the genesis, or creation of a regime; *effectiveness* concerns its present validity. *Together,* they account for the *continuity* and *evolution* occurring between the creation of law and the present.

The method is primarily an interdisciplinary tool that accounts for creation by discerning the effective Military Regime:
(1) by understanding (a) why outer space was not initially reserved exclusively for peaceful and scientific purposes as UN Res. 1148 (f) (XII) of November 14, 1957, suggested, (b) why nuclear testing was prohibited in outer space while it is allowed underground, (c) why

* D.E.A Droit Maritime, Aérien et Spatial; M.A. International Politics and Outer Space; Doctorat d'Etat candidate; Member I.I.S.L.

1 This first section provides an overview of the assumptions and definitions used in this chapter, the legal and political problems and questions the study intends to answer. The theoretical foundations of the Method of Genetic Effectiveness will also be touched upon.

2 R. Keohane, *Theory of World Politics: Structural Realism and Beyond* in Political Science: The State of the Discipline 503-540 (A.W. Finifter, editor, 1983).

the orbiting of nuclear weapons was prohibited as compared to the non-prohibition of ICBM's potentially transiting through or tested in outer space, (d) why reconnaissance satellites were not prohibited, (e) why Fractional Orbital Bombardment Systems (FOBS) developed by the Soviets, although technically not covered by Article 4 (1) of the Outer Space Treaty, were gradually abandoned, dismantled and finally prohibited by the SALT II Treaty, and (f) why anti-satellite (ASAT) weapons tests were undertaken although, according to the minimum common-ground interpretation, "peaceful" meant "non-aggressive".

(2) by analysing two major legal and political controversies, namely (a) whether the term "peaceful" means "non-military" (civilian) or "non-aggressive" and (b) whether the ABM Treaty (under Article V and "agreed statement D") permits the testing and development of "ABM systems based on other physical principles" (than those existing at the time).

The use of the Method in the way it has just been suggested - as a means of discerning the effective Military Regime - yields three important benefits. The first is the understanding of the Military Regime's creation and maintenance conditions. Given that the future of the Military Regime is very likely to be characterized by the same conditions of maintenance or change (creation) that led to its present situation, their understanding should consequently permit to undertake some valid and well-based projections about its future. The second benefit is the achievement of an objective interpretation of the Regime's provisions.

The final benefit is a follow-up of the previous benefits and is twofold. On the one hand, the identification of the effective Military Regime, the understanding of the conditions of its creation and maintenance, and the ability of making projections about the future, demonstrate the efficacy and the usefulness of the Method of Genetic Effectiveness. On the other, the ability of the Method to supply an objective interpretation suggests that it may be used as a means of interpretation complementary to the existing methods codified in Article 31 and 32 of the Vienna Convention on the Law of Treaties (1969).[3]

Having set the theoretical framework of the study and having clarified the purpose and the way the Method of Genetic Effectiveness was intended and, consequently, conceived to be used, I turn now to the phenomenon to be observed, namely the Military Regime of Outer Space. A "regime" is a set of principles, rules and procedures around which actor-expectations converge.[4] The Space Regime contains two sub-regimes: the Military Regime and the Regime of the Civilian Uses of Outer Space (hereinafter the Civilian Regime). The principles, the procedures and the rules forming the Space Regime, as well as the internal structure of the Regime, are displayed in Table 3.

---

[3] The need for an additional interpretative tool or the inadequacies of the existing legal methods are not demonstrated here.

[4] Keohane, *The Demand for International Regimes*, 36 International Organisation 325-355 (2, Spring 1982).

In the international order, Keohane argues that the major function of international regimes is: "to facilitate the making of specific agreements on matters of substantive significance within the issue-area covered by the regime". This function results from an "investigation over the sources of specific agreements" which "reveals that they are not, in general, made on an *ad hoc* basis, nor do they follow a random pattern. Instead, they are "nested" within more comprehensive agreements, covering more issues". The overall "nest" agreements are "related to military-security relations among the major states".[5]

The nesting phenomenon also applies to the Space Regime as illustrated in *Table 1*. In constructing it, I took under consideration all the specific references made in each agreement to previous and more general ones.

Table 2 addresses the relation of the "nest" agreements with the major states and asks two questions: first, who had the initiative or which nation's input was dominant in the creation of those agreements; second, who are the depositary governments.

Table 3 shows that the Military and the Civilian Regime share the principles and procedures of the Space Regime, hence demonstrating that the conditions of creation for one of the two might account for both.

The answer to the two questions reveal the pre-eminent roles of the USA and the USSR in the elaboration of these agreements.[6] It also reveals that, although the two countries had a monopoly on global security issues and on laying down the basic nest agreements, when it comes to specific issues such as liability, registration, or even the Moon Agreement, their monopoly is broken.

What has thus far been illustrated is only the relationship between the "nest" agreements with the major states, not a relationship and their military-security relations. The relationship between military-security relations and the Military Regime is explored in the next section, after the presentation of the Method of Genetic Effectiveness. The Method is employed in order to identify the effective Military Regime by revealing the relationship between the military-security relations and the Military Regime's creation. The operation will be undertaken indirectly by examining the relationship between its specific rules and the military-security relations. This is done for three reasons. Firstly because it is those rules that shape the Military Regime; secondly because the specific rules are much more clear compared to the relatively vague general principles and consequently offer a solid frame of reference; and finally because these rules express and put into effect the general

5 *Ibid.*, at 334.

6 Great Britain, which appears to have played a role in this process, did not, however, follow a different line than that of the USA.

principles. The last section attempts to project some future developments in two directions: *maintenance* of the existing regime and *change.*

Table 1: Nesting Phenomenon of the UN Space Agreements

	Int'l Law	UN Charter	Space Treaty	Rescue Agrmt.	Liability Conv.	Registr. Conv.	Moon Agrmt.	Remote Sensing
Int'l Law								
UN Charter	+							
Space Treaty	+	+						
Rescue Agreement	+	+	+					
Liability Convention	+	+	+					
Registration Convention	+	+	+	+	+			
Moon Agreement	+	+	+	+	+	+		
Remote Sensing	+	+	+			+		

Table 2 : Agreements and UN Resolutions related to Outer Space

	UN Charter	Res. 1472	Res. 1884	Res. 1962	Test Ban Treaty	Space Treaty
Initiative (Countries)	USA-USSR-UK	common proposal (1)	common proposal (2)	USA-USSR and others	USA-UK-USSR	USA-USSR
Depository Govts.	USA				USA-UK-USSR	USA-UK-USSR

	Rescue Agrmt.	Liability Conv.	ABM Treaty	Registr. Conv.	Moon Agreement
Initiative (Countries)	joint USA-USSR paper	USA-USSR & others (3)	USA-USSR	France-USA-USSR	USA-USSR-Argentina-Austria
Depository Govts.	USA-UK-USSR	USA-UK-USSR	USA-USSR	UN Secretary General	UN Secretary General

1. Establishing the COPUOS and regulating its membership. Based on a "common understanding" between the USA and the USSR.
2. Based on the "declaration of intention" between the USA and the USSR not to station nuclear weapons or other weapons of mass destruction in outer space.
3. Canada, Iran, Japan and Sweden abstained from the votings in the COPUOS, the 1st committee, and the G.A, because they wished to have included provisions more favourable to the claimant states; the agreement seems to have favoured the space powers.

Table 3: The International Regime of Outer Space

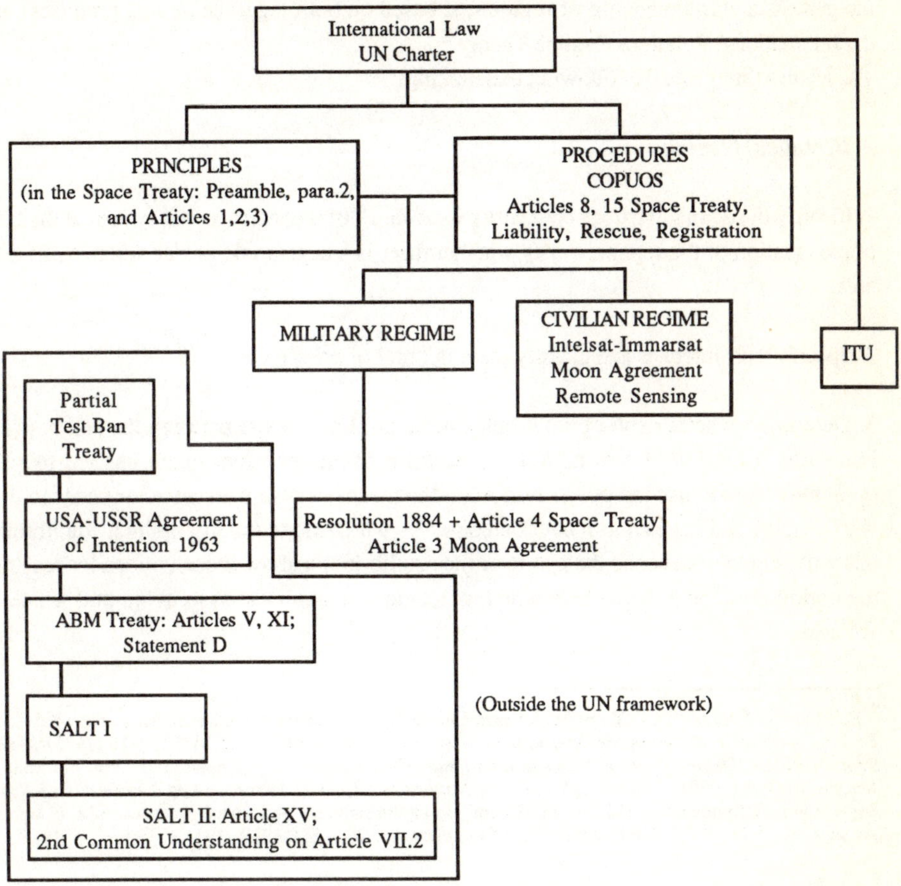

2. THE METHOD OF GENETIC EFFECTIVENESS

I. The Method of Genetic Effectiveness

The Method of Genetic Effectiveness, as a method of inquiry concerning the conditions of the genesis and maintenance of regimes, is based on both legal theoretical premises[7] and the International Relations Regime Theory.[8]
The Method suggests the following undertakings:

A. (Creation) Genesis

1. Identify the actors in the space/security issue-area[9] of the international system at the time of the creation of the regime; verify whether there is a hegemonic power within this issue-area.

2. Specify their interests and classify them in order of priority.

3. Determine whether sub-optimal outcomes/equilibria[10] exist between the actors in the issue-area. Examine, from the outset, the form of competition which has led to sub-optimality. Recognise the power resource - the means or resources an actor needs to deal with an issue and have control over outcomes [11]- which led to the sub-optimal equilibrium; this will help to understand the nature of the equilibrium and the preconditions for reaching the optimal outcome. Recognise which outcomes the actors tried to avoid and which to achieve.

---

[7] R.J. Dupuy, *Préface* in J. Touscoz, Le principe de l'effectivité dans l'ordre international (1964); G. Tunkin, *International Law in the International System*, IV Receuil des Cours 147, 1 - 218 (1975); Matte, *Droit Maritime, Droit Aérien, et Droit International: Quel Rapport?*, V Annuaire de Droit Maritime et Aérien 301-354 (1980); J. Sztucki, *Security of Nations and Cosmic Space*, in Legal Problems of Space Exploration: A Symposium, US Senate, Committee on Aeronautics and Space Sciences; 87th Congress, 1st session, U.S.G.P.O., Washington D.C., Document no. 26, 1164-1210 (1961).

[8] a) *Supra* note 4;
b) Keohane, *The Theory of Hegemonic Stability and Change in the International Economic Regimes, 1967-1977*, in Changes in the International System 131-162 (O.R. Holsti, R.Siverson & A.George, editors, 1980);
c) Stein, *Coordination and Collaboration: Regimes in an Anarchic World*, 36 International Organization 299-324 (2, Spring 1982).

[9] "Since issues are defined subjectively, so are issue-areas. When the governments active on a set of issues see them as closely interdependent and deal with them collectively, we call that set of issues an issue-area. When we do so, we are making a statement about actors' beliefs and behavior, not about the objective reality of the problems themselves". In R. Keohane & J. Nye Jr., *Power and Interdependence* (1977).

[10] *Supra* note 8c, at 304-307.

[11] *Supra* note 9, at 11.

4. Consider if any of the following conditions exist:
a. The need for norms and principles or a "generalised commitment" to such a need or recognition of the latter as a " public good."
b. The creation of a regime would permit lower transaction costs or the "issue density" [12] is high.
c. The need for information in general and especially in the specific issue area.

5. Examine the role of third or disadvantaged actors.

B. Maintenance

1. Examine whether any of the conditions of creation have changed.

2. Examine whether the regime fulfills its aims.

3. Examine whether:
a. States have reassessed their power-resources and their interest in the regime.
b. they have a vested interest in it.
c. the regime has obtained legitimacy and traditionality.
d. there has been any shift in the criteria of decision making.

Following the Method of Genetic Effectiveness *point by point,* I shall seek to demonstrate the relationship between military-security relations and the Military Regime by examining the conditions of the genesis and maintenance of the latter. If this correlation is demonstrated, it will also serve to illustrate the validity of the Method of Genetic Effectiveness.

II. Application of the Method of Genetic Effectiveness

Genesis - Demonstration of the Relationship

1 (a) *Time*: The preparatory period for the creation of the Space Regime was from 1957, after the first testing of an ICBM (August), and the launching of Sputnik (October) by the USSR through 1962. On 5 August 1963 the Partial Test Ban Treaty (PTBT) was signed, the negotiations having begun early in that year. Also Resolutions 1884 (XVIII) and 1962 (XVIII), containing a "Declaration of legal principles governing the activities of states in the exploration and use of outer space", were adopted.

(b) *Actors*: By the end of 1962 only two states - the USA and the USSR - had reached outer space and had developed considerable launching and space capabilities. The two

[12] *Supra* note 9; *supra* note 4, at 339.

states were also the major military actors in the international system. These two powers were hegemonic in their own camps but not hegemonic overall. They could be described as co-hegemonic in the issue-area of nuclear weapon systems and in outer space.

2. The major interest of these two powers was and still is security. In the military sphere, security may be satisfied by achieving military superiority over other states, by prohibiting its (their) military superiority, and/or by prohibiting military competition through arms control or disarmament.

3. *Sub-optimal outcome - equilibrium.* The issue-area of outer space is related to the existence of nuclear weapons systems, thus the security area. Humanity at first reached outer space in order to demonstrate military nuclear capabilities. Khrushchev made this point several times: "The Soviet Union launched an intercontinental ballistic missile, the testing of which yielded positive results. We can now send a missile to any point on the globe, carrying, if necessary, a hydrogen warhead. Our announcement to this effect was greeted with disbelief and regarded as an attempt by the Soviet leaders to attack confidence in their own people and intimidate the Western governments. But then the Soviet Union, using the intercontinental ballistic missile, launched an artificial satellite...".[13] After World War II the USA was far superior to the USSR in economic[14], military and political terms.[15] The only area of Soviet superiority was the size of its conventional forces in Europe. The USA had superiority in its nuclear capacity and the air power to deliver nuclear weapons. The race towards an equilibrium or for better security started immediately after World War II. The USSR obtained nuclear and thermonuclear weapons but it still lacked the intercontinental delivery means to threaten the sanctuary of the USA (as the USSR was threatened). The solution was found in the intercontinental ballistic missile (ICBM).

By the end of 1962, the power resource in both outer space and the security "issue-areas" purely concerned military capability: ICBM's which could either put a satellite into orbit or, traveling through outer space, deliver a thermonuclear warhead to its target. If one defines *equilibrium* as the capacity of an actor to avert a nuclear attack by its own means, then both actors, through competition, had reached an equilibrium in the security "issue-area". The Soviet Union had denied the USA superiority, without being able to claim its own, since the latter had also built ICBM's. As ICBM's were also the power resource in the outer space "issue-area", an equilibrium was reached within that area as well.

---

13 N.S. Khrushchev, *For Victory in Peaceful Competition with Capitalism* (1960).

14 Th.G. Patterson, *Soviet American Confrontation* (1979).

15 a) Alperovitz, *Atomic Diplomacy - Hiroshima and Potsdam* (1980);
b) Rowe, *The United States, the United Nations and the Cold War*, XXV International Organisation 59-78 (1, 1971).

There are two ways to prove that such an equilibrium situation did exist at the end of 1962. This can be done by firstly taking into account the power equation as it was then perceived and secondly by reviewing the declarations of officials and the strategic policy they followed. A brief examination of the specialised and general literature of the time[16] shows that the USSR had acquired a retaliatory capacity. Of course, it can be argued that government estimates of the opponent's strength are different from those stated in literature. In September 1962, US Defense Secretary McNamara doubted that the USA would maintain nuclear superiority; in November 1962, he accepted that the USSR would reach a full retaliatory power and that "when both sides have a sure second-strike capability then you might have a more *stable* balance of terror".[17]

Another indirect sign can be found in strategic policy. Although the Department of Defense was trying for two years to formulate a counterforce strategy, early in 1963 McNamara gave signs of searching for a countervalue strategy[18], saying that this change was necessary due to the increase in the Soviet arsenal. Hence, the equilibrium of security was a sub-optimal outcome, achieved through competition, based on nuclear weapons and intercontinental/space launching capabilities: offensive capability. The outcome to be avoided was the achievement of superiority by the other side. The optimal outcome result was the enhancement of security by stabilising or limiting the arms race.

The 1962 equilibrium was the first upon which the Military Regime has been edified. Yet, as the arms race continued, new equilibria at higher levels of forces have appeared. Those equilibria, which can be proved by undertaking a comparison of strategic forces, are equally manifested by changes in the American nuclear strategy/posture. In 1962 we enter the era of Mutual Assured Destruction (MAD): a "counterforce strategy" and a "damage limitation posture" are adopted; in 1966, "parity" with the Soviet Union is recognised and a "countervalue posture" is adopted; then, in 1971/'72 there is a shift to the concept of "sufficiency" and in 1977/'78 to that of "essential equivalence".[19]

Table 4 examines the number of US-USSR security related agreements signed over thirty years, since 1957. One may observe that agreements are created just after the appearance of an equilibrium of forces; the PTBT, the Outer Space Treaty, the ABM Treaty, the SALT I and II Treaties are among them. Consequently, the elaboration of agreements in the space-security area is very highly linked with the existence of a US-USSR equilibrium of nuclear forces.

---

16 a) *The Western Alliances and the Communist Bloc*, Institute for Strategic Studies (1962); b) E. Bottome, *The Missile Gap* (1971).

17 McNamara as cited in D. Ball, *Politics and Force Levels: The Strategic Missile Program of the Kennedy Administration* at 198 (1980).

18 *Ibid.*, at 199.

Table 4: Equilibria of Strategic Forces and Creation of Agreements

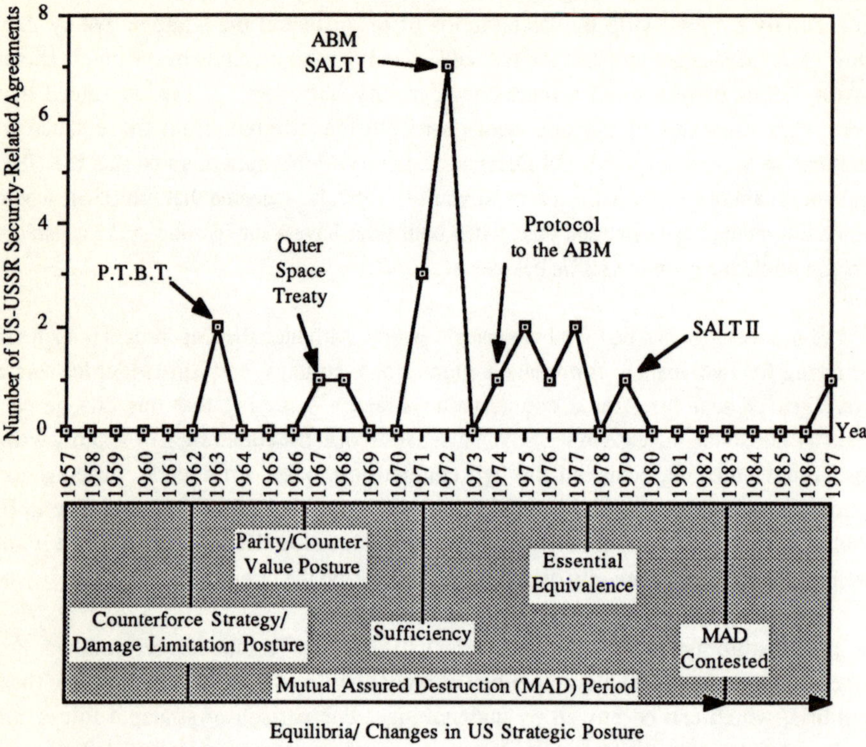

4 (a) The desire to control the arms race was obvious after the Cuban missile crisis. The need for *détente* was publicly acknowledged and as can also be observed in table 4 most of the agreements were elaborated during the period of *détente* (1963-1979); *détente* is a condition for agreements and agreements are a proof of *détente*. The need for norms and principles was also recognised; This is connected to :

(b) The opening of outer space as the new medium for activities and regulations. The "issue-density" was and still is high. The subjects for regulation were abundant. A look at the contents of the UN Resolutions of 1958-1963 and those of other international bodies[20] demonstrates this very clearly. *Ex post facto*, this may be proven by the number of agreements elaborated in the thirty years of space activity.

(c) The need for information concerning the other side's activities has been crucial for the formulation of policies. In 1962, the USA had just recovered from the infamous "missile

20 *I.e.*, Institut de Droit International, International Law Association.

gap" controversy, which was due to information provided by satellites.[21] Moreover, in order to achieve *détente*, information for verification was crucial.
The function of deterrence or the maintenance of equilibrium has gradually been entrusted to Early Warning Satellite systems. Prior to the existence of Early Warning Satellite systems, the warning time in the case of a nuclear attack by ballistic missiles provided by radar was only 15 minutes. Thus, the USA used to maintain a large percentage of its Strategic Air Command force on airborne alert. Satellites are capable of detecting an ICBM attack at the outset: the warning time has therefore been doubled. Consequently, each actor could be sure that it could at least partially retaliate before the attacking forces destroyed all or part of its own.

5. Our theoretical premises are confirmed by the behaviour of third actors. On 31 December 1985, 88 countries had ratified the Outer Space Treaty and 110 the PTBT. Most of those states do not or will not conduct space activities. By ratifying the Outer Space Treaty they had everything to win and nothing to lose; if they did not ratify the agreement, they were going to lose even the small benefits that the agreement offered them. By ratifying the PTBT they were at least protecting themselves against radioactive fallout resulting from nuclear weapons tests.

In the case of the PTBT, the behaviour of two actors, China and France, confirms the equilibrium precondition in the specific issue-area of nuclear testing. These two States did not stop their atmospheric tests until no further tests were required. China has ratified the Treaty but France still reserves the right to conduct tests.

III. The Effective Military Regime

A. Exegesis

The Space Regime was created to regulate space activities during peacetime and, in particular, the security relations of the superpowers. In any case, the idea of regulating war in the nuclear and space age is absurd.

Why was outer space not exclusively preserved for peaceful purposes as Resolution 1148 (XII) suggested in 1957? The answer is now clear: such a Resolution would have deprived the USSR of its ICBM's and of its capacity to threaten the sanctuary of the US. The USSR countered this proposal by demanding that the US should first dismantle the US bases surrounding and threatening the USSR before reserving outer space exclusively for peaceful purposes.

---

[21] *Supra* note 16 (b); Ball, *supra* 17.

Why was nuclear testing prohibited in outer space? First, the two superpowers had completed a series of tests in the upper atmosphere and in outer space. Second, there was the threat of radioactive fallout and of the destruction of the ozone layer. Third, they had to prove their commitment to *détente*.[22] Fourth, nuclear explosions in outer space would damage satellites. Finally, with a new generation of satellites, each side had the capacity to monitor compliance with the agreement.[23]
It is often explained that ICBM's are not prohibited because they do not, according to Article 4 of the Outer Space Treaty, complete a full orbit. This would be correct if the Space or the Military Regime were applied in time of war or if we were referring only to the testing of ballistic missiles. Since, however, the Space Regime applies only during peacetime, and since missiles during their testing do not carry nuclear warheads, the "full orbit" interpretation is not valid. Moreover, their testing started before the Military Regime's creation, and their continuation was necessary in order to maintain their security equilibrium.

The orbiting of nuclear weapons was prohibited, while ICBM's were not, because ICBM's were the basis of the security equilibrium and because ICBM's are a more effective strategic system than orbiting bombs. ICBM's need less throw-weight (launching power) than the missiles required to put the bombs into orbit; they can carry a larger payload; they can undertake a completely co-ordinated attack; they are less vulnerable targets; they have greater accuracy; they are less expensive to build and maintain, and they present no risk of accidental deorbiting.[24] As ICBM's are the basis of the security equilibrium between the two superpowers they are not prohibited under the Military Regime.

A similar exegesis can be offered as regards the dismantling and the final prohibition of FOBS's. Compared with ICBM's, FOBS's were inaccurate, more expensive and destabilising since they could surprise the opponent's defences: their launch would be similar to a space launching, and could attack unexpectedly from a different direction (*e.g.* from the south, unlike ICBM's, which come from the north).

The reason for the non-prohibition of reconnaissance satellites is clear: they provide necessary information for the maintenance of the equilibrium and of the Military Regime. Moreover, they can provide information for other agreements not related with outer space.

The case of ASAT weapons is more complicated. ASAT's did not exist at the time of the initial creation of the regime; and even now, it is dubious whether they have become fully

---

22 A. Coussins, *The Improbable Triumvirate* 124 (1972).

23 J.F. Kennedy, *address*, in UN Document ENDC/102 (30/7/1963).

24 a) Th. Shelling, *Military uses of Outer Space* in World Politics 97-113 (Goldsen, editor, 1963); b) Sponsler, *The Military Role in Space*, Bulletin of the Atomic Scientists 23-26 (June 1964).

developed and form part of the arsenals, even of the USSR. It is true, though, that the Soviets performed a series of tests during the 1970's and that the USA has also tested ASAT's recently. Their use by the superpowers is prohibited by the rule of non-interference, and especially by their function: to provide information essential to the equilibrium's stability. An attack against a simple reconnaissance satellite might be reciprocated, and one against a military telecommunications or an early warning satellite may be considered as a sign of an all-out attack; further, attacking a civilian satellite in peacetime seems illogical. ASAT use, at least against the other superpower, falls under the rules of deterrence, is subjected and related to the philosophy of mutual destruction, and therefore deterred in a similar way as the use of nuclear weapons.

Their deployment in outer space is prohibited because (a) such prohibition is conform to the spirit of maintaining the stability of the equilibrium, (b) their deployment would be contrary to the "non-aggressive use of space" obligation, resulting from the interpretation of the term "peaceful", and (c) to our knowledge, and under the assumption that they are operational, states have not deployed them in outer space. ASAT testing, however, as with testing of ICBM's, and according to the observed practice of states, should be considered as permitted.

B. *Interpretation*[25]

1. *Peaceful.* In the aftermath of the Outer Space Treaty, two schools of thought existed; one arguing that "peaceful" meant "non-aggressive"[26] and the other that the term meant "non-military".[27] Today, according to the above exegesis of the nature of the Military Regime, the meaning of the term "peaceful" as "non-aggressive" should be confirmed.[28] On the one hand, the fact that space was conquered by military means and for military purposes, and on the other, the need of military testing in space and collecting intelligence from military non-aggressive satellites, made a non-military use of space and the adoption of an

---

25 Interpreting the term "peaceful" of the Outer Space Treaty and "Statement D" of the ABM Treaty has led to controversies, notwithstanding the fact that the opposing sides have basically used the same canons of interpretation, provided by Articles 31 and 32 of the Vienna Convention on the Law of Treaties. The problem is how one can identify the law, when the negotiating records are classified, and when even those who have access to them reach different conclusions, as in the case of the State Department's legal advisor, Sofaer, and senator Nunn (The New York Times, at 1 (12/3/1987); The Economist, at 21 (21/3/1987)); moreover, how could an international judge decide over an issue, if he needed to consult a classified negotiating record? In similar cases, the exit from the traditional legal means of interpretation seems necessary. On exiting the legal system, *see supra* note 7 (d).

26 Galloway, in Herczeg, *Introductory Report,* in Proceedings of the 10th Symposium on the Law of Outer Space 106-107 (1967), U.C. School of Law, Davis- Ca., (1968).

27 a) *Ibid.*, at 106;
b) Zhukov, *ibid.*, at 115.

28 "Aggressive" is defined as the activities or systems that can undertake and accomplish an attack; it is not the intention that counts, it is their objective capability.

analogous interpretation of the term "peaceful" impossible.[29] This interpretation was confirmed by Professor Vereshchetin, who declared that "no serious writer in the Soviet Union argues today that 'peaceful' means 'non-military'".[30]

Thus the definition of peaceful as meaning non-aggressive is applicable *ratione loci* to outer space; *ratione modi* to activities conducted in orbit (in order to remain in space they have to be in orbit); *ratione temporis* to activities conducted in peacetime. Aggressive (capable of undertaking and accomplishing an attack by themselves) activities such as the testing of ballistic missiles and ASAT systems, which are permissable constitute an exception to this rule. The prohibition of the testing of ABM systems is an exception to the exception (thus offensive weapons tests are allowed, whilst defensive weapons tests are prohibited).

The scope of the obligation for a non-aggressive use of outer space resulting from this interpretation is, however, limited to that of the Outer Space Treaty; it is limited only to orbital activities and it is limited only during peacetime. Consequently, only ASAT, ICBM and ABM space deployment should be considered as prohibited by the obligation of non-aggressive use of outer space; their testing is free.[31]

2. *Other Principles*. The international character of outer space (which is not subject to appropriation) was established by the first satellites' navigation and was codified by the Outer Space Treaty. The principle of the exploration and use of outer space as "province of all mankind", "for the benefit and in the interests of all countries" and for the "maintenance of peace and security" were shaped and put into practice according to the perceptions of the two powers who had the military and space capabilities to create and enforce them.The concepts of peace and security could not diverge from those expressed by the equilibrium of the superpowers. Since that equilibrium has contributed to the avoidance of a major war, according to this logic all countries benefit. Other benefits resulting from such international co-operation accordingly depend upon the good will or the discretion of the space powers.

3. *"Statement D"*. The controversy over the meaning of the Statement has broken up when officials of the American administration argued for a "broad" interpretation of the ABM Treaty.[32] Given that Article II of the Treaty provides a definitive enumeration of "ABM

---

29 The term "peaceful" in the Outer Space Treaty does not have the meaning of "exclusively peaceful" either, as Kolosov and Stashevskii argue in *The Struggle for Peaceful Outer Space* 202, ISRO Satellite Center (ISAC), Bangalore, India (1986). If that were so, the term "exclusively peaceful" would have been redundant.

30 Vereshchetin, *intervention* (recorded by the author) 29th Colloquium on the Law of Outer Space (1986).

31 During their testing they do not undertake an attack, and they do therefore not constitute an "aggressive" activity.

32 This new interpretation is called "broad" or "revisionist" as opposed to the "restrictive", "strict" or "traditional" interpretation. One could distinguish two rounds of the controversy; one in October 1985

systems and components", "Statement D", they argue, allows development and testing of all ABM systems and components, including space-based, "based on other physical principles" than those existing at the time of the Treaty's conclusion; accordingly, even their deployment could be negotiated.[33]

There should be no doubt about the meaning of the "Statement". The equilibrium of forces achieved between the US and the USSR and the spirit of the Military Regime reflect an attitude of offence.[34] The 1972 ABM Treaty was intended to ban defensive weapons in order to prevent destabilising the equilibrium of offensive ones.[35] The parties to the Treaty decided that their security would rely only on offensive weapons; only one ABM system was allowed after the 1974 Protocol to the Treaty, and the United States decided not to exercise this right and to dismantle all their ABM systems.

The Treaty limits the number of existing ABM systems, prohibits the development, testing and deployment of any space-based ABM systems and conditions upon negotiations the deployment of future land-based ABM systems.

"Statement D" refers only to Article III and does not introduce any exceptions to Article V, prohibiting the development, testing and deployment of all ABM space-based systems, present or future. What it provides is that the parties must negotiate in order to work out the details of a deployment of weapons based on "other physical principles" capable of substituting only those allowed by Article III: land-based ABM systems and components.[36] "Statement D" does not allow therefore the development and testing of any type of space-based ABM systems, nor does it provide for any negotiations of their deployment.

(International Herald Tribune, at 2 (10/10/1985)) and the other in February 1987 (*see* The New York Times (5/2-12/2/1987)); in both cases, and although the administration found it "justified", the "broad" interpretation was not officially adopted.

33 For a legal analysis, *see* the *statement* by Sofaer, Legal Advisor, Department of State, before the Subcommittee on Arms Control, International Security and Science of the House Foreign Affairs Committee, Washington D.C., (22/10/1985) in *The ABM Treaty and the SDI Program*, U.S. Department of State, Bureau of Public Affairs (excerpted from 755 Current Policy).

34 When President Reagan declares that offence is immoral, he reminds us of Premier Kossygin who in 1967 said that "defence is moral; offence is immoral" (Time, at 35 (20/10/1986)). In 1972, the USA persuaded the USSR to abandon defences.

35 *See* Bundy, Kennan, McNamara, & Smith, *The President's Choice: Star Wars or Arms Control*, in Foreign Affairs 264-278 (Winter '84/'85)

36
a) *See* V. Vereshchetin, E. Vasilevskaya, and E. Kamenetskaya, *Outer Space: Politics and Law* 36 (1987);
b) In September 1987, the US Senate adopted an amendment imposing to the administration the observance of the "strict" interpretation; *see* Le Monde, at 1, 5 (19/9/1987).

3. THE FUTURE OF THE MILITARY REGIME.

The aim of this study was not to specify rules that will have to be elaborated in order to limit the militarisation of outer space; such rules may already be found in numerous UN resolutions or agreement proposals made within the Conference on Disarmament. The aim was to observe and explain the creation, maintenance or change, and, accordingly, to make some projections into the future of the Military Regime.

I. First Direction: *Maintenance*

1 (a) In the military field there has been little qualitative change in the actors that can influence the Military Regime. Great Britain and France have developed ballistic missile capabilities, but in the overall equation they side with the US. China has developed ICBM capabilities but has also accepted the Space Regime in general. [37]

In civilian matters, the situation is different. The European Space Agency provides its member states with a space (launching) capability. China and Japan have developed space capabilities and start providing commercial services. India has some space capabilities and is working towards their extension; which might provide India with at least an intermediate range ballistic missile capability. Brazil is also currently working towards the acquisition of a space capability.

(b) There has been no real change in the interests of the actors, though the way in which the USA perceives the realisation of its objectives may have changed.

(c) The power resource of the main actors remains the same; the equilibrium has been solidified and has created higher levels of confidence. This was first achieved through the increase in the respective arsenals, and then by the agreements which laid down the rules for the type and the extent of these arsenals of offensive weapons. The SALT I and II Treaties set numerical limits on the arsenals and emphasised their nature: offensive weapons of one type, ballistic missiles, "no bombs in space", no "fractional orbital missiles". Meanwhile, the two actors have enhanced their capabilities by augmenting their experience in outer space through several space missions and by testing ASAT systems. The latter fact plus the power-instruments envisaged in projects such as SDI, could double the nuclear power resource by adding a real space power in pursuit of the control of outer space, analogous to attempts to control the seas.

(d-1) The "generalised commitment" to a regime for outer space still seems to exist. Only the commitment to the nature of the power resource behind the regime seems to be contested, at least by one side with the SDI project.

---

[37] It seems that these actors do not have the intention to violate the Space Regime.

(d-2) The issue-density is still high and it will continue to be so as day-by-day mankind makes its presence in outer space more permanent; *e.g.* space stations or colonies.

(d-3) The need for information exists and will continue to exist.

2. In terms of the enforcement of specific rules, the Space Regime has fulfilled its aims. In terms of general principles and guidelines, such as the exploration and use of outer space for the benefit of all mankind, one may say that it had been satisfactory but not entirely successful. This assessment, however, depends on one's point of view. The space powers probably consider the regime a success, since they are expected to co-operate. From the point of view of a third world country, this may be considered unsatisfactory.

3 (a) At least one country, the USA, has reassessed its power resource: it envisages a new power resource namely the SDI program. The USA has also reassessed its interests towards the Space Regime. After having contributed over several years to the elaboration of the Moon Agreement, it did not finally ratify it; in this last instance the USSR has acted in the same way.

(b) Naturally all countries have some vested interests in a regime, the elaboration of which started only thirty years ago. The USSR seems to have especially invested in it, since it opposes any change in the nature of the power equilibrium supporting it. But the USA also possesses an interest in the maintenance of a regime that presently satisfies its needs; this will be noted below in 3 (d).

(c) The Space Regime has obtained legitimacy and traditionality. Having reconnaissance satellites in outer space is now considered normal, and even a security system based on missiles which could come from the sky has been accepted.

(d) A shift in the decision-making criteria may be observed within the USA; but this shift may be connected to changes in the relationship of the forces within a specific issue area, such as voting in the UN, and not with a shift in attitude. The report of the National Commission on Space, for example, has recommended to the US government that: "The United States avoid accepting international arrangements that give broad jurisdiction over American activities in space to international bodies in which adversaries have an undue influence or in which decisions will be made by majorities with little current competence in the space field. In addition we recommend against U.S. support for any global organisation that purports to regulate broadly the utilisation of outer space".[38]

---

38 *Pioneering the Space Frontier*, Report of the National Commission on Space 165 (1986).

II. Second Direction: *Change*

Our findings suggest that future political developments, combined with technological developments (which are contrary to existing law) introducing a military-security system of a different nature, will upset the current equilibrium of forces, and consequently destroy most of the Military Regime, as it is basically expressed in its specific rules. An indication of one direction that the regime might take may be discerned from the discussions between the USA and the USSR on disarmament, in particular as regards the elimination or drastic cuts in the number of ICBM's.[39]

Change in the regime will depend on the number and nature of the changes in the military-security equation. The outbreak of war or a drastic change of the balance of power would mean the disappearance of the entire regime. If, for example, one country achieves absolute superiority, then even the rule of free navigation in outer space could be challenged. If a change in the spirit of the military-security equation occurs, then, according to the findings of the Method of Genetic Effectiveness, a new Military Regime will not appear before a new equilibrium of forces, with different characteristics, has solidified.[40]

The new actors in the civilian space activities issue-area do not seem to be able to directly influence the transformation of the present or the creation of a new Military Regime; in any case, they cannot provoke a radical change of it. Although they are capable of developing some primitive space weapons [41], their overall military space power, even sided with one of the two superpowers, cannot modify the equilibrium of forces established between the two superpowers. The way they may influence the evolution of the Military Regime is indirect[42]: either by exercising diplomatic or public opinion pressure on the two superpowers, together with other third/non-space actors, or, and most important, by linking developments in the Civilian Regime with those in the military.

What would be the future of the Civilian Regime and how would a change of the Military Regime affect it, since the former is related to the latter by virtue of being based on common principles? The issue-area of the civilian use of outer space has become semi-independent from the military uses, with its own power resource: civilian space launching capabilities. In recent years the latter has become separated from the initial ICBM military power resource. Today more countries have entered the space arena and compete quite successfully with the two major powers. In the remote sensing area it is not military power that counts but remote sensing capabilities; the role played by France in the elaboration of

---

39 Time, at 20 (20/10/1986).

40 According, also, to both the "market failure" and the "prisoners dilemma" models; *see*: *supra* note 4, at 334-335 and *supra* note 8 c, at 307, respectively.

41 *E.g.* ASAT's functioning on the basis of small nuclear explosions in space.

42 The importance of this influence and its impact cannot be easily determined and measured.

the last remote sensing "draft agreement" supports this argument. Thus, only a change in the general principles will have an effect; simple changes in the rules of the Military Regime would not seem to alter the Civilian Regime. This line of argument does not by any means suggest that the USA - USSR role is not important for the Civilian Regime. The endorsement of an agreement on the civilian use of outer space by them is still a condition for its effectiveness, since they possess the most important space capabilities; the ineffectiveness of the Moon Agreement provides enough evidence for this argument.

IV. CONCLUSION

We cannot predict the future of the Military Regime. We can only identify basic factors conditioning its future and alternative directions that might be taken. The Method of Genetic Effectiveness has indicated that an equilibrium of strategic forces and an active involvement of the two superpowers were essential for the creation and maintenance of the present regime, and will very likely continue to be for any future evolution. Yet, these two factors were not, and will not be sufficient if a new Military Regime or changes to the present are to occur. Independently of the level at which the equilibrium is established, co-operation, information and benefits[43] for third actors are necessary.

In the age of thermonuclear weapons, it does not appear probable that "exotic" technologies and space weapons will lead to the creation of an absolute hegemony, although their possession by only two countries might lead to a co-hegemonial situation. Whatever the outcome of the arms race for the mastery of space will be, a new equilibrium will be reached which will again require collaboration in order to avert war and co-operation in order to form and maintain a new regime. Would it not be wiser for such co-operation to start now?

---

43 In order that the Regime is respected and gains legitimacy.

THE PROGRESSIVE DEVELOPMENT OF SPACE LAW: NEW OPPORTUNITIES AND RESTRAINTS

Gennady M. Danilenko*

1. INTRODUCTION

International space law, just as international law in general, is in a process of constant change, reflecting changes within the international community. The future development of space law is and will continue to be determined by a number of factors, including political, economic, military and cognate interests of states in the exploration and use of outer space and its resources, the development of technology and the overall state of political and economic relations in the world.

The complexity of factors which directly or indirectly influence the formation of international space law makes any prediction about its future hazardous. However, because space law has traditionally been based on anticipatory regulation, a number of future problems have already been outlined by existing normative structures and policy trends. Additionally it is important to be aware of the fact that the development of space law does not take place in a legal vacuum. Therefore, some future problems may be assessed in the light of existing trends in international law in general. Of particular importance in this respect is the existing experience in the regulation of analogous problems in other fields of international law. Thus, the negotiations in the framework of the Third United Nations Conference on the Law of the Sea concerning areas and resources beyond the limits of national jurisdiction can give an indication of problems that may arise in future negotiations concerning outer space.

Within the confines of a brief article it is not possible to analyse all the major problems concerning the progressive development of international space law. Therefore, this article focusses on some general trends which, if realised, could change the whole structure of existing space law. These trends relate to (a) the establishment of a more equitable international space order, (b) the determination of adequate mechanisms for international cooperation and (c) the maintenance of space for peaceful purposes. It is submitted that these areas not only open new opportunities for the progressive development of space law, but also show political, economic and legal realities that determine the prospects for their realisation.

2. ESTABLISHMENT OF A MORE EQUITABLE SPACE ORDER

The dominant factor which will influence the future development of space law is the increasing economic value of outer space. The growing economic benefits to be gained

---

* Research Fellow, Institute of State and Law, Moscow, USSR.

from conducting space activities will lead to the emergence of conflicting interests and claims of various states regarding outer space. With the advances of space technology in such areas as telecommunications and remote sensing, and emerging prospects for its application in other spheres, particularly energy production, materials processing and the mining of precious metals available on the Moon and asteroids, problems relating to political-economic principals of space utilisation will definitely be pushed to the fore. Against the background of ongoing negotiations and discussions concerning the global rearrangement of existing economic relations and the establishment of a New International Economic Order (NIEO), future law-making negotiations for space will have to address a number of difficult questions relating to resource management and the distribution of derived benefits.

Reflecting the demands of the developing countries, the aim of a NIEO with respect to resources outside national jurisdiction is to establish a regime that would redress existing inequalities concerning the allocation of access to these resources. The developing countries, lacking the necessary technological and financial capabilities to exploit space recources, seek to use political-legal means to gain participation in the management and exploitation of these resources and the resulting benefits.

The Outer Space Treaty[1], although adopted at a time when the concept of a NIEO did not yet exist, stipulates that "the exploration and use of outer space, including the Moon and other celestial bodies, shall be carried out for the benefit and in the interests of all countries, irrespective of their degree of economic or scientific development".[2]
Even during the negotiations leading to the Outer Space Treaty, the developing countries pressed for the adoption of more concrete obligations in this area.[3] Within the context of demands by the developing countries for a more equitable redistribution of the world's resources, their current aim is to advocate the incorporation into space law of new principles and rules that would narrow the gap between developing and developed countries and guarantee factual equality as regards access to outer space and its resources.

Dissatisfaction with the present conditions of access to the resources of outer space has given rise to unilateral claims to a resource that currently has the greatest economic value.

---

[1] Treaty on Principles Governing the Activities of States in the Exploration and Use of Outer Space, Including the Moon and Other Celestial Bodies, 1967, 610 UNTS 205.

[2] Article 1.

[3] Thus, the representative of the United Arab Republic in the Legal Sub-Committee of the United Nations Committee on the Peaceful Uses of Outer Space (UNCOPUOS) has stated that a future outer space treaty should contain concrete norms that would provide "possibilities to non-space powers to enable them to participate in and to draw benefits from the exploration and use of outer space with the aim of deriving practical benefits relating to their economic and social development", UN DOC. A/AC. 105/C.2/SR 65, 8 (1966).

In their joint Bogotà Declaration of 1976[4], seven equatorial countries claimed that the geostationary orbit is a natural resource over which subjacent states have complete and exclusive sovereignty. On the other hand, various ideas have been developed aimed at a complete internationalisation of space activities. In this respect the concept of the "common heritage of mankind" plays a major role. The negotiations relating to the regime of the Moon, which were considered by the developing countries as a major step towards the establishment of a NIEO[5], resulted in the adoption of the Moon Agreement[6], which proclaimed that the Moon and its resources belong to the "common heritage of mankind".[7] Although the Moon Agreement states the legal consequences of the concept of the "common heritage of mankind" only in the most general terms, it is considered by the developing countries as a major achievement in their efforts to obtain real participation in the development of and benefits from the resources of the Moon.

As space activities move from exploration to commercial exploitation, the demands for the promotion of specific regimes which in one form or another guarantee benefits for states lacking space technology will intensify. In view of the increasing commercialisation of outer space, a number of countries have already articulated the necessity for "those countries that do not have space technology to have access to such commercialisation and to be able to participate in the benefits to be derived therefrom".[8]

Underlying the demands for a more equitable space order as regards the resource management and distribution of the derived benefits is the concept of equity. There has been a call for equitable access to resources of outer space, their equitable use and equitable distribution of benefits derived therefrom. Considered in the context of distributive justice, the new concept of equity requires the granting of such access to space resources or distribution of benefits as recognises the preferential rights of the developing countries, thus promoting *de facto* equality. Consequently, in the course of negotiations concerning specific problems of space law, there exists a strong pressure to regard as equitable only such legal regimes that take into account in the first place the special interests and needs of the developing countries.

---

[4] Declaration of the First Meeting of Equatorial Countries, signed in Bogotà, Colombia, December 3, 1976, by Brazil, Colombia, Ecuador, Indonesia, Kenya, Uganda, and Zaire. For an English translation of this document, *see* 6 Journal of Space Law 193 *ff.* (1978).

[5] *See, e.g.*, the statements in the COPUOS of the representatives of Venezuela (UN Doc. A/AC. 105/PV 171, 68 (1977)), Brazil (UN Doc. A/Ac. 105/PV 172, 26 (1977)) and Colombia (UN Doc. A/AC. 105/C.2/SR 291, 6 (1978)).

[6] Agreement Governing the Activities of States on the Moon and Other Celestial Bodies, 1979, UN Doc. A/3420.

[7] *Id.*, Article 11 (1).

[8] UN Doc. A/AC. 105/370, 7 (1986).

From a political-legal perspective, the desire of a large number of countries to endow space law with broad functions relating to the reallocation of space resources and benefits in order to achieve factual equality amounts to a fundamental revision of the existing system of space law which mandates *de jure* equality of states.[9] It is not surprising , therefore, that some states are directly calling for the creation of "a new international order in outer space"[10] or for a "new space law guaranteeing the equitable use of outer space".[11]

Although under the given circumstances the demands for the creation of a new space law are unlikely to succeed, it is reasonable to assume that the insistence of a large number of states, constituting the majority of the international community, on the establishment of a NIEO in general and of a more equitable space order in particular will have an impact on the content of the future law of outer space.

In this connection, a number of difficult problems arise in view of the political and economic realities prevailing in the international community and specific characteristics of the international law-making process. From a broad perspective, there are serious doubts as to whether it is possible to provide space law with functions aimed at creating factual equality as long as the international community is based on the co-existence of states with different socio-economic systems. From a policy perspective, of particular importance is the fact that any attempt to establish a new space order can only be successful if it is based on a realistic assessment of existing power structures within the international community. From this point of view, a greater participation of a large number of developing countries lacking space capabilities in the process of decision-making concerning outer space may create situations in which the potential legal significance of the majority view may be easily inflated. Experience indicates that if states lacking space capabilities but commanding numerical superiority try to control the process of law-creation, various impractical proposals inevitably find their way into multilateral legal instruments. Combined with the traditional tendency towards anticipatory regulation in space law this may result in excessive legal regulation having an adverse effect on emerging space activities.[12]

---

[9] According to Article 1 of the Outer Space Treaty, "outer space , including the Moon and other celestial bodies, shall be free for exploration and use by all states without discrimination of any kind on a basis of equality".

[10] The statement in the Legal Sub-Committee of the UNCOPUOS of the representative of Colombia, UN Doc. A/AC. 105/C.2/SR 405, 6 (1984).

[11] The statement in the UNCOPUOS of the representative of Indonesia, UN Doc. A/AC. 105/SR 289, 6 (1986).

[12] During the negotiations leading to the Moon Agreement, the Soviet representative pointed out the dangers of such an unnecessary excessive regulation, particularly as regards the exploitation of lunar resources and distribution of benefits. He stated, among other things, that "there was a danger that legal norms lacking any practical value might be adopted, norms that would have no relationship to the real tasks and trends of Moon exploration and would therefore hamper rather than stimulate that activity thus having a retrogressive effect" UN Doc. A/AC 105/C.2/SR 226, 8 (1975).

Consequently, there is a danger that negotiated legal instruments, even if adopted through consensus, would not eventually receive sufficient support, especially on the part of states whose interests are specially affected.

It is evident, however, that without the participation of the specially affected states, notably the major space powers, the establishment of a universal and effective legal regime for outer space is impossible. Just as before, the interests of space powers will in the years to come be the major factor in the process of elaboration of any new principles, concepts and concrete rules of space law. Thus, notwithstanding the strong pressure to consider equity exclusively in terms of special interests and needs of the developing countries, existing space law in defining concepts of "equitable access" or "equitable distribution" also takes into account the interests of states directly participating in space activities. According to Article 33 of the International Telecommunications Convention[13], "equitable access" to the geostationary orbit requires that not only the special needs of the developing countries be taken into account, but also a number of other factors, notably considerations of efficient and economical use, which protect the interests of states having a real need for the use of the orbit. Similarly, providing for "an equitable sharing" of benefits from lunar resources, the Moon Agreement stipulates that special consideration shall be given not only to the interests and needs of the developing countries, but also to the efforts of those countries which have contributed either directly or indirectly to the exploration of the Moon.[14] In view of this trend, it seems reasonable to assume that new developments in the area of translating general notions of equity into specific rules and procedures which will guarantee equitable access to space resources and equitable sharing of the derived benefits will be practicable only if they accomodate the interests of all countries, including those of states carrying out space activities.

Political and legal realities will also determine the prospects of the realisation of a number of specific steps aimed at restructuring existing space law. Thus, unilateral claims to the geostationary orbit are unlikely to succeed because of their unacceptability to the overwhelming majority of states supporting the existing principle of freedom of exploration and use of outer space. Not only developed, but also developing states seem to share the view that the establishment of the exclusive control of equatorial countries over segments of the geostationary orbit would be incompatible with the general policy aimed at guaranteeing equitable access to space resources for all states. An additional consideration is the fact that the geostationary orbit is definitely located in outer space which is free for exploration and use by all states.[15]

---

[13] International Telecommunications Convention, Nairobi, 1982.

[14] Article 11 (7).

[15] The emergence of claims to the geostationary orbit reflects existing experience, especially in the law of the sea, that in situations where there is no precise boundary between zones of national jurisdiction and international areas the increasing economic value of the resources of adjacent areas

A more complex situation arises in the case of the concept of the "common heritage of mankind". Although as such this concept has already received certain recognition in space law, the prospects of its implementation depend on a number of factors, including legal ones. The most important legal issue that the international community will have to address in this connection is whether the existing law recognising the legitimacy of unilateral exploitation of space resources should be abrogated. The existing consensus in this respect is based on the Outer Space Treaty which proclaimed the freedom of exploration and use of outer space, including the Moon and other celestial bodies.[16] The negotiating history of the Outer Space Treaty[17], subsequent actual practice and official statements of various states[18] indicate that the notion of "use" also includes exploitation of space resources.

From a policy perspective, how this issue will be settled in the future will determine the nature and specific content of an international regime for the natural resources of the Moon envisaged in the Moon Agreement.[19] Effective implementation of the concept of the "common heritage of mankind", particularly the creation of a regime providing for the factual equality of states in the management and exploitation of lunar resources, is possible only in a situation where states do not have the right to exploit these resources in accordance with their national programmes. Only in such a legal situation will states possessing space technology be inclined to agree to a number of essential conditions, including possible financial payments and technology transfers.

It is the realisation of this fact that has led the proponents of the concept of the "common heritage of mankind" to press for the adoption of such political-legal principals as would restrict or exclude unilateral access to the resources of the Moon. During the negotiations leading to the Moon Agreement, suggestions were made that the exploitation of lunar

---

creates a danger of unilateral extention of territorial jurisdiction. In this case existing customary law defining the limits of outer space at the lowest perigees of orbiting satellites (For details *see* Vereshchetin & Danilenko, *Custom as a Source of International Law of Outer Space*, 13 Journal of Space Law 22 *ff.* (1985)) is sufficient to refute claims that the geostationary orbit was not in outer space. However, the potential significance of the establishment of a precise boundary for the future development of space law should not be underestimated. It appears that the traditional arguments against the treaty determination of a boundary between air and outer space, namely that there were no practical problems in this area and no scientific basis for defining a boundary (*See e.g.*, UN Doc. A/AC. 105/370, 21 (1986)) do not take this into account. Such arguments are also largely irrelevant because they fail to recognise the fact that every delimitation is not a scientific, but, as the Chamber of the International Court of Justice put it, a "legal-political operation". Even in cases where it is possible to discern a natural boundary, stressed the Chamber, the political delimitation has not necessarily "to follow the same line", I.C.J. Reports 277 (1984).

16 Article 1.

17 *See e.g.* the statement in the Legal Sub-Committee of the UNCOPUOS of the representative of France (UN Doc. A/AC. 105/C.2/SR 57, 16 (1966).

18 *See e.g.* the statements of the representatives of Italy (UN Doc. A/AC. 105/C.2/SR 202, 78 (1973)) and the GDR (UN Doc. A/AC. 105/C.2/SR 246, 7 (1976)).

19 Article 11 (5).

resources should be carried out only as "part of an international effort".[20] There was also strong pressure to establish a moratorium on the exploitation of the resources of the Moon prior to the establishment of the international regime.[21] However, in contrast to the law of the sea where the tendency towards an "exclusive" character of the "common heritage of mankind" regime initially led to the adoption of the Moratorium Resolution[22] and resulted in the Law of the Sea Convention[23] which stipulates that no state may exercise rights with respect to minerals recovered from the seabed except in accordance with the Convention[24], existing space law does not contain any prohibition on the unilateral exploitation of space resources. It remains to be seen what direction future space law will take in this respect. For the time being, it is important to note that the provisions of the Outer Space Treaty providing for the freedom of use of outer space and the absence of any explicit norms establishing a moratorium on lunar exploitation in the Moon Agreement are likely to be major legal factors influencing the outcome of future law-making activities. Even if the Moon Agreement will be interpreted as establishing a moratorium, as long as it remains practically ineffective due to the non-participation of the leading space powers, attempts to declare the unilateral exploitation of the resources of the Moon illegal would encounter serious political and legal difficulties.

3. NEW MECHANISMS FOR INTERNATIONAL COOPERATION IN SPACE

The implementation of a more equitable space order will depend to a large extent on the determination of adequate machinery for international cooperation in the use of outer space. New opportunities provided by the advances in space technology and the resulting requirement for intensified international cooperation are pushing to the fore problems related to the creation of an effective institutional framework for such cooperation.

Various proposals in this respect have been made right from the beginning of the space age.[25] Although a number of international institutions dealing with outer space activities

---

[20] The statement of the representative of Lebanon (UN Doc. A/AC. 105/C.2/SR 188, 21 (1973)).

[21] *See e.g.* the statements of the representatives of India (UN Doc. A/AC. 105/PV 123, 6 (1973)) and Mexico (UN Doc. A/AC. 105/PV 173, 41 (1977)).

[22] UN Doc. A/Res. 2574 (1969).

[23] United Nations Convention on the Law of the Sea, UN Doc. A/Conf. 62/122 (1982).

[24] Article 173 (3). Under the Convention state parties, state entities, natural or juridical persons do not have a direct access to the seabed. According to Article 153 of the Convention, exploration and exploitation of the resources of the seabed can be carried out only under a contract between potential miners and the International Seabed Authority which organises, carries out and controls activities on the seabed "on behalf of mankind as a whole".

[25] Already during the negotiations on the Outer Space Treaty the representative of the United Arab Republic pointed out the necessity of "institutionalising certain forms of cooperation" in order to "ensure real equality of all countries", UN Doc. A/AC. 105/C.2/SR 70, 10 (1966).

already exist, in the light of new developments new proposals were advanced outlining the direction which might be taken in a search for organisational solutions acceptable to all states.

During the negotiations leading to the Moon Agreement, various states pressed for a complete internationalisation of the activities relating to the exploitation of the resources of the Moon. Using the model adopted in the ongoing law of the sea negotiations, proponents of the concept of the "common heritage of mankind" proposed that the exploitation of the lunar resources should be, as the representative of Argentine put it, "subject to an international authority which, in the name of mankind, would apply laws and jurisdiction designed to solve possible conflicts".[26] Suggestions were made that an international authority should collect and distribute the benefits from the development of the resources of the Moon. However, notwithstanding the views to the contrary[27], in its present form the Moon Agreement does not provide for any international organisation. It only creates an obligation to "establish an international regime, including appropriate procedures, to govern the exploitation of the natural resources of the Moon".[28] Future negotiations will determine whether the term"appropriate procedures" would simply denote a system of concrete rules regulating the exploitation of the resources or a new international institution and, if so, what form such an institution would take.

In any event, in the light of present experience it appears to be clear that proposals aimed at a complete internationalisation of space activities would be impracticable. It seems that in the future only ideas seeking an effective coordination of national space programmes in order to attain the rational use of existing resources and technology will be of practical relevance. Proceeding from such considerations, the Soviet Union recently put forward two concrete proposals relating to institutional aspects of international cooperation in the peaceful uses of outer space. These concerned the establishment (a) of a World Space Organisation[29] and (b) of an international space centre.[30] Both proposals are based on the assumption that fruitful cooperation in space calls for the strict observance of the principles

---

[26] UN Doc. A/AC. 105/C.2/SR 190, 42 (1972). *See also* UN Doc. A/AC. 105/PV 169, 31-35 (1976). For similar proposals on the doctrinal level *see e.g.*, Nesgos, *The Proposed International Sea-Bed Authority as a Model for the Future Outer Space International Regime*, 5 Annals of Air and Space Law 549 (1980).

[27] *See* Cocca, *Introduction to the Study of the Legal Framework for Economic Activity in Space* (Encuadre juridico de la actividad economica en el espacio) 113 (1982). C.Q. Christol, *The Modern International Law of Outer Space* 357 (1982).

[28] Article 11 (5).

[29] *See* the letter of N.I. Ryzhkov, Chairman of the Council of Ministers of the USSR, to the UN Secretary General. Pravda, 13 June 1986. *See also* UN Doc. A/41/470, 34-38(1986).

[30] *See* the statement of M.S. Gorbachev, the General Secretary of the CPSU Central Committee, Pravda, November 28, 1986. *See also* the statement of N.I. Ryzhkov, Pravda, 7 January 1987.

of equality and mutual benefit and should take into account the present possibilities and prospects for the development of space technology and the real needs of participating states.

(a) Realisation of the proposal relating to the creation of a World Space Organisation would result in the establishment of a universal international organisation which would coordinate national space programmes and carry out large-scale international projects in various areas of space science and technology. This would ensure that all states, in particular the developing countries, which would participate in these projects under preferential conditions, would be granted access to scientific and technical achievements in the exploration and use of outer space. The Soviet project provides for a gradual increase in cooperation in the framework of a new organisation, leading to the joint manufacture of spacecraft and exploitation of circumterrestrial space.

(b) The proposal concerning the creation of an international space centre aims at promoting closer cooperation between developing and developed countries in space. Established by the leading space powers, such a centre would develop space technology at the request of developing countries and provide opportunities for training of their technical personnel. It would also have its own launch facilities and provide launch services.

At this stage it is difficult to predict the forms of institutional arrangement which will be acceptable to all states in the future. It is, however, clear that as space activities intensify, the need for an effective universal institutional framework for international cooperation will become more evident.

4. MAINTAINING OUTER SPACE FOR PEACEFUL PURPOSES

In the course of the ongoing debates concerning a more equitable international space order, there is a growing recognition of the fact that efforts aimed at establishing such an order will only be meaningful if outer space is preserved for peaceful purposes. It is generally acknowledged that averting an arms race in outer space is a prerequisite for fruitful international cooperation. Recognising the close link between the prevention of an arms race in outer space and the development of international cooperation, the Second United Nations Conference on the Exploration and Peaceful Uses of Outer Space of 1982 (UNISPACE 2) stressed that "the prevention of an arms race and hostilities in outer space is an essential condition of international cooperation and use of outer space for peaceful purposes".[31]

---

[31] UN Doc. A/Conf. 101/10, paragraph 14 (1982).

The urgency of adopting measures to stop the trend towards militarisation of outer space is heightened by rapid technological advances resulting in the feasibility of developing and deploying specific weapons systems intended for use in outer space. The materialisation of the SDI programme (commonly known as "Star Wars") adopted by the present US administration[32] would transform existing technological possibilities into political and military reality.

Besides the negative military and political consequences relating to strategic stability and increased tension, the introduction of space weapons would have devastating effects on civilian space programmes. As in any other new field of human endeavour, space exploration and exploitation require the existence of favourable conditions at national and international level. An arms race in outer space would inevitably divert intellectual and material resources that are essential to the economic development of space. The use of orbital resources, including the limited resources of the geostationary orbit, for stationing hundreds and thousands of military satellites needed to implement the "Star Wars" programme would severely reduce the opportunities for civilian utilisation.[33]

Any perspective on the further development of space law in the domain of preserving outer space for peaceful purposes will be determined by the interest of the international community in adopting effective measures aimed at averting an arms reace in outer space and by the changing international political environment. Clarification of legal issues in this regard involves the assessment of existing law and the elaboration of specific proposals. In discussing relevant legal aspects, it is important to note that existing space law does not exclude all military uses of outer space. Admittedly, there is much to be said for the view that the provision of the Outer Space Treaty according to which the exploration and use of outer space "shall be carried out for the benefit of mankind and in the interests of all countries"[34] can be interpreted as entailing a prohibition on uses of outer space for military purposes.[35]

However, the Outer Space Treaty specifically forbids only the stationing of nuclear weapons or any other kind of weapons of mass destruction in outer space.[36] According to

---

[32] *See* 19 Weekly Compilation of Presidential Documents 442 (1983, No. 12).

[33] It has been suggested that as the result of the deployment of thousands of military satellites in space having their own protective keep-out zones of hundreds and thousands km in diameter "space will likely become too crowded with literary no room for satellites to move" *SDI: Progress and Challenges* 38, US Congress, Senate, Defence Appropriation Committee, Staff Report, Washington (1986).

[34] Article 1.

[35] *See* Marcoff, *Principes Fondamentaux du droit international de l'espace,* in 10 Air and Outer Space Law 253 *ff.* (D.S. Constanstopoulos, editor, Thessaloniki 1981).

[36] Article IV.

the Treaty any military activity is excluded only on the Moon and other celestial bodies.[37] The Moon Agreement does not contain anything new in this respect.[38] Consequently, whereas the testing and deployment of a space-based anti-missile system envisaged by the SDI programme would clearly violate the provisions of the US-Soviet ABM-Treaty[39], the existing multilateral treaty framework only provides concrete legal obstacles to its realisation if it is to be based on weapons systems that can be designated as nuclear weapons or weapons of mass destruction.

In view of the inadequacy of existing law, it is clear that real progress in the area of non-militarisation of outer space requires elaboration of new concrete legal rules that would effectively limit or prevent military uses of outer space. Because of the destabilising effect that the introduction of space weapons would have on the overall political and military situation, discussions and law-making efforts relating to non-militarisation of outer space tend to focus on measures to prevent its weaponisation.

Recognising the importance of bilateral negotiations in this field, the Soviet Union has also put forward at the UN a number of concrete proposals aimed at preventing all kinds of weapons in outer space. These include a Draft Treaty on the Prohibition of the Stationing of Weapons of any Kind in Outer Space[40] and a Draft Treaty on the Prohibition of the Use of Force in Outer Space and from Space against the Earth[41] which envisage the prohibition on testing, deployment and use of space weapons.

It is important to note that by advancing these far-reaching proposals the Soviet Union stresses the need for strict international verification of compliance with the negotiated agreements. In the view of the Soviet Union, the proposed World Space Organisation could fulfil important functions in this respect. For monitoring purposes the World Space Organisation could initially use technical means provided by the space powers, and later its own facilities.

Analysis of bilateral and multilateral negotiations indicates that progress in the development of space law in the sphere of non-weaponisation of outer space has been impeded primarily

---

37 *Id.*

38 *See* Article 3.

39 United States of America and Union of Soviet Socialist Republics. Treaty on the Limitation of Anti-Ballistic Missile Systems, 1972, 944 UNTS 13. Under Article V of the Treaty each party "undertakes not to develop, test, or deploy ABM systems or components which are sea-based, air-based, space-based or mobile land-based". For details *see* Vereshchetin, *"Strategic Defense Initiative" and International Law*, Proceedings of the 29th Colloquium on the Law of the Outer Space 94-99 (1987).

40 *See* Pravda, 12 August 1981, *See also* UN Doc. A/36/192 (1981).

41 *See* Pravda, 22 August 1983. *See also* UN Doc. A/38/194 (1983).

by an unfavourable political climate. It is quite clear that a successful outcome to negotiations on the prevention of an arms race in outer space requires a display of political will on the part of those states whose participation is crucial for the resolution of the issue. The political commitment to space armament programmes, especially to SDI, on the part of the United States is a major obstacle in this area. If internal and international processes should lead to a change in United States' attitude, the interest of the international community in the prevention of an arms race in outer space could be easily transformed into effective legal obligations of a universal character.

5. CONCLUSION

The rapid development of space technology, the advent of economic utilisation of outer space and the growing interests of various states in the application of space technology heighten the need for adequate legal rules governing the use of outer space. In the years to come space law faces a serious challenge in establishing a legal order in space that would guarantee equitable allocation of space resources and benefits resulting from their exploitation.

Whether or not new developments in space law and policy will result in a more equitable space order depends both on the ability of the international community to preserve outer space for peaceful purposes and on the ability to establish new legal rules that provide for the orderly utilisation of outer space and facilitate international cooperation in the interests of all mankind.

Chapter Four

The Changing Role of States in the Regulation of Space Activities

THE CONTRIBUTION OF THE DEVELOPING COUNTRIES TO THE LEGAL FORMULATION OF FUTURE SPACE LAW

Ida Bagus Rahmadi Supancana*

1. INTRODUCTION

Three decades after the first human venture into space with the launching of Sputnik I, space science and technology have reached an advanced stage. A whole series of successes has been achieved in this fourth dimension of human activity[1], including the landing of man on the Moon in the Apollo II mission; the construction of a space platform/station and space laboratory to carry out scientific research; the landing of an unmanned spacecraft on the surface of Mars; and also the launching of the Space Shuttle, regarded as marking a new era in space activity.
Space science and technology have brought improvements in human life. Many satellites have been launched into outer space for a variety of functions such as telecommunications, meteorology, remote sensing, navigation *etc*.. More diverse activities are being considered. These range from constructing large space structures for industry[2], to burying the dead in a certain orbit in outer space.[3] Now, people are enjoying the benefits achieved by space science and technology: direct television broadcasting by satellites placed in outer space enables the direct transmission of pictures of international events from all over the world; direct telephone links via satellite connect people from different countries; the use of meteorological satellites for weather forecasts; the use of remote sensing satellites to detect natural resources on earth and as an early warning system against natural disasters.

Besides improving human life and prosperity, space activities may also threaten human life and the environmental balance. The re-entry of the Soviet nuclear powered satellite "Cosmos 954" into Canadian territory on 24 January 1978 highlights the danger of such activities.[4] With the rapid growth of satellites launched into outer space using nuclear power sources, the threat to human life increases. Environmental harm may also result from such other activities as the continued and unregulated use of high energy laser beams; high frequency microwave emissions; ozone destroying aerosols and the introduction of

---

* Asst. Legal Expert, The Minister Coordinator for Political Affairs and Security, Jakarta, Indonesia.

1 Land was the first dimension of human activity; the second started when man turned his activities to the water, and the third dimension began when aircraft as a means of air transportation was invented.

2 A certain chemical process in non-gravitational conditions can be applied to convert alloy into precious metal.

3 A private enterprise called 3M has even offered to bury human bodies by putting them in a capsule and placing it in a certain orbit in outer space. With the natural characteristics of outer space, it is hoped that the bodies would not decay.

4 *See* Christol, *Protection of Space from Environmental Harms*, Annals of Air and Space Law 433 (1979). *See also* Bhatt, *An Ecological Approach to Aerospace Law*, *id*., at 385.

disease laden objects into space. Weather modification activities may also be fitted into this category.

Such contamination and pollution may result from planned activities or experiments, or a result from accidents.[5] Still fresh in the mind is the "Challenger" disaster which took the lives of all its crew members. However, this was not the first accident. Virgill Grissom, Edward White and Robert Chafee died on 27 January 1967 whilst undergoing a test for an Apollo flight. Also, on 30 June 1971, the crew of Soyuz II (Georgy Dobrovolsky, Victor Patsayev and Vladislaw Volkov) were found dead in their cabin.[6] Furthermore, the stationing of satellites in the geostationary satellite orbit (GSO) can cause radio frequency interference and could result in collisions between space objects.

Although the 1967 Treaty on Principles Governing the Activities of States in Exploration and Use of Outer Space was designed to guarantee that such activities should be for the benefit of and in the interest of all countries, and should be for peaceful purposes, it may be observed that 75% of the activities in outer space have been conducted for military purposes.[7] Space Powers are competing to gain military superiority with the aid of space science and technology. Much space research has been directed at developing sophisticated weapons and space defence systems such as anti-satellite weapons, laser beams and particle beams. An arms race in space increases the potential threat to human lives and the environment.

So far, space activities have been dominated by "the Space Powers" (USA and USSR) and "the Potential Space Powers" (Europe, Japan, India, China and Canada), while most of the developing countries are "Late Comers" and as a consequence, the achievements of space technology have largely been enjoyed by the developed countries. For example, in the field of communications, it was stated at the Second United Nations Conference on the Exploration and Peaceful uses of Outer Space that as of 31 December 1981 a total of about 220 satellites have been launched into the geostationary orbit (GSO) for various telecommunications purposes (including broadcasting, meteorology, and other services, as well as for scientific experimentation) or had been notified to the ITU as being planned. Of these, 63 satellites are intended for international public telecommunications services (INTELSAT, INTERSPUTNIK, INMARSAT). Of the 157 remaining satellites, 128 have

---

[5] *See* Lay and Taubenfeld, *Modification of the human environment*, in IV The Future of the International Legal Order : The Structure of the International Environment 124-154 (C.E. Black and R.A. Falks, editors, 1972).

[6] *See* Manfred Lachs, *The Law of outer Space* 2 (1972).

[7] *See* Jasani, *The Military Use of Outer Space*, in World Armament and Disarmament 351 (SIPRI Yearbook, 1984).

been notified by the developed countries and 29 by the developing countries.[8] This imbalance is a cause of specific concern for the developing countries.

The purpose and objective of this chapter is to analyse several areas of existing space law as regards the experience, needs and interests of developing countries and to examine whether existing space law has met the needs of all states in a just, equitable and rational way. Several questions need to be asked concerning existing space law:

- Are the legal principles laid down by existing space law able to accommodate the interests and needs of all countries, irrespective of their degree of economic or scientific development?
- Are there any doctrines which are no longer relevant in accommodating the needs and interests of all countries in a just, equitable and rational way?
- In what ways have the developing countries so far taken part in the legal formulation of space law?

The answers to these questions may be useful when considering the future development of space law. In order to formulate future space law, we must be able to predict future space activities, for these will throw up new legal problems. Participation of private enterprises in space, for example, deserves urgent consideration to guarantee that such activities will be covered by law. Several methods may be applicable in formulating future rules governing space activities.[9] One may:

a. Commence with international law and apply its principles by way of analogy to relationships in space; and
b. Create new principles of law based on the characteristic nature of space activities.

2. THE DEVELOPMENT OF INTERNATIONAL SPACE LAW

Before analysing the present law, it is important, briefly, to trace the development of international space law, in order to obtain a comprehensive picture of how it was formulated, including the participation of developing countries and the problems involved.

The development of international space law is closely related to the successful mission of Sputnik I to orbit the Earth on 4 October 1957. Immediately after that historic success, the General Assembly of the United Nations issued resolution 1148 (XII) which stressed the

---

[8] *See* Paragraph 62 of the *Report of the Second United Nations Conference on the Exploration and Peaceful Uses of Outer Space* (Vienna, 9-21 August 1982; hereinafter Unispace Report).

[9] *See* Sierra Vasques, *Cosmic International Law*, Translated by Elaine Malley, Wayne State University Press 19 (Detroit 1965)

need to draw up an international treaty on disarmament including a provision that any object launched into outer space should be for peaceful purposes.[10]

The development of space law should not be separated from the role of international law and international cooperation. International law has codified some fundamental principles, while international cooperation guides this activity towards the benefit of mankind and international peace.[11] The establishment of several international organisations, including the Committee on Space Research (COSPAR), the World Meteorological Organisation (WMO), the International Astronautical Federation (IAF), the International Telecommunication Union (ITU) and even the United Nations Committee on the Peaceful Uses of Outer Space (UNCOPUOS) are the result of international cooperation.

Space law has developed in two forms; firstly in the form of a series of resolutions, either multilateral or unilateral; secondly, by the negotiation of international conventions.[12]

Several resolutions are worth noting. General Assembly resolution 1721 of 20 December 1961 states that international law including the Charter of the United Nations shall apply to all activities in outer space, including the Moon and other celestial bodies. It also stresses that the exploration and use of outer space should be for peaceful purposes. Resolution 1802 (XVII) of 14 December 1962 urged for an immediate effort to formulate legal principles governing the activities of states in the exploration and use of outer space, including the Moon and other celestial bodies. The resulting principles also contain provisions on international liability for damage caused by aircraft accidents, on the giving of assistance to astronauts and the return of astronauts and space objects in case of accident, distress or emergency landing.[13] Resolution 1884 (XVIII) of 1963 contains provisions prohibiting the placing of nuclear weapons and weapons of mass destruction in outer space. This resolution prohibits military activities, and also confirms the principle that outer space, including the Moon and other celestial bodies, should be used for peaceful purposes.

Resolution 1962 (XVIII) of 13 December 1963 is to be regarded as the most important, since it lays down fundamental principles of law concerning state activities in outer space, including the Moon and other celestial bodies. These principles were later adopted in the

---

10 *See* Lachs, *supra* note 6. *See also* Dembling, *Treaty on Principles Governing the Activities of States in the Exploration and Use of Outer Space, including the Moon and other Celestial Bodies,* I Manual on Space Law 1 (N. Jasentuliyana and R. A. K. Lee, editors, 1979).

11 *See* Priyatna Abdurrasyid, *Pengantar Hukum Ruang Angkasa dan Space Treaty 1967* (BPHN, Jakarta 1972).

12 *Ibid.*, at 15.

13 G.A. Res. 1802 (XVII), 14 December 1962, Paragraph 3 of the Consideration and part I of the Dictum.

form of a Treaty on Principles Governing the Activities of States in the Exploration and Use of Outer Space, Including the Moon and Other Celestial Bodies.[14]

We should not ignore contributions from several independent bodies such as the "David Davies Memorial Institute for International Studies" and the "Institut de Droit International" which have made draft proposals for the formulation of Space Law.[15]

The above resolutions, though not as binding as international conventions, have played an important moral role, since they reflect the state of development of legal thought at that time.

The Outer Space Treaty of 1967 was the first international convention of a general character applied to outer space.[16] It also marked a new trend in the development of International Law, because it is universal in scope and character.[17] The Outer Space Treaty laid down broad, fundamental principles applicable to the use and exploration of outer space. It was understood that further conventions would be needed to provide more specific rules as outer space activities progressed. The Rescue Agreement of 1968[18], the Liability Convention of 1972[19], the Registration Convention of 1975[20] and the Moon

---

[14] The 9 fundamental principles are:

- Freedom of Exploration and Use of Outer Space and Celestial Bodies
- Non-appropriation of Outer Space or Celestial Bodies
- Exploration and Use of Outer Space and Celestial Bodies in Accordance with the Fundamental Principles of International Law, including the Charter of The United Nations
- Partial Demilitarisation of Outer Space
- Retention by States of Sovereign Rights over Space Objects Launched into Outer Space
- International Responsibility of States for National Activities in Space, including Liability for damage caused by Space Objects
- Prevention of Potentially Harmful Consequences of Experiments in Outer Space and on Celestial Bodies
- Assistance to Personnel of Spacecraft in the Event of Accident, Distress or Emergency Landing
- International Cooperation in the Peaceful Exploration and Use of Outer Space and Celestial Bodies.

[15] The Study Group on The Law of Outer Space of the David Davies Memorial Institute has drafted provisions governing the exploration and use of outer space. Also the Institut de Droit International drafted a resolution on 11 September 1963 on the Law of Outer Space. For details, *see also Law and Politics in Space* 153 *ff.* and 181 *ff.* (Maxwel Cohen, editor, 1964).

[16] *See* Dembling, *supra* note 11, at 1.

[17] *See* Christol, *supra* note 4, at 433 *ff.*

[18] The Agreement on the Rescue of Astronauts, the Return of Astronauts and the Return of Objects Launched into Outer Space of 1968 was based on the principle that astronauts are the envoys of mankind as laid down in the Outer Space Treaty of 1967.

[19] This convention was based on Articles 6 and 7 of the Outer Space Treaty of 1967.

[20] The Convention on Registration of Objects Launched into Outer Space of 1975, based on Article 8 of the Outer Space Treaty of 1967.

Agreement of 1979[21] are all international conventions which have been based on the principles laid down in the Outer Space Treaty of 1967. Meanwhile, additional principles concerning particular space activities have been developed within UNCOPUOS, such as, for example, the use of nuclear power sources by space objects, direct broadcasting by satellite and remote sensing.

3. ANALYSIS

There are those who claim that developing countries have contributed very little during the legal formulation of existing Space Law. This was due to a lack of technical knowledge and information on the part of developing countries concerning space activities. Consequently, the legal principles that have been laid down accommodate the interests of the developed countries more than they protect the interests of the developing countries.

It is our task to analyse whether existing space law has covered the needs and interests of all countries, including the needs and interests of the developing countries. Key questions arise. Firstly, are all states satisfied with the content of existing space law? Secondly, did most of the countries participate in its formulation? Finally, we should also analyse whether existing space law is able to solve legal problems that may arise from future space activities; this will be useful in verifying the validity of existing space law.

As was explained previously, existing space law in a broad sense comprises all the regulations governing space activities, starting with the resolutions of the General Assembly, followed by the Outer Space Treaty of 1967 (The Magna Charta) and including any further conventions or agreements based on the principles laid down in the Outer Space Treaty.
However, existing space law has several weaknesses, which will be discussed below.

a. The meaning of "peaceful uses"

Scholars have noted that the meaning of "peaceful uses" is still open to various interpretations, since there is no official explanation or criterion concerning the meaning.

At the beginning of the space age, several views were advanced as to its meaning.[22] One view holds that military activities in space can never be peaceful. The opposing position is that non-aggressive military uses are peaceful. The latter interpretation was applied by

---

21 The Agreement Governing the Activities of States on the Moon and other Celestial Bodies of 1979 was designed to govern the activities in the exploration and use of natural resources on the Moon.

22 *See* Carl Q. Christol, *The Modern International Law of Outer Space* 22 (1982). *See also: National Paper Indonesia, overview on international space science and technology and space application in Indonesia*, Unispace Report, *supra* note 8, at 5.

President Reagan to support his proposal for a Strategic Defence Initiative. This proposal aims at developing a space defence system involving sophisticated technologies such as laser beam weapons, particle beam weapons, anti-satellite weapons, and the establishment of military bases/fortifications in outer space *etc.*. The objective of this space defence system is to make strategic nuclear missiles "impotent and obsolete".

The continuation of arms race activities in outer space is pushing mankind further away from peace. The situation increases the concern of developing countries that they will be potential victims of such space activities. Meanwhile, the idea of discussing military activities in outer space at UNCOPUS was supported mostly by the developing countries and opposed by some of the space powers.

At the Second United Nations Conference on the Peaceful Uses of Outer Space (UNISPACE '82), debates about the legal competence of this forum to discuss military activities in outer space coloured the proceedings.[23] The Space Powers asserted that the Committee of Disarmament is the only body with the competence to discuss all matters concerning disarmament, including military activities in outer space. On the other hand, most developing countries were of the opinion that UNCOPUOS is legally competent, since almost all international treaties governing the activities of states in the exploration and use of outer space were concluded by this Committee.

Most arms talks have been dominated by the superpowers, with the result that the agreements that have been concluded mainly refelct their interests. The interests of other countries have not, however, been satisfactorily accommodated. Therefore, the efforts to give UNCOPUOS legal competence to discuss military activities in outer space reflects a new consciousness among developing countries to play an active role in protecting human life from ultra-hazardous activities and maintaining international peace and security. Therefore, the refusal to discuss military activities in outer space, based on the opinion that this body was established merely to govern the exploration and use of outer space in peace-time, seems to be unreasonable and exaggerated.

b. Non-appropriation of outer space or celestial bodies

So far, this principle has been applied in favour of the developed countries. In the field of communications, for example, this can be seen in the formulation of Article 33(2) of the ITU Convention of 1973 (Malaga-Torremolinos). This article provides that "in using frequency bands for space radio services, members shall bear in mind that radio frequencies and the geostationary satellite orbit are limited natural resources, which must be used efficiently and economically so that member states may have equitable access to

---

23 *See* Unispace Report, *supra* note 8.

both in conformity with the provisions of the radio regulations according to their needs and the technical facilities at their disposal".[24]

This Article illustrates the "first come, first served" principle. Consequently, developed countries are able to fully capitalise the fruits of space science and technology and their spin-offs, further improving their standards of living. The developing countries, earthbound by their limited technological capabilities, have to continue to live of their dwindling natural resources whilst buying high-priced products from the rich nations. Of the currently operational civilian communications satellites operating in the 6/4 and 14/11 Gigahertz frequency bands, 49 belong to developed countries, 15 to the 109 member consortium INTELSAT, and only 4 to developing countries.[25]

As Dr Jasentuliyana has stated[26], the concerns of the developing countries are essentially twofold; firstly, concerning access to the geostationary orbit, and secondly, concerning the fact that they cannot cope with the technical and financial burdens imposed by the technical requirements involved in satellites and earth stations. With regard to access to the geostationary orbit, the "Bogotà Declaration" of 1976 by the equatorial countries stated that the claim to the geostationary orbit was not intended as a "territorial claim" but more as an expression of concern from developing countries about their opportunity to benefit from this limited natural resource. Although this declaration was opposed by most of the developed countries and several developing countries, it has in fact raised a new consciousness amongst developing countries that the formulation of provisions concerning the exploration and use of outer space should take into account the needs and interests of developing countries. At UNISPACE '82 this new consciousness was witnessed in the consideration of the special needs of developing countries with respect to the geostationary orbit, such as the goal of increasing effective communications capacity through technological advances, in order to accommodate the communications needs of all countries, which may conflict with the goal of the developing countries to increase their self-reliance in space technology. The conference finally recommended that any future plan and/or arrangement should not result in the unnecessary hastening of the implementation of plans to the detriment of the financial interests and self-reliance of the developing countries.[27]

---

[24] *See* Priyatna Abdurrasyid, *Facts and Issues Concerning the Geostationary Orbit (a Legal View)* 2 (1985).

[25] *See* Jasentuliyana, *The Developing Countries and The Geostationary Orbit*, Thirteenth Annual Friedman Conference on The Global Telecommunications Revolution: An Emerging Challenge and Opportunity for International Law 2 (Columbia University School of Law, 29 March 1985).

[26] *Ibid.*

[27] *See The Feasibility of Obtaining Closer Spacing of Satellites in the Geostationary Orbit*, G.A., Distr. General A/AC.105/3401 Rev 1, Committee on the Peaceful Uses of Outer Space.

As a result of increasing effort by the developing countries, Article 33(2) of the ITU Convention of 1973 (Malaga-Torremolinos) was amended at the Plenipotentiary conference held in Nairobi in 1982. The reformulated Article 10,3c (mod 67) reads as follows[28]:

"The essential duties of the International Frequency Registration Board shall be (among others) to furnish advice to members with a view to the operation of the maximum practicable number of radio channels in those portions of the spectrum where harmful interference may occur, and with a view to the equitable, effective and economical use of the geostationary orbit, taking into account the needs of members requiring assistance, the specific needs of developing countries as well as the special geographical situation of particular countries."

Concerning the application of the "non-appropriation" principle, some scholars have asked whether this means that a state is not allowed to claim certain exclusive rights over a site which it discovered and physically occupied first, and that it is not permitted to assert exclusive rights concerning lunar exploration and use the same site if no other favourable landing spot exists in the area.[29]

c. International responsibility of states for national activities in space, including liability for damage caused by space objects

This principle is contained in Articles 6 and 7 of the Outer Space Treaty of 1967 and was later formulated in detail by the Convention on International Liability for Damage Caused by Space Objects of 1972, popularly known as the "Liability Convention". The Convention emphasised the need to elaborate international rules and procedures concerning liability for damage caused by space objects and to ensure, in particular, the prompt payment of a full and equitable measure of compensation to victims of such damage. Thus, this treaty was "victim-oriented". The application of the principle of absolute liability for damage on the surface of the Earth or to aircraft in flight[30] illustrates this "victim-oriented" character of the Convention.

Though the Liability Convention aims at protecting the interests of the victim, if one reads carefully, it seems that some of the articles contain loopholes regarding legal problems that may arise in the future:

---

[28] *See* Priyatna, *supra* note 24, at 2.

[29] O.O. Ogunbanwo, *International Law and Outer Space Activities* 73 (1975); *See also* Vlasic, *The Space Treaty: preliminary evaluation*, 55 California Law Review 512/513.

[30] Article 2 of the Liability Convention of 1972.

- The term "damage" as mentioned in Article 1(a) is limited to physical and direct damage and does not cover indirect damage or non-physical damage. Future space activities involving the use of nuclear power sources will increase the possibility of the occurrence of indirect and non-physical damage. Space law should anticipate regulating such a possibility.
- The Space Shuttle, which, as a means of future space transportation, shows characteristics of both a spacecraft and an aircraft, is not covered by the definition of "Space Object".
- The government-to-government procedure for claiming compensation cannot ensure the prompt payment of compensation. Moreover, this procedure does not cover liability arising from activities of private enterprises.
- The effectiveness of international cooperation clauses in cases of large scale danger where different interpretations have been raised may be in some doubt, as shown by the diplomatic communications between the USSR and Canada in the case of "Cosmos 954".

Since the Liability Convention is open to amendment, it is still possible to incorporate such amendments, particularly with regard to the participation of private enterprises in the commercial use of outer space, to meet the requirements governing future space activities as described above.

With regard to future commercial space transportation, the question is whether the Liability Convention should be amended by adding some provisions to cover this activity or whether a new convention should be formulated, specifically designed to cover all problems that may arise. It may be useful in this respect to draw an analogy with the "Warsaw System" governing international air transport.

The Indonesian experience in launching its telecommunications satellite "Palapa B-2" may also provide a useful experience in formulating future rules on space law. This satellite failed to reach its orbit after separation from the shuttle orbiter. Without going into the technical aspects of this failure, it is interesting to note the terms of the launching contract between NASA and the Department of Tourism, Post and Telecommunication of the Republic of Indonesia, in particular concerning "inter-party waiver liability" and "third party liability".

The waiver of inter-party liability was based on the "NASA Shared Launch Agreement for Payloads Launch and Associated Service" issued by the NASA office of space transportation operation on 8 March 1979. It stipulates that the "user" of the shuttle service should agree to its provisions. Article V, paragraph 3 of this "Cargo Launch Agreement" on the allocation of certain risks, states:

"NASA and the user agree that, with respect to damage to persons or property involved in a Space Transportation System (STS) operation, neither NASA or the User, nor any person who has contracted with NASA or the user for STS services or who owns property or employs a person to be flown on the Shuttle, shall make any claim with respect to injury to or death of its contractor's property or personnel caused by NASA, the User or any other persons involved in STS operations during such operation, whether such injury, death or damage arises through negligence or otherwise."

As a consequence of this provision, each party has to insure its own property in order to cover possible damage during the operation. A similar provision applied to Palapa B-2 which was lost in space.

Indonesia considered the waiver of the liability provision to be unjust and unequal. Technically, the possibility of fault or contributory negligence on the part of the User (Indonesia) was very small. If the space shuttle is used much more frequently as a means of space transportation and used commercially either by states or private enterprises, the launching contracts which determine the rights and obligations of the parties should be negotiated on a more equal basis.

On the problems of "third party liability", Article V of the Liability Convention provides:

"1. Whenever two or more states jointly launch a space object, they shall be jointly and severally liable for any damage caused."

The above provision was applicable to the launching of Palapa B-2 since it was a joint launching. According to paragraph 2 of Article V, the participants in a joint launching may conclude an agreement apportioning among themselves the financial obligations for which they are jointly and severally liable. After separation of the satellite from the shuttle orbiter, the burden of the third party liability was placed on the user (the owner of the satellite). This may be implied from Article V(2) of the "NASA Shared Shuttle Launch Agreement and Associated Services" which states:

"The user shall obtain, at no cost to NASA, insurance protecting the US government and its contractors from any third party for any damage resulting from a free-flying payload after separation of the payload from the shuttle."

From the above provisions it can be concluded that the obligation concerning third party liability before the separation was placed upon NASA.

4. CONCLUDING REMARKS

1. As existing space law cannot cover all legal problems arising from future space activities, a comprehensive study should be conducted by the international community in order to contribute towards the legal formulation of future space law that will meet the needs of future space activities.

2. The effectiveness of future space law depends upon whether it takes into account the need and interests of all countries, based on the principles of equality, justice and rationality, including consideration of the future capabilities of the developing countries in space science and technology.

3. Active participation and contributions from the developing counties is absolutely necessary to formulate future space law.

4. There should be close and mutual cooperation between the developed and developing countries in the fields of law, science and technology.

THE FUTURE ROLE OF MUNICIPAL LAW IN REGULATING SPACE-RELATED ACTIVITIES

Phillip Dann*

Before any of the UN space treaties were signed, the United States had enacted two major items of space-related legislation. These were the National Aeronautics and Space Act 1958[1] and the Communications Satellite Act 1962.[2] It is perhaps surprising, therefore, that there is still a need to attack the misconception that space law is only international law.[3] Even among those writers who acknowledge the relevance of municipal law, there is a tendency to regard it as by far the lesser part of space law.[4]

The aim of this contribution is to show that municipal law is already an important part of space law, and that its relative importance is likely to increase. This view is based on a particular understanding of the term 'space law', which should be stated at the outset: space law is not a coherent or self-contained body of law. The term is purely a functional one, used to describe the sum of all legal rules, whatever their source, which are applicable to space-related activities.[5]

There are two important consequences of this rough definition. The first has already been noted: that space law is not only international law. It includes relevant rules of other legal systems, such as those of municipal law, or for that matter, European Community law.[6] The second consequence is that space law is not always special law. It includes rules which are not exclusively applicable to space-related activities. Indeed, it includes rules which came into force long before the first rocket was launched. The appropriate test is whether a given rule is capable of applying to some space-related activity.

---

* MA, LL.M. (Cantab.), Barrister, Asst. Legal Adviser, INMARSAT, London, UK.

1 42 USC Section 2451 *et seq.*

2 47 USC Section 701 *et seq.*

3 *See*, for example, the observations of Eilene Galloway in Proceedings of the 29th Colloquium on the Law of Outer Space 293-4 (1987).

4 *See*, for example, Diederiks-Verschoor, *Space Law as it affects Domestic Law*, 7 Journal of Space Law 39 (1979); *and also* Bakotic, *A Note on a Basic Problem in the Teaching of Space Law*, Proceedings of the 29th Colloquium on the Law of Outer Space 205-206 (1987).

5 *See* Bakotic, *ubi supra.*

6 For a discussion of the impact of European Community law on international satellite broadcasting, *see* Mestmacker, *The Impact of Deregulation on Trade in Services Agreements and on Telecommunication Monopolies in Europe*, 53 Telecommunication Journal 639, at 642 (XI/1986).

This approach can be supported by reference to Article 3 of the Outer Space Treaty of 1967, which states the following:

"States parties to the treaty shall carry on activities in the exploration and use of outer space, including the moon and other celestial bodies, in accordance with international law, including the Charter of the United Nations, in the interests of maintaining international peace and security and promoting international co-operation and understanding."

This provision not only dispels any suggestion that the geographical scope of public international law is limited to the Earth and its atmosphere: it also makes clear that general rules of international law are potentially applicable to activities in outer space. Such rules supplement the provisions of the space treaties.

Similarly, the municipal law component of space law does not consist only of specific enactments, such as the US National Aeronautics and Space Act. It includes rules of more general application. Once this has been grasped, it is obvious that municipal law is an important part of space law. Consider, for example, the many space-related activities which are conducted pursuant to contracts governed by some domestic system of law. There are the commercial launch contracts made with NASA and Arianespace. Associated with a commercial launch, there will typically be insurance policies covering third party liability, loss of payload, consequential loss of profits and other risks. Satellite transponders are frequently sold, leased or hired-out. There are agreements for the conduct of commercial research in space, such as the one between NASA and the 3M Corporation.[7] Orders are placed for the construction of satellites and launch vehicles, and for the provision of telemetry, command and monitoring services.

It is true that certain provisions of such contracts may reflect specific legal requirements. For example, in a launch contract it is usual to allocate responsibility for registration of the launch vehicle and of any space object to be carried on that launch vehicle. Subject to this, however, the various contracts referred to are negotiated and drafted within no other framework than the general law of contract.

Many other branches of municipal law must be considered, in the same sense, to be part of space law. For example, physical injuries and damage to property may occur in space, or be caused on Earth by a space object. In such cases it may be possible for the injured party to bring a claim in tort (delict) or under product liability laws; although such a claim may raise formidable problems of jurisdiction and applicable law.[8] It should be remembered

[7] Aviation Week & Space Technology 102 (12 January 1986).

[8] *See*, for example, Croft Jr., *Manufacturers' Liability under United States Law for Products used in Commercial Space Activities*, 14 Journal of Space Law 113 (1986).

that, even where there is liability on the international plane, under the provisions of the Liability Convention, claims may still be pursued under domestic law.[9]

Public as well as private law must be taken into account. For example, national laws which restrict the export of sensitive technology have a double impact on the launch of objects into space. On the one hand, a country may prohibit the shipping of satellites to certain other countries for launch.[10] On the other, a country may consider that a launch from within its territory amounts to an export of the launch vehicle and/or its payload, and require that a licence be obtained.[11]

There is undoubtedly scope for great ingenuity in seeking to apply general rules to this relatively new field of activity. One may perhaps be sceptical about the Texas savings and loans institution which applied to the Texas Savings and Loan Department, a state regulatory agency, for authority to open a branch on the Moon.[12] Of much greater practical interest is the prospect of anti-trust and anti-monopoly laws (including the relevant provisions of European Community law) being applied in this context. This may be of particular importance while there are still relatively few providers of space-related equipment and services.

A final, and important, example of the application of general municipal law in this context is that of industrial and intellectual property law. There are already several cases in which patent rights have been claimed in space-related inventions. These include the RCA patent on a new method of launching spin-stabilised spacecraft from the bay of the Space Shuttle.[13] The United States is currently being sued by the Hughes Aircraft Co. for alleged infringement of its satellite patents; although the United States is contending that US patent law does not apply outside the territorial United States.[14] Questions of copyright can also arise: the Austrian Supreme Court has had to decide whether the transmission by satellite of a television programme from one fixed point to another, for the purpose of subsequent

---

9 Convention on International Liability for Damage Caused by Space Objects (entered into force 1972), Article XI (2).

10 Satellites made with US parts may not at present be shipped to the Soviet Union for launch: Wall Street Journal (7 January 1987).

11 This was formerly true of the United States: *see* Dula, *Private Sector Activities in Outer Space*, 19 The International Lawyer 159 at 170 (1985). However, in the case of private launches this has been reversed by the Commercial Space Launch Act of 1984: *see* note 17 below.

12 Dula, *op. cit.*, at 180.

13 Satellite Week 8 (3 November 1986).

14 Office of Technology Assessment, *Space Stations and the Law: Selected Legal Issues* 37 (1986). The original decision on the merits is reported in 717 F.2d 1351, Fed. Cir. (1983).

distribution by cable, amounts to a "broadcast" within the meaning of Austrian copyright legislation.[15]

Such examples illustrate a further point. This somewhat casual application of general municipal law to space-related activities may appear undesirable. It is arguable that States should enact comprehensive and specific legislation to regulate such activities.[16] However, as the US and Austrian cases show, legal issues will have to be resolved as and when they arise, whether or not they have been anticipated by law makers.

Of course, there is already a considerable amount of national legislation which relates expressly to space activities. Two examples from the United States have already been given, to which may be added two more. The Commercial Space Launch Act of 1984[17] was enacted to give effect to the Reagan Administration's policy of encouraging the commercialisation of expendable launch vehicles.[18] The Act requires private launch operations to be licensed, and designates the Department of Transportation as the licensing agency. The Land Remote-Sensing Commercialization Act of 1984[19], as its title suggests, provides for the transfer to the private sector of the US LANDSAT Remote Sensing System. The Act also provides for the licensing, by the Secretary of Commerce, of all private remote sensing systems; and it lays down certain principles of non-discriminatory access to unenhanced data.

The United Kingdom has enacted the Outer Space Act 1986, the purpose of which is accurately summarised by its long title:

"An act to confer licensing and other powers on the Secretary of State to secure compliance with the international obligations of the United Kingdom with respect to the launching and operation of space objects and the carrying on of other activities in outer space by persons connected with this Country."

The activities referred to may only be carried out under the authority of a licence issued by the Secretary of State, who may impose such conditions as he thinks fit. Such conditions may, for example, relate to the prevention of contamination of outer space, or require the

---

15 *See* Marie Helen Pichler, *Copyright Problems of Satellite Transmissions of Programme-Carrying Signals in Western Europe*, Proceedings of the 29th Colloquium on the Law of Outer Space 128, at 129 (1987).

16 For a contrary view, however, *see* the report referred to in note 14 above, at 7.

17 49 USC Section 2601 *et seq.*

18 *See* Myers, *Federal Government Regulation of Commercial Operations using Expendable Launch Vehicles*, 12 Journal of Space Law 40, at 41 (1984-5).

19 15 USC Section 4201 *et seq.*

licensee to insure himself against third party liability.[20] The Secretary of State is also required to maintain a register of space objects.

To take one further example from the United Kingdom: the regulation and licensing of satellite telecommunications are for the most part carried out under the general provisions of the Telecommunications Act 1984 and the Wireless Telegraphy Act 1949. However, direct broadcasting by satellite (DBS) will be regulated under specific provisions contained in the Cable and Broadcasting Act 1984.[21]

The above is no more than an outline of the present role of municipal law in regulating space-related activities. It remains to offer some speculations on the future development of municipal law in this context.

The existing space treaties will doubtless have an effect on the development of municipal law, although this will be limited. The treaties contain scarcely any provisions which require the Parties to adopt specific rules within their domestic legal systems. One of the few examples is in Article 8 of the Outer Space Treaty, which in effect prescribes a rule of private international law:

"Ownership of objects launched into outer space, including objects landed or constructed on a celestial body, and of their component parts, is not affected by their presence in outer space or on a celestial body or by their return to Earth."

There are also provisions in the space treaties to which the parties can scarcely give effect without enacting domestic legislation; although this is not an express requirement. For example, Article 6 of the Outer Space Treaty provides in part that, "The activities of non-governmental entities in outer space, including the moon and other celestial bodies, shall require authorization and continuing supervision by the appropriate State Party to the Treaty". It is difficult to imagine that a Party could discharge these responsibilities without introducing a system of licensing and regulation, as the United States and the United Kingdom have already done. Similarly, in order to establish a national register of objects launched into outer space, as envisaged in the Registration Convention[22], it will typically be necessary to enact domestic legislation. It may be expected that an increasing number of States will introduce such legislation as their activities in space, and those of their nationals, increase. It should be noted, however, that the space treaties prescribe nothing of the form or content of such legislation.

---

20 Section 5.

21 Sections 37-52. These sections are not yet in force.

22 Convention on Registration of Objects Launched into Outer Space (entered into force 1976), Article II.

The space treaties also affect municipal law in that they define in part the limits of national jurisdiction in relation to activities in space. The most important rule is that contained in Article 2 of the Outer Space Treaty:

"Outer space, including the moon and other celestial bodies, is not subject to national appropriation by claim of sovereignty, by means of use of occupation, or by other means."

In general, therefore, State jurisdiction over activities in space will be on a personal, rather than territorial, basis. However, Article 8 of the Outer Space Treaty provides for quasi-territorial jurisdiction over space objects:

"A State party to the treaty on whose registry an object launched into outer space is carried shall retain jurisdiction and control over such object, and over any personnel thereof, while in outer space or on a celestial body."

These provisions only define the extent of permitted jurisdiction. It does not follow that the existing municipal law of a particular State will necessarily apply to the activities of nationals of that State in outer space, or to activities on board a space object carried on the registry of that State. That is a matter to be determined by the law of the State in question. For example, English criminal law does not in general apply to acts committed outside English territory, even by British nationals.[23] It has been necessary to enact specific legislation in order to extend the application of the criminal law to British ships[24], British-controlled aircraft[25] and the United Kingdom Continental Shelf.[26] No such legislation has been enacted in relation to space objects on the United Kingdom registry - interestingly, the point is ignored in the Outer Space Act 1986 - and it may be said with confidence that English criminal law will not in general apply to activities on United Kingdom-registered space objects.

However, in certain cases the English courts will exercise jurisdiction over British nationals in respect of crimes committed outside English territory. For example, the Offences Against the Person Act 1861 provides that, where murder or manslaughter are committed by a British national "out of the United Kingdom, whether within the Queen's dominions or without...", the offence may be tried in England.[27]

---

[23] *See Board of Trade v. Owen* [1957] A.C. 602, 625.

[24] Merchant Shipping Act 1984, section 687, as amended.

[25] Tokyo Convention Act 1967, section 1.

[26] Continental Shelf Act 1964, section 3.

[27] Section 9.

It would seem, therefore, that if a British national commits murder in outer space, the English courts would exercise jurisdiction.

It is likely that several States will enact legislation in order to extend the application of their domestic laws to space, or perhaps to declare that such laws already apply. This process has already begun in the United States. The "special maritime and territorial jurisdiction" was enlarged in 1981 so as to apply to space vehicles on the registry of the United States.[28] As a result, certain activities committed on space vehicles, including murder and arson, would amount to Federal crimes.

It has already been noted that the applicability of US patent laws in outer space is controversial.[29] A second attempt is at present being made to resolve this issue by legislation.[30] The proposed legislation would provide that an invention made, used or sold in outer space on an aeronautical or space vehicle under the jurisdiction or control of the Untied States would be considered to be made, used or sold within the United States for patent purposes. There has also been an attempt to introduce a "Tax Status of Space Act" in Congress, which would give to space business a legal status similar to that of business done on the earth's surface.[31]

What is important in this context is that there should be no legal vacuum in relation to activities in outer space. It does not follow that existing domestic laws must be applied without modification. For example, it may not be appropriate to extend industrial safety legislation and employer's liability laws to activities on a space vehicle or space station. Given the still hazardous nature of manned space flight, it may be impossible to comply with the letter of safety regulations designed to protect factory workers. However, there will be a need for appropriate safety standards; and it will remain necessary to provide a system of compensation for astronauts who may be injured in the course of a space flight.

In other cases, the direct application of existing domestic laws may be wholly desirable. In the present writer's view, there can be no good reason why any State which restricts the performing of experiments on live animals should not apply its relevant legislation unaltered to such experiments in outer space. This raises the interesting question of whether, if launch services became cheaper, certain activities might not be conducted in space so as to avoid the domestic law restrictions which are of merely territorial application.

---

28 18 U.S.C.A., Section 7.

29 *See* note 14, above.

30 United Nations Monthly Survey of Selected Events in the Peaceful Exploration of Outer Space 27 (February 1987).

31 *See* Dula, *op. cit.*, at 163.

A commercial enterprise might, for example, wish to conduct experiments in genetic engineering which are illegal in its country of residence. At first sight, the likelihood might seem remote: it would in most cases be cheaper to conduct the same activity in another country with less strict legislation. However, it may be advantageous for other reasons to carry out the activity on a space object registered in the country of residence: there may be favourable tax treatment, or the protection of resulting industrial property rights may be more secure. This anomalous situation is entirely possible, given the piecemeal way in which domestic laws are applied to activities in space. Furthermore, national legislatures may be quick to recognise abuses of the law, but they are not always quick to take remedial action.

How fast can municipal law be expected to develop in relation to space activities? This will depend on the volume of such activities, and the rate of technological progress. The reason why the United States is at present considering the extension of its patent laws is because experiments are already being conducted in space, and patented inventions are being used in space. In due time it may become common for persons to remain for long periods on space stations, or even the Moon. At that stage it will be necessary to consider how the concepts of domicil and residence apply in such cases. If colonies are established on the Moon or other celestial bodies, many branches of the law will have to be transplanted, such as matrimonial law and even electoral law. It is appropriate, however, that the law should react to change, at the risk of sometimes lagging behind, rather than trying to anticipate change. One can only admire the initiative of those who wish to open a bank on the Moon; but it cannot be certain that retail banking will exist on the Earth in its present form in thirty years time.

A final matter to be considered is whether there will be a great drive to harmonise national laws governing space-related activities. There has been a persistent assumption held by certain academic lawyers that the unification of laws is in itself desirable, and moreover, is greatly desired by the public. In many cases this is true; but diversity may also be an attractive thing. This is well illustrated in the case of launch contracts. It can be predicted with confidence that, at future space law conferences, there will be proposals to standardise launch contracts, presumably by international treaty. It will be said that, as launchings become increasingly common, space transport will become comparable to air and sea transport, and should have its own equivalent of the Warsaw Convention of 1929 or the Athens Convention of 1974.

Such proposals may exaggerate the probable growth in space transport; but that is not the real objection. Uniform conditions of carriage, whether of passengers or goods, often favour the carrier unduly. There is already considerable concern at the modest limits of liability established under certain international conventions, a concern which has been heightened by the recent disaster involving a car ferry at Zeebrugge.[32] It happens that both NASA and Arianespace have so far insisted on transferring the risk of launch failure to their customers.[33] There is now an increasing demand for launch service providers to accept at least a part of this risk.[34] In the near future there may be greater competition in the provision of launchers[35], and it may become possible for customers to negotiate a more favourable allocation of risks. There is also no reason why many other provisions in launch contracts should be standardised: for example, clauses dealing with cancellation, ancillary services and satellite storage. In this context uniformity of contract terms is highly undesirable; but a call to impose uniformity by international convention may well appeal to governments wishing mutually to protect their national launch agencies, whether public or private.

There are good reasons, therefore, to oppose any general move towards the unification of municipal laws relating to space. However, there are cases in which some harmonisation of laws may be desirable. It has already been noted that, in the context of private international law, space-related activities will give rise to difficult questions of jurisdiction and choice of law.[36] Professor Hamilton DeSaussure has argued that an international body of lawyers should consider such questions:

"Their objective would not be to develop a new code of space law, but to establish a common consensus as to how to allocate jurisdiction for extraterrestrial activity, how to choose the applicable substantive law, and how to provide for some judicial uniformity."[37]

This is an attractive suggestion: the problem will be to find a body which has both the expertise to undertake this study and the influence to ensure that its proposals are implemented.

Although it may be difficult to make firm predictions about the future development of space law, it is possible to draw some conclusions about the future practitioners of space law. At one time it might have appeared that space law was a highly specialised and esoteric area of practice. Now it can be seen that the space lawyer must be extremely versatile. He or she should ideally have a sound knowledge of both public international law and at least one

---

32 *See* Gaskell, *The Athens Convention 1974 - the Concept of Limitation*, 137 New Law Journal 383 (1987).

33 *See* Myers & Hanes, *A New Approach to Launch Contracts*, Satellite Communications 58 (October 1986).

34 *See* note 32 above.

35 *See* Parker, *Where now for ELV's?*, 2 Space 5 (Dec. 1986 - Feb. 1987).

36 *See* note 8 above.

37 DeSaussure, *An Integrated Legal System for Space*, 6 Journal of Space Law 179, at 191 (1978).

system of municipal law. This should include a broad understanding of several different branches of municipal law, including contract, tort, industrial and intellectual property, private international law, criminal law, and so on. Above all, the space lawyer will need to develop that skill which is desirable for all lawyers: the ability to recognise the relevance of branches of law which at first sight do not seem to apply to the problem in hand. The practice of space law will not be dull.

THE SCOPE OF VALIDITY AND EFFECTIVENESS OF ENVIRONMENT-RELATED NORMS IN OUTER SPACE LAW

Reinhard Müller*

1. INTRODUCTION

It is universally accepted that scientific and technological progress can have negative impacts on the human environment and that "the interaction between man and environment as well as the maintenance of the ecological balance on our Planet" are among the most important issues facing mankind today as a global problem.[1]
Taking into account the increasingly intensive exploration and use of outer space involving technologies of the highest scientific level, and with a view to the possibility that all countries of the world may be affected by adverse consequences of outer space activities, it seems to be justified to extend this thesis to outer space.[2]
In international law publications[3], the issue of "environmental protection in outer space" was called to attention very early. Apart from problem catalogues[4] comprising aspects calling for regulation as well as analyses of the pertaining international law[5] currently operative, a number of scientific attempts have been made to classify the sources of environmental pollution in outer space with a view to assessing the effectiveness of instruments of international law in combatting them.[6] For example, Winogradow[7] and Vassilevskaja[8] come to the conclusion to distinguish between negative consequences of legitimate exploration and use, and negative consequences due to "armament" of outer

* Dr. sc. jur.; Professor of International Law, Martin-Luther-University Halle, GDR; Member IISL.

1 Inposemzew, *Sozialismus und weltumspannende Probleme unserer Zeit*, 10 Horizont 25 (1979).

2 Mention is not made of the advantages of outer space use for understanding also terrestrial environmental problems. *Cf.* A.S. Piradov, *inter alia ,Weltraumrecht* 193 (1978).

3 Evaluating the literature prior to state practice is in my view normally not justified. The order was chosen in order to permit a complex presentation and evaluation of the codification process.

4 *Inter alia* Fasan, *Legal problems of the terrestrial environment*, Proceedings of the 14th Colloquium on the Law of Outer Space (1971); Krause-Ablass, *Protection of the Terrestrial Environment in Outer Space, a Principle of International Law, ibid.*

5 Sand, *Space programs and international environmental protection*, 1 International and Comparative Law Quarterly (1972); G. Gal., *Space Law* 169 (1969).

6 Gorove, *Pollution and Outer Space; A legal analysis and appraisal*, 1 International Law and Politics 53 (1972); Diederiks-Verschoor, *Harm producing events caused by fragments of space objects debris*, Proceedings of the 24th Colloquium on the Law of Outer Space (1982).

7 Winogradow, *Tätigkeit im Weltraum und Umweltschutz*, Weltraum und Recht 123 (1985).

8 E.Schuwkowa-Vassilevskaja,*Völkerrechtlicher Schutz der kosmischen Umwelt* (Original: Russian) VIth Intercosmos Seminar for Lawyers, Budapest 1986.

space. In my view this approach is fully justified since it shows clearly that the causes of pollution may be of entirely contrasting character and will result in principally different legal consequences.

2. THE INTERRELATION BETWEEN THE PREVENTION OF AN ARMS RACE IN OUTER SPACE AND ENVIRONMENTAL PROTECTION.

All environment-related norms of outer space law have as a common characteristic that they can contribute to the reduction of hazards of pollution in outer space. Thus, for example, the conclusion of and adherence to the Moscow Nuclear Test Ban Treaty of 1963[9] promoted essentially the decrease in radioactivity of the atmosphere. A similarly positive assessment has to be given to the effect achieved through the Convention on the Prohibition of Military and other Hostile Application of Means on the Environment of 1977 (Environmental Modification Convention).[10]

It is therefore of paramount importance to emphasise the relationship between the preservation of peace, disarmament, arms control and environmental protection[11] in order to prove that the policy of arms race does not only greatly endanger peaceful and mutually beneficial cooperation among states in exploring and using outer space, but also results in serious negative phenomena in the cosmic environment.

Already during the research and development phase of the SDI programme, most of the early detection and communications satellites within this space weapons system take positions in the geostationary orbit and worsen the situation in this already crowded limited natural resource which should be used for the benefit of all mankind. With regard to the utilisation of the geostationary orbit it could even be assumed that *e.g.* the services of the ITU may be abused for the SDI programme. Laser experiments may affect the optical sensors of meteorological and remote sensing satellites. The debris of space objects destroyed in the course of anti-satellites systems tests constitute a real danger for other space objects in the low earth orbit.

The list of negative consequences of an arms race in outer space could be continued. It illustrates the absolute necessity of preventing the danger of an arms race in outer space.

There exist a number of important agreements on this issue in international law. Thus, the Nuclear Test Ban Treaty of 1963; Article IV of the Outer Space Treaty of 1967; the Environmental Modification Convention of 1977; Article 3 of the Moon Agreement of 1979, the bilateral treaties between the USSR and the USA (SALT I of 1972, SALT II of 1979, ABM of 1972, later of 1974). There are also a number of initiatives within and

---

[9] *Völkerrecht*, Dokumente, vol. 2, 526 (Berlin 1980) .

[10] *Völkerrecht*, Dokumente, vol. 3, 1. c., 1022.

[11] *Cf.* Kotezka & Pauke, *Zusammenarbeit im Umweltschutz. Beitrag zur friedlichen Koexistenz*, 7 Deutsche Außenpolitik 107 (1982).

the UN-System and especially the Geneva Conference on Disarmament aimed at a complete ban on the deployment of arms in outer space[12], and at the same time naturally at the prevention of negative environmental implications in the course of the development, testing, deployment or even application of these arms systems.

Of absolute priority, however, is the ban on the deployment of arms as a key to the preservation of world peace and of international security. It is absolutely vital to emphasise this priority.

3. THE EXISTING INTERNATIONAL LAW CONCERNING THE PROTECTION OF THE COSMIC AND TERRESTRIAL ENVIRONMENT FROM NEGATIVE CONSEQUENCES OF PEACEFUL OUTER SPACE ACTIVITIES

We must now consider the environmental norms of outer space law, which exclusively relate to the negative consequences of basically peaceful activities for the exploration and use of outer space.

Considering the historically short period of codification and development of outer space law, the existing norms governing the protection of the cosmic and terrestrial environment from negative consequences of outer space activities are in my view a model for legal regulations relating to other spheres of scientific and technological activities.

Incorporating par. 6 of the Declaration on Legal Principles for the Activities of States in Exploring and Using Outer Space of December 13, 1963[13], Article IX of the Outer Space Treaty of 1967[14] obliges the member states to avoid harmful contamination in outer space, on the Moon and other celestial bodies as well as adverse changes in the surroundings of the Earth as a consequence of introducing extraterrestrial matter and to take adequate steps. This regulation is supplemented by the obligation to inform and to consult with the potentially affected states which a potentially damage-inflicting state has to fulfil. It has to be added that the fulfilment of this obligation can be requested by the potentially affected states at any time.

According to Article VI of the Outer Space Treaty, the member states are held responsible to secure the compliance of these obligations, independent of whether an activity is carried out by governmental agencies or by non-governmental entities.[15]

---

[12] *Cf.* More in detail: Müller, *The prevention of an arms race in outer space - the present international law and aspects of its necessary improvement*, Proceedings of the 29th Colloquium on the Law of Outer Space 62 (1987); *cf.* particularly on the ABM Treaty; Vereshchetin, *"Strategic Defense Initiative" and International Law, ibid.*, at 94.

[13] Res. A/XVIII, 1962.

[14] Res. A/XXI, 2222 Annex of December 13, 1966.

[15] *Cf.* - concerning remote sensing - Vereshchetin & Postyshev, *Responsibility of States for Remote Sensing Activities*, Proceedings of the 27th Colloquium on the Law of Outer Space 247 (1985).

Article 7 (2) of the Moon Agreement of 1979[16] extends the information system. According to it, member states are obliged to inform the UN Secretary General on all measures taken to protect the environment and, to the maximum extent feasible, to notify in advance of any intended placements of radioactive material on the Moon as well as of the purposes of such placements. Finally, Article 7 (3) provides for the establishment of scientific protective areas - probably bearing in mind the efficient Antarctic Treaty system.[17]
An important role in preventing damage is finally attached to Article 5 (4) of the Cosmonaut Rescue Agreement of 1968[18], with the obligation of the launching state to prevent threats originating from its space object for a potentially affected state on the initiative and under control of the latter and to Article 4 (3) of the Registration Convention of 1974[19], with the obligation of the registrating state to inform the UN Secretary General on registered space objects which are no longer orbiting the Earth.
In cases where damage does occur during the performance of space activities, the launching states have to bear international liability in accordance with Article VII of the Outer Space Treaty, the modalities being laid down in the Liability Convention of 1972[20]:

- Damage inflicted by space objects on the surface of the Earth as well as to aircraft in flight are dealt with according to the strict liability principle (Article II);
- Damage inflicted by space objects elsewhere than on the surface of the Earth to a space object of another launching State are dealt with according to the liability-by-fault principle (Article III).[21]

Article III of the Outer Space Treaty of 1967 provides the basis for supplementing this set of norms by principles of general international law. In my opinion it is, however, not very promising to resort to these in this connection. Thus, for example the obligation for the cooperation of states in science and technology is laid down in much more concrete terms in Article IX of the Outer Space Treaty than in the Declaration of Principles of 1970.[22] And the same has to be taken into consideration with regard to the so-called generally recognised principles of international law. As it has been pointed out in a similar context[23],

---

16 Res. A/34/168 Annex of December 5, 1979.

17 *Handbook of Measures in Furtherance of the Principles and Objectives of the Antarctic Treaty*, 2301, 1106, 2263 (J. Heap, editor, 1985).

18 Res. A/XXII, 2345 Annex of December 19, 1967.

19 Res. A/XXIX, 3225 Annex of November 12, 1974.

20 Res. A/XXVI, 2777 Annex of November 29, 1971.

21 *Cf.* for this rough summary of the content, Buecling, *Weltraum, Grundsätze des Weltraumrechts;* Lexikon des Rechts, 4/1220 (November 22, 1985).

22 German text in: *Völkerrecht*, Dokumente, 1.c., vol. 3, 713.

23 Müller, *Völkerrecht und globale Probleme der Menschheit - am Beispiel des internationalen Umweltschutzes*, Wiss. Z., Univ. Halle, XXXV '86 G., H. 1, 43.

the principles of customary international law existing side by side with international contractual law, such as the principles of good-neighbourly relations, the prohibition of legal abuse, the principle of good offices *etc.*, are too vague in their content to derive from them the necessary concrete structures of rights and obligations. This is also true with regard to the results of international environmental conferences which are eventually quoted. They are not legally binding themselves, but are merely providing some stimuli for the further development of international law.

If state practice is chosen as a yardstick for the efficiency of environment-related norms in outer space law, both activities for the peaceful exploration and use of outer space as well as the relationship between countries engaged in these activities and those affected by it, then it will be shown that the set of norms used at present is adequate.

- There are no scientifically established (and published) analyses to prove that serious or even irreparable damage has occurred in the cosmic environment, on celestial bodies or on the Earth due to the exploration and use of outer space.[24]
- Not a single case is known where justified claims for compensation by affected countries were not fulfilled or a request to avert damage was not met by the launching state.[25]

I do not share the view that, as a framework, Article IX of the Outer Space Treaty of 1967 is ineffective, or that the absence of a regulation providing that consultations should result in definite solutions makes Article IX[26] impracticable.

Of course Article IX of the Outer Space Treaty is of framework character. This framework is, however, filled out by Article VI and VII as well as by the Liability Convention. Where necessary, *e.g.* for the exploration and use of the Moon, the framework character allows the establishment of specific constellations of rights and obligations.

I hold that if it is really impossible to reconcile diverging opinions concerning a certain space activity, the norms of peaceful settlement according to Article 33 of the UN Charter should be applied.

---

24 At UNISPACE '82 the following environment-related aspects were mentioned which could have effects in the future: nuclear energy sources on board of satellites, a growing number of so-called non-operative "waste objects", effects of fuel emission on atmosphere and ionosphere, hazards from chemical and biological experiments in outer space; effects from future ion-driven units; *cf.* annex II to the Final Document, No. 296, 333 and, commenting on it, Szeplabi, *UNISPACE und Weltraumrecht, Ergebnisse und Perspektiven der 2. Weltraumkonferenz der Vereinten Nationen*, 31 Zeitschrift für Luft- und Weltraumrecht 326 (no. 4, 1982).

25 *Cf.* damage settlement USSR - Canada by Treaty between the two states of January 2, 1981; International Legal Materials 689 no. 20 (1981); *cf. also* the assessment of the effectiveness of the Registration Convention by Kopal, Proceedings of the 27th Colloquium on the Law of Outer Space 252-253 (1985).

26 *Inter alia* Jenks, *Space Law* 278 (1965), and A. Buecling, *Völkerrechtliche Haftung für Raumfahrtschäden nach dem Weltraumhaftungsabkommen vom 29-3-1972* 18 (1982).

Whether it is advisable to confer functions of arbitration to COPUOS/LSC[27] seems doubtful because of the working rhythm and working methods of this body. On the other hand it seems highly plausible to entrust such functions to a UN Outer Space Organisation, as it was suggested by the USSR in 1985.[28]

Most important, however, is to what extent all states are actually willing to fulfil their present legally-binding obligations.[29] This does not deny the existence or the emergence of new needs for regulation. But the elaboration of draft principles by COPUOS/LSC relevant to the use of nuclear power sources in outer space[30] proves that the "Magna Charta" of outer space could be specified also in this respect.

Another issue that has been discussed frequently over the last few years is that of so-called space debris. Often these are small and smallest fragments from inactive and also active space objects. Some debris rapidly enters the Earth's atmosphere and burns up, while some debris stays in the low earth orbit for a longer period of time.[31]
It seems to be advisable to refrain from speculating on possible dangers caused by space debris, since the data available on this point differ widely.[32] However, I hold the view that the alleged gaps in outer space law concerning the legal treatment of these debris are insubstantial.

What in my opinion should be clarified is only whether such debris should or could still be considered to be space objects and therefore are covered by the Liability Convention of 1972: Article I (d) explicitly includes components of a space object. Identifying the origin of a small part from a certain object, however, may lead to difficulties.[33]

27 For proposals of this kind *see* Winogradow, *op. cit.*, at 129.

28 Neues Deutschland of Aug. 17/18, 1985, 5; *see also* supplementary proposals by the USSR in the letter of the President of the Council of Ministers of the USSR, Ryschkow, to the UN Secretary General of June 10, 1986.

29 Thus we find in a list compiled by Perek in the supplement to his contribution *Strengthening the Registration Convention*, Proceedings of the 27th Colloquium on the Law of Outer Space 189 (1985), examples of non-registered or incompletely registered US-American space objects.

30 Report by COPUOS/LSC on the work at the 25th session, A/AC. 105/370, 16 (May 5, 1986).

31 Wolfe, *Orbital debris - current issues as they impact on an expanding manned presence in Space*, Proceedings of the 27th Colloquium on the Law of Outer Space 260 (1985).

32 *Cf.* the discussion on the Wolfe contribution, *ibid.*, 288-289.

33 *Also* Majorski, *ibid.*, 288.

A possible further development can at best be seen in substantiating a common duty of all states concerned to minimise space debris, provided the technical and economical means are available.

Stating a "general pollution ban"[34] is unrealistic in any case and also inconsistent with Article I (2) of the Outer Space Treaty of 1967, covering the freedom of exploration and use of outer space for all states.

In this context the question arises whether inactive satellites, *e.g.* in the geostationary orbit, should be regarded as outer space debris at all. Even in their inactive state they remain registered property of the registrating state which retains its jurisdiction and control and has certainly to take liability in the case of damage according to the Liability Convention.

In my opinion it is more sensible at least not to consider inactive satellites in the geostationary orbit as "environmental pollutants", but as a form of using the orbit for which the legal regulation has been worked out for years by the ITU, and with a certain degree of success.[35] To come to unanimous conclusions in this way is more promising than by proclaiming general prohibitions on pollution.

4. CONCLUSION

How can "space environmental law" be further developed? Certainly not by postulating new facts of liability. These already exist and the Liability Convention is capable of interpretation. A desirable step would be closer cooperation both in the sphere of prevention of any kind of pollution and in the exploration and use of outer space for the benefit of all interested states.

Again, attention should be paid to the USSR proposal to establish a universal Outer Space Organisation which would provide a suitable framework for this.

Finally, it is essential for all member states of the Outer Space Treaty strictly to fulfil their obligation laid down in Article VI: to bear international responsibility for all national enterprises, governmental and non-governmental, and to place any activity concerning the exploration and use of outer space by non-governmental entities under authorisation requirement and continuing supervision.

---

34 *Also* Vitt, *Auf Kollisionskurs im All*, 35 Zeitschrift für Luft- und Weltraumrecht 42 (no. 1, 1986).

35 *Cf.* Jakhu, *A legal analysis of the ITU Space Conference Report*, Proceedings of the 28th Colloquium on the Law of Outer Space (1986).

EPILOGUE

Henri A. Wassenbergh*

In 1957, at the dawn of the space age, outer space was a field completely free for human activity in the absence of specific legal rules applying to outer space. It was therefore a play-ground for legal experimentation on a world level, but merely on paper. The agreed objectives of law are peace, progress and well-being. The legal regime to be framed for outer space should serve these purposes. It is rather unusual to have an opportunity to devise legal rules for human activities in an unknown environment where no authority is present or can be exercised.

It becomes even more unusual when it is considered that only a few privileged States will be able to engage in and control outer space activities. It was only natural that at the beginning idealist theories prevailed: that outer space is "the province of all mankind", the use and exploration of outer space shall be "for the benefit and in the interests of all countries", the natural resources of outer space shall be "the common heritage of mankind", *etc*.. Legally the most important rule which was laid down in a legal instrument, is that of the freedom of outer space, the absence of nationality and sovereignty, the prohibition of national appropriation, and the applicability of international law and the Charter of the United Nations.

It is understandable that only States were made subjects of outer space law in the early stages of law-making. It is only recently that the tenability of this basis has been questioned in view of the increasing interest of non-governmental entities and the capability to undertake space activities on a commercial basis. For, it is States who have to implement Article VI of the Outer Space Treaty of 1967 and provide in their national legislation for authorisation and supervision of space activities of non-governmental entities.

From the viewpoint of positive law, space law is imperfect in many ways and fields: the pace with which space technology is developing and in its wake the commercialisation of outer space activities that is taking place, together with the growing possibilities of the inhabitation of outer space (space stations), the (de-)militarisation of outer space and the further exploration of outer space are all factors which invite and necessitate new, amended and additional rules of positive international space law.
To enumerate a number of obvious imperfections of present-day space law: there is no delimitation of outer space, no definition of a space object, of a launching State and launching vehicle, of natural space resources, of the common heritage of mankind, of the meaning of Articles I and II of the Outer Space Treaty, of peaceful purposes, nor is there an agreed legal regime for the geostationary orbit, nor for the regime for the exploitation of the natural resources of outer space.

---

* Chairman of the International Institute of Air and Space Law and Professor of Air and Space Law, Leiden University, The Netherlands.

These are among the subjects which deserve the further special attention of lawyers, politicians and scientists. But there are many more. It is therefore highly gratifying that in the present publication the editors have compiled views from all over the world on the future of space law.

The contributions speak for themselves and merit close reading by all those responsible for and active in the use of outer space, engaged in space activities and concerned about our future.

One thing is becoming ever more clear: what is required is a gradual deregulation of outer space activities to liberate private enterprise from governmental bondage when wishing to become active in outer space.

To do so requires close international intergovernmental agreement on what should *not* be done in outer space (by States, international organisations or private enterprise).

An interesting aspect in this respect is the possible advantage of *international* appropriation of (parts of) outer space to avoid the commercialisation of outer space activities by private enterprise leading to the assertion of sovereignty-claims with respect to outer space. (*cf.* the 1976 Bogotà Declaration!)

Indeed, the contribution by the editor-in-chief seems of special interest for the *lex ferenda:* the creation of sub-divisions of outer space law each with their *own* principles, rules and regulations. Launching services (*i.e.* transport to and from outer space), space activities such as the construction of space stations and their use in outer space (for instance materials-processing in outer space), and, finally, earth-related space activities such as DBS, Remote Sensing, satellite communications (INTELSAT) may require different and special legal rules. In addition, and closer to home, are the problems of copyright law, protection of patents, industrial property rights, liability, insurance.

The idealists are being replaced by pragmatists: the law has to serve and balance the interests of the parties involved.

Law applies wherever people live together and are active, regardless of the environment. The environment only influences the way in which people act and interact. Only where scarcity occurs (shortage of necessities, a lack of means or resources to supply the needs of everybody) has individual freedom to be curtailed and is the enforcement of the rules concerned necessary.

The freedom of outer space was established when outer space was still practically "empty" of human activity. Now earth orbits are beginning to become somewhat crowded. The use of the freedom has accordingly to be regulated. The great advantage, however, of space law over terrestrial law is that, so far, outer space has not been divided into sovereign territories and is still treated as one single common environment.

The impending limitation on the use of the freedom of outer space in view of a possible (further) militarisation of outer space and a certain further commercialisation of outer space activities, need not lead to the introduction of national sovereignty in outer space. If a workable legal space regime of "regulated freedom" proves to be politically possible, it will also offer an example of an alternative way in which the development of international law on our planet could be approached.

The present book offers a wealth of ideas and suggestions as to the development of outer space law. Let us hope that many people and especially the members of the UNCOPUOS will study this material and make use of it to shape the space law of the future and so guarantee peace, progress and well-being both in space and on earth.

APPENDICES

APPENDIX I

TREATY ON PRINCIPLES GOVERNING THE ACTIVITIES OF STATES IN THE EXPLORATION AND USE OF OUTER SPACE, INCLUDING THE MOON AND OTHER CELESTIAL BODIES OF 27 JANUARY 1967

The States Parties to this Treaty,

Inspired by the great prospects opening up before mankind as a result of man's entry into outer space,

Recognizing the common interest of all mankind in the progress of the exploration and use of outer space for peaceful purposes,

Believing that the exploration and use of outer space should be carried on for the benefit of all peoples irrespective of the degree of their economic or scientific development,

Desiring to contribute to broad international co-operation in the scientific as well as the legal aspects of the exploration and use of outer space for peaceful purposes,

Believing that such co-operation will contribute to the development of mutual understanding and to the strengthening of friendly relations between States and peoples,

Recalling resolution 1962 (XVIII), entitled "Declaration of Legal Principles Governing the Activities of States in the Exploration and Use of Outer Space", which was adopted unanimously by the United Nations General Assembly on 13 December 1963,

Recalling resolution 1884 (XVIII), calling upon States to refrain from placing in orbit around the earth any objects carrying nuclear weapons or any other kinds of weapons of mass destruction or from installing such weapons on celestial bodies, which was adopted unanimously by the United Nations General Assembly on 17 October 1963,

Taking account of United Nations General Assembly resolution 110 (II) of 3 November 1947, which condemned propaganda designed or likely to provoke or encourage any threat to the peace, breach of the peace or act of aggression, and considering that the aforementioned resolution is applicable to outer space,

Convinced that a Treaty on Principles Governing the Activities of States in the Exploration and Use of Outer Space, including the Moon and Other Celestial Bodies, will further the Purposes and Principles of the Charter of the United Nations,

Have agreed on the following:

Article I

The exploration and use of outer space, including the moon and other celestial bodies, shall be carried out for the benefit and in the interests of all countries, irrespective of their degree of economic or scientific development, and shall be the province of all mankind.

Outer space, including the moon and other celestial bodies, shall be free for exploration and use by all States without discrimination of any kind, on a basis of equality and in accordance with international law, and there shall be free access to all areas of celestial bodies.

There shall be freedom of scientific investigation in outer space, including the moon and other celestial bodies, and States shall facilitate and encourage international co-operation in such investigation.

Article II

Outer space, including the moon and other celestial bodies, is not subject to national appropriation by claim of sovereignty, by means of use or occupation, or by any other means.

Article III

States Parties to the Treaty shall carry on activities in the exploration and use of outer space, including the moon and other celestial bodies, in accordance with international law, including the Charter of the United Nations, in the interest of maintaining international peace and security and promoting international co-operation and understanding.

Article IV

States Parties to the Treaty undertake not to place in orbit around the earth any objects carrying nuclear weapons or any other kinds of weapons of mass destruction, instal such weapons on celestial bodies, or station such weapons in outer space in any other manner.

The moon and other celestial bodies shall be used by all States Parties to the Treaty exclusively for peaceful purposes. The establishment of military bases, installations and fortifications, the testing of any type of weapons and the conduct of military manoeuvres on celestial bodies shall be forbidden. The use of military personnel for scientific research or for any other peaceful purposes shall not be prohibited. The use of any equipment or facility necessary for peaceful exploration of the moon and other celestial bodies shall also not be prohibited.

Article V

States Parties to the Treaty shall regard astronauts as envoys of mankind in outer space and shall render to them all possible assistance in the event of accident, distress, or emergency landing on the territory of another State Party or on the high seas. When astronauts make such a landing, they shall be safely and promptly returned to the State of registry of their space vehicle.

In carrying on activities in outer space and on celestial bodies, the astronauts of one State Party shall render all possible assistance to the astronauts of other States Parties.

States Parties to the Treaty shall immediately inform the other States Parties to the Treaty or the Secretary-General of the United Nations of any phenomena they discover in outer space, including the moon and other celestial bodies, which could constitute a danger to the life or health of astronauts.

Article VI

States Parties to the Treaty shall bear international responsibility for national activities in outer space, including the moon and other celestial bodies, whether such activities are carried on by governmental agencies or by non-governmental entities, and for assuring that national activities are carried out in conformity with the provisions set forth in the present Treaty. The activities of non-governmental entities in outer space, including the moon and other celestial bodies, shall require authorization and continuing supervision by the appropriate State Party to the Treaty. When activities are carried on in outer space, including the moon and other celestial bodies, by an international organization, responsibility for compliance with this Treaty shall be borne both by the international organization and by the States Parties to the Treaty participating in such organization.

Article VII

Each State Party to the Treaty that launches or procures the launching of an object into outer space, including the moon and other celestial bodies, and each State Party from whose territory or facility an object in launched, is internationally liable for damage to another State Party to the Treaty or to its natural or juridical persons by such object or its component parts on the Earth, in air space or in outer space, including the moon and other celestial bodies.

Article VIII

A State Party to the Treaty on whose registry an object launched into outer space is carried shall retain jurisdiction and control over such object, and over any personnel thereof, while in outer space or on a celestial body. Ownership of objects launched into outer space, including objects landed or constructed on a celestial body, and of their component parts, is not affected by their presence in outer space or on a celestial body or by their return to the Earth. Such objects or component parts found beyond the limits of the State Party to the Treaty on whose registry they are carried shall be returned to that State Party, which shall, upon request, furnish identifying data prior to their return.

Article IX

In the exploration and use of outer space, including the moon and other celestial bodies, States Parties to the Treaty shall be guided by the principle of co-operation and mutual assistance and shall conduct all their activities in outer space, including the moon and other celestial bodies, with due regard to the corresponding interests of all other States Parties to the Treaty. States Parties to the Treaty shall pursue studies of outer space, including the moon and other celestial bodies, and conduct exploration of them so as to avoid their harmful contamination and also adverse changes in the environment of the Earth resulting from the introduction of extraterrestrial matter and, where necessary, shall adopt appropriate measures for this purpose. If a State Party to the Treaty has reason to believe that an activity or experiment planned by it or its nationals in outer space, including the moon and other celestial bodies, would cause potentially harmful interference with activities of other States Parties in the peaceful exploration and use of outer space, including the moon and other celestial bodies, it shall undertake appropriate international consultations before proceeding with any such activity or experiment.A State Party to the Treaty which has reason to believe that an activity or experiment planned by another State Party in outer space, including the moon and other celestial bodies, would cause potentially harmful interference with activities in the peaceful exploration and use of outer space, including the moon and other celestial bodies, may request consultation concerning the activity or experiment.

Article X

In order to promote international co-operation in the exploration and use of outer space, including the moon and other celestial bodies, in conformity with the purposes of this Treaty, the States Parties of the Treaty shall consider on a basis of equality any requests by other States Parties to the Treaty to be afforded an opportunity to observe the flight of space objects launched by those States.

The nature of such an opportunity for observation and the conditions under which it could be afforded shall be determined by agreement between the States concerned.

Article XI

In order to promote international co-operation in the peaceful exploration and use of outer space, States Parties to the Treaty conducting activities in outer space, including the moon and other celestial bodies, agree to inform the Secretary-General of the United Nations as well as the public and the international scientific community, to the greatest extent feasible and practicable, of the nature, conduct, locations and results of such activities. On receiving the said information, the Secretary-General of the United Nations should be prepared to disseminate it immediately and effectively.

Article XII

All stations, installations, equipment and space vehicles on the moon and other celestial bodies shall be open to representatives of other States Parties to the Treaty on a basis of reciprocity. Such representatives shall give reasonable advance notice of a projected visit, in order that appropriate consultations may be held and that maximum precautions may be taken to assure safety and to avoid interference with normal operations in the facility to be visited.

Article XIII

The provisions of this Treaty shall apply to the activities of States Parties to the Treaty in the exploration and use of outer space, including the moon and other celestial bodies, whether such activities are carried on by a single State Party to the Treaty or jointly with other States, including cases where they are carried on within the framework of international inter-governmental organizations.

Any practical questions arising in connexion with activities carried on by international inter-governmental organizations in the exploration and use of outer space, including the moon and other celestial bodies, shall be resolved by the States Parties to the Treaty either with the appropriate international organization or with one or more States members of that international organization, which are Parties to this Treaty.

Article XIV

1. This Treaty shall be open to all States for signature. Any State which does not sign this Treaty before its entry into force in accordance with paragraph 3 of this Article may accede to it at any time.

2. This Treaty shall be subject to ratifications by signatory States. Instruments of ratification and instruments of accession shall be deposited with the Governments of the United Kingdom of Great Britain and Northern Ireland, the Union of Soviet Socialist Republics and the United States of America, which are hereby designated the Depositary Governments.

3. This Treaty shall enter into force upon the deposit of instruments of ratification by five Governments including the Governments designated as Depositary Governments under this Treaty.

4. For States whose instruments of ratifications or accession are deposited subsequent to the entry into force of this Treaty, it shall enter into force on the date of the deposit of their instruments of ratification or accession.

5. The Depositary Governments shall promptly inform all signatory and acceding States of the date of each signature, the date of deposit of each instrument of ratification of and accession to this Treaty, the date of its entry into force and other notices.

6. This Treaty shall be registered by the Depositary Governments pursuant to Article 102 of the Charter of the United Nations.

Article XV

Any State Party to this Treaty may propose amendments to this Treaty. Amendments shall enter into force for each State Party to the Treaty accepting the amendments upon their acceptance by a majority of the States Parties to the Treaty and thereafter for each remaining State Party to the Treaty on the date of acceptance by it.

Article XVI

Any State Party to the Treaty may give notice of its withdrawal from the Treaty one year after its entry into force by written notification to the Depositary Governments. Such withdrawal shall take effect one year from the date of receipt of this notification.

Article XVII

This Treaty, of which the English, Russian, French, Spanish and Chinese texts are equally authentic, shall be deposited in the archives of the Depositary Governments. Duly certified copies of this Treaty shall be transmitted by the Depositary Governments to the Governments of the signatory and acceding States.
IN WITNESS WHEREOF the undersigned, duly authorised, have signed this Treaty.

APPENDIX II

AGREEMENT ON THE RESCUE OF ASTRONAUTS, THE RETURN OF ASTRONAUTS AND THE RETURN OF OBJECTS LAUNCHED INTO OUTER SPACE OF 22 APRIL 1968

The Contracting Parties,

Noting the great importance of the Treaty on Principles Governing the Activities of States in the Exploration and Use of Outer Space, including the Moon and Other Celestial Bodies, which calls for the rendering of all possible assistance to astronauts in the event of accident, distress or emergency landing, the prompt and safe return of astronauts, and the return of objects launched into outer space,

Desiring to develop and give further concrete expression to these duties,

Wishing to promote international co-operation in the peaceful exploration and use of outer space,

Prompted by sentiments of humanity,

Have agreed on the following:

Article 1

Each Contracting Party which receives information or discovers that the personnel of a spacecraft have suffered accident or are experiencing conditions of distress or have made an emergency or unintended landing in territory under its jurisdiction or on the high seas or in any other place not under the jurisdiction of any State shall immediately:

(a) Notify the launching authority or, if it cannot identify and immediately communicate with the launching authority, immediately make a public announcement by all appropriate means of communication at its disposal;

(b) Notify the Secretary-General of the United Nations, who should disseminate the information without delay by all appropriate means of communication at his disposal.

Article 2

If, owing to accident, distress, emergency or unintended landing, the personnel of a spacecraft land in territory under the jurisdiction of a Contracting Party, it shall immediately take all possible steps to rescue them and render them all necessary assistance. It shall inform the launching authority and also the Secretary-General of the United Nations of the steps it is taking and of their progress. If assistance by the launching authority would help to effect a prompt rescue or would contribute substantially to the effectiveness of search and rescue operations, the launching authority shall co-operate with the Contracting Party with a view to the effective conduct of search and rescue operations. Such operations shall be subject to the direction and control of the Contracting Party, which shall act in close and continuing consultation with the launching authority.

Article 3

If information is received or it is discovered that the personnel of a spacecraft have alighted on the high seas or in any other place not under the jurisdiction of any State, those Contracting Parties which are in a position to do so shall, if necessary, extend assistance in search and rescue operations for such personnel to assure their speedy rescue. They shall inform the launching authority and the Secretary-General of the United Nations of the steps they are taking and of their progress.

Article 4

If, owing to accident, distress, emergency or unintended landing, the personnel of a spacecraft land in territory under the jurisdiction of a Contracting Party or have been found on the high seas or in any other place not under the jurisdiction of any State, they shall be safely and promptly returned to representatives of the launching authority.

Article 5

1. Each Contracting Party which receives information or discovers that a space object or its component parts has returned to Earth in territory under its jurisdiction or on the high seas or in any other place not under the jurisdiction of any State, shall notify the launching authority and the Secretary-General of the United Nations.

2. Each Contracting Party having jurisdiction over the territory on which a space object or its component parts has been discovered shall, upon the request of the launching authority and with assistance from that authority if requested, take such steps as it finds practicable to recover the object or component parts.

3. Upon request of the launching authority, objects launched into outer space or their component parts found beyond the territorial limits of the launching authority shall be returned to or held at the disposal of representatives of the launching authority, which shall, upon request, furnish identifying data prior to their return.

4. Notwithstanding paragraphs 2 and 3 of this Article, a Contracting Party which has reason to believe that a space object or its component parts discovered in territory under its jurisdiction, or recovered by it elsewhere, is of a hazardous or deleterious nature may so notify the launching authority, which shall immediately take effective steps, under the direction and control of the said Contracting Party, to eliminate possible danger of harm.

5. Expenses incurred in fulfilling obligations to recover and return a space object or its component parts under paragraphs 2 and 3 of this Article shall be borne by the launching authority.

Article 6

For the purposes of this Agreement, the term "launching authority" shall refer to the State responsible for launching, or, where an international inter-governmental organization is responsible for launching, that organization, provided that that organization declares its acceptance of the rights and obligations provided for in this Agreement and a majority of the States members of that organization are Contracting Parties to this Agreement and to the Treaty on Principles Governing the Activities of States in the Exploration and Use of Outer Space, including the Moon and Other Celestial Bodies.

Article 7

1. This Agreement shall be open to all States for signature. Any State which does not sign this Agreement before its entry into force in accordance with paragraph 3 of this Article may accede to it at any time.

2. This Agreement shall be subject to ratification by signatory States. Instruments of ratification and instruments of accession shall be deposited with the Governments of the United Kingdom of Great Britain and Northern Ireland, the Union of Soviet Socialist Republics and the United States of America, which are hereby designated the Depositary Governments.

3. This Agreement shall enter into force upon the deposit of instruments of ratification by five Governments including the Governments designated as Depositary Governments under this Agreement.

4. For States whose instruments of ratification or accession are deposited subsequent to the entry into force of this Agreement, it shall enter into force on the date of the deposit of their instruments of ratification or accession.

5. The Depositary Governments shall promptly inform all signatory and acceding States of the date of each signature, the date of deposit of each instrument of ratification of and accession to this Agreement, the date of its entry into force and other notices.

6. This Agreement shall be registered by the Depositary Governments pursuant to Article 102 of the Charter of the United Nations.

Article 8

Any State Party to the Agreement may propose amendments to this Agreement. Amendments shall enter into force for each State Party to the Agreement accepting the amendments upon their acceptance by a majority of the States Parties to the Agreement and thereafter for each remaining State Party to the Agreement on the date of acceptance by it.

Article 9

Any State Party to the Agreement may give notice of its withdrawal from the Agreement one year after its entry into force by written notification to the Depositary Governments. Such withdrawal shall take effect one year from the date of receipt of this notification.

Article 10

This Agreement, of which the English, Russian, French, Spanish and Chinese texts are equally authentic, shall be deposited in the archives of the Depositary Governments. Duly certified copies of this Agreement shall be transmitted by the Depositary Governments to the Governments of the signatory and acceding States.
IN WITNESS WHEREOF the undersigned, duly authorised, have signed this Agreement.

APPENDIX III

CONVENTION ON INTERNATIONAL LIABILITY FOR DAMAGE CAUSED BY SPACE OBJECTS OF 29 MARCH 1972

The States Parties to this Convention,

Recognizing the common interest of all mankind in furthering the exploration and use of outer space for peaceful purposes,

Recalling the Treaty on Principles Governing the Activities of States in the Exploration and Use of Outer Space, including the Moon and Other Celestial Bodies,

Taking into consideration that notwithstanding the precautionary measures to be taken by States and international intergovernmental organizations involved in the launching of space objects, damage may on occasion be caused by such objects,

Recognizing the need to elaborate effective international rules and procedures concerning liability for damage caused by space objects and to ensure, in particular, the prompt payment under the terms of this Convention of a full and equitable measure of compensation to victims of such damage,

Believing that the establishment of such rules and procedures will contribute to the strengthening of international co-operation in the field of the exploration and use of outer space for peaceful purposes,

Have agreed on the following:

Article I

For the purposes of this Convention:

(a) the term "damage" means loss of life, personal injury or other impairment of health; or loss of or damage to property of States or of persons, natural or juridical, or property of international intergovernmental organizations;

(b) the term "launching" includes attempted launching;

(c) the term "launching State" means:

(i) A State which launches or procures the launching of a space object;

(ii) A State from whose territory or facility a space object is launched;

(d) The term "space object" includes component parts of a space object as well as its launch vehicle and parts thereof.

Article II

A launching State shall be absolutely liable to pay compensation for damage caused by its space object on the surface of the earth or to aircraft in flight.

Article III

In the event of damage being caused elsewhere than on the surface of the earth to a space object of one launching State or to persons or property on board such a space object by a space object of another launching State, the latter shall be liable only if the damage is due to its fault or fault of persons for whom it is responsible.

Article IV

1. In the event of damage being caused elsewhere than on the surface of the earth to a space object of one launching State or to persons or property on board such a space object by a space object of another launching State, and of damage thereby being caused to a third State or to its natural or juridical persons, the first two States shall be jointly and severally liable to the third State, to the extent indicated by the following:

(a) If the damage has been caused to the third State on the surface of the earth or to aircraft in flight, their liability to the third State shall be absolute;

(b) If the damage has been caused to a space object of the third State or or to persons or property on board that space object elsewhere than on the surface of the earth, their liability to the third State shall be based on the fault of either of the first two States or on the fault of persons for whom either is responsible.

2. In all cases of joint and several liability referred to in paragraph 1 of this article, the burden of compensation for the damage shall be apportioned between the first two States in accordance with the extent to which they were at fault; if the extent of the fault of each of these States cannot be established, the burden of compensation shall be apportioned equally between them. Such apportionment shall be without prejudice to the right of the third State to seek the entire compensation due under this Convention from any or all of the launching States which are jointly and severally liable.

Article V

1. Whenever two or more States jointly launch a space object, they shall be jointly and severally liable for any damage caused.

2. A launching State which has paid compensation for damage shall have the right to present a claim for indemnification to other participants in the joint launching. The participants in a joint launching may conclude agreements regarding the apportioning

among themselves of the financial obligation in respect of which they are jointly and severally liable. Such agreements shall be without prejudice to the right of a State sustaining damage to seek the entire compensation due under this Convention from any or all of the launching States which are jointly and severally liable.

3. A State from whose territory or facility a space object is launched shall be regarded as a participant in a joint launching.

Article VI

1. Subject to the provisions of paragraph 2 of this article, exoneration from absolute liability shall be granted to the extent that a launching State establishes that the damage has resulted either wholly or partially from gross negligence or from an act or omission done with intent to cause damage on the part of a claimant State or of natural or juridical persons it represents.

2. No exoneration whatever shall be granted in cases where the damage has resulted from activities conducted by a launching State which are not in conformity with international law including, in particular, the Charter of the United Nations and the Treaty on Principles Governing the Activities of States in the Exploration and Use of Outer Space, including the Moon and other Celestial Bodies.

Article VII

The provisions of this Convention shall not apply to damage caused by a space object of a launching State to:
(a) Natonals of that launching State;
(b) Foreign nationals during such time as they are participating in the operation of that space object from the time of its launching or at any stage thereafter until its descent, or during such time as they are in the immediate vicinity of a planned launching or recovery area as the result of an invitation by that launching State.

Article VIII

1. A State which suffers damage, or whose natural or juridical persons suffer damage, may present to a launching State a claim for compensation for such damage.

2. If the State of nationality has not presented a claim, another State may, in respect of damage sustained in its territory by any natural or juridical person, present a claim to a launching State.

3. If neither the State of nationality nor the State in whose territory the damage was sustained has presented a claim or notified its intention of presenting a claim, another State may, in respect of damage sustained by its permanent residents, present a claim to a launching State.

Article IX

A claim for compensation for damage shall be presented to a launching State through diplomatic channels. If a State does not maintain diplomatic relations with the launching State concerned, it may request another State to present its claim to that launching State or otherwise represent its interests under this Convention. It may also present its claim through the Secretary-General of the United Nations, provided the claimant State and the launching State are both Members of the United Nations.

Article X

1. A claim for compensation for damage may be presented to a launching State not later than one year following the date of the occurrence of the damage or the identification of the launching State which is liable.

2. If, however, a State does not know of the occurrence of the damage or has not been able to identify the launching State which is liable, it may present a claim within one year following the date on which it learned of the aforementioned facts; however, this period shall in no event exceed one year following the date on which the State could reasonably be expected to have learned of the facts through the exercise of due diligence.

3. The time-limits specified in paragraphs 1 and 2 of this article shall apply even if the full extent of the damage may not be known. In this event, however, the claimant State shall be entitled to revise the claim and submit additional documentation after the expiration of such time-limits until one year after the full extent of the damage is known.

Article XI

1. Presentation of a claim to a launching State for compensation for damage under this Convention shall not require the prior exhaustion of any local remedies which may be available to a claimant State or to natural or juridical persons it represents.

2. Nothing in this Convention shall prevent a State, or natural or juridical persons it might represent, from pursuing a claim in the courts or administrative tribunals or agencies of a launching State. A State shall not, however, be entitled to present a claim under this Convention in respect of the same damage for which a claim is being pursued in the courts

or administrative tribunals or agencies of a launching State or under another international agreement which is binding on the States concerned.

Article XII

The compensation which the launching State shall be liable to pay for damage under this Convention shall be determined in accordance with international law and the principles of justice and equity, in order to provide such reparation in respect of the damage as will restore the person, natural or juridical, State or international organization on whose behalf the claim is presented to the condition which would have existed if the damage had not occurred.

Article XIII

Unless the claimant State and the State from which compensation is due under this Convention agree on another form of compensation, the compensation shall be paid in the currency of the claimant State or, if that State so requests, in the currency of the State from which compensation is due.

Article XIV

If no settlement of a claim is arrived at through diplomatic negotiations as provided for in Article IX, within one year from the date on which the claimant State notifies the launching State that it has submitted the documentation of its claim, the parties concerned shall establish a Claims Commission at the request of either party.

Article XV

1. The Claims Commission shall be composed of three members: one appointed by the claimant State, one appointed by the launching State and the third member, the Chairman, to be chosen by both parties jointly. Each party shall make its appointment within two months of the request for the establishment of the Claims Commission.

2. If no agreement is reached on the choice of the Chairman within four months of the request for the establishment of the Commission, either party may request the Secretary-General of the United Nations to appoint the Chairman within a further period of two months.

Article XVI

1. If one of the parties does not make its appointment within the stipulated period, the Chairman shall, at the request of the other party, constitute a single-member Claims Commission.

2. Any vacancy which may arise in the Commission for whatever reasons shall be filled by the same procedure adopted for the original appointment.

3. The Commission shall determine its own procedure.

4. The Commission shall determine the place or places where it shall sit and all other administrative matters.

5. Except in the case of decisions and awards by a single-member Commission, all decisions and awards of the Commission shall be by majority vote.

Article XVII

No increase in the membership of the Claims Commission shall take place by reason of two or more claimant States or launching States being joined in any one proceeding before the Commission. The claimant States so joined shall collectively appoint one member of the Commission in the same manner and subject to the same conditions as would be the case for a single claimant State. When two or more launching States are so joined, they shall collectively appoint one member of the Commission in the same way. If the claimant States or the launching States do not make the appointment within the stipulated period, the Chairman shall constitute a single-member Commission.

Article XVIII

The Claims Commission shall decide the merits of the claim for compensation and determine the amount of compensation payable, if any.

Article XIX

1. The Claims Commission shall act in accordance with the provisions of article XII.

2. The decision of the Commission shall be final and binding if the parties have so agreed; otherwise the Commission shall render a final and recommendatory award, which the parties shall consider in good faith. The Commission shall state the reasons for its decision or award.

3. The Commission shall give its decision or award as promptly as possible and no later than one year from the date of its establishment unless an extension of this period is found necessary by the Commission.

4. The Commission shall make its decision or award public. It shall deliver a certified copy of its decision or award to each of the parties and to the Secretary-General of the United Nations.

Article XX

The expenses in regard to the Claims Commission shall be borne equally by the parties, unless otherwise decided by the Commission.

Article XXI

If the damage caused by a space object presents a large-scale danger to human life or seriously interferes with the living conditions of the population or the functioning of vital centres, the States Parties, and in particular the launching State, shall examine the possibility of rendering appropriate and rapid assistance to the State which has suffered the damage, when it so requests. However, nothing in this article shall effect the rights or obligations of the States Parties under this Convention.

Article XXII

1. In this Convention, with the exception of articles 24 to 27, references to States shall be deemed to apply to any international intergovernmental organization which conducts space activities if the organization declares its acceptance of the rights and obligations provided for in this Convention and if a majority of the States members of the organization are States Parties to this Convention and to the Treaty on Principles Governing the Activities of States in the Exploration and Use of Outer Space, including the Moon and other Celestial Bodies.

2. States members of any such organization which are States Parties to this Convention shall take all appropriate steps to ensure that the organization makes a declaration in accordance with the preceding paragraph.

3. If an international intergovernmental organization is liable for damage by virtue of the provisions of this Convention, that organization and those of its members which are States Parties to this Convention shall be jointly and severally liable; provided, however, that:

(a) any claim for compensation in respect of such damage shall be first presented to the organization;

(b) only where the organization has not paid, within a period of six months, any sum agreed or determined to be due as compensation for such damage, may the claimant

State invoke the liability of the members which are States Parties to this Convention for the payment of that sum.

4. Any claim, pursuant to the provisions of this Convention, for compensation in respect of damage caused to an organization which has made a declaration in accordance with paragraph 1 of this article shall be presented by a State member of the organization which is a State Party to this Convention.

Article XXIII

1. The provisions of this Convention shall not affect other international agreements in force in so far as relations between the States Parties to such agreements are concerned.

2. No provision of this Convention shall prevent States from concluding international agreements reaffirming, supplementing or extending its provisions.

Article XXIV

1. This Convention shall be open to all States for signature. Any State which does not sign this Convention before its entry into force in accordance with paragraph 3 of this article may accede to it at any time.

2. This Convention shall be subject to ratification by signatory States. Instruments of ratification and instruments of accession shall be deposited with the Governments of the Union of Soviet Socialist Republics, the United Kingdom of Britain and Northern Ireland and the United States of America, which are hereby designated the Depositary Governments.

3. This Convention shall enter into force on the deposit of the fifth instrument of ratification.

4. For States whose instruments of ratification or accession are deposited subsequent to the entry into force of this Convention, it shall enter into force on the date of the deposit of their instruments of ratification or accession.

5. The Depositary Governments shall promptly inform all signatory and acceding States of the date of each signature, the date of deposit of each instrument of ratification of and accession to this Convention, the date of its entry into force and other notices.

6. This Convention shall be registered by the Depositary Governments pursuant to Article 102 of the Charter of the United Nations.

Article XXV

Any State Party to this Convention may propose amendments to this Convention. Amendments shall enter into force for each State Party to the Convention accepting the amendments upon their acceptance by a majority of the States Parties to the Convention and thereafter for each remaining State Party to the Convention on the date of acceptance by it.

Article XXVI

Ten years after the entry into force of this Convention, the question of the review of this Convention shall be included in the provisional agenda of the United Nations General Assembly in order to consider, in the light of past application of the Convention, whether it requires revision. However, at any time after the Convention has been in force for five years, and at the request of one third of the States Parties to the Convention, and with the concurrence of the majority of the States Parties, a conference of the States Parties shall be convened to review this Convention.

Article XXVII

Any State Party to this Convention may give notice of its withdrawal from the Convention one year after its entry into force by written notification to the Depositary Governments. Such withdrawal shall take effect one year from the date of receipt of this notification.

Article XXVIII

This Convention, of which the Chinese, English, French, Russian and Spanish texts are equally authentic, shall be deposited in the archives of the Depositary Governments. Duly certified copies of this Convention shall be transmitted by the Depositary Governments to the Governments of the signatory and acceding States.
IN WITNESS WHEREOF the undersigned, duly authorized, have signed this Convention.

APPENDIX IV

CONVENTION ON REGISTRATION OF OBJECTS LAUNCHED INTO OUTER SPACE OF 14 JANUARY 1975

The States Parties to this Convention,

Recognizing the common interest of all mankind in furthering the exploration and use of outer space for peaceful purposes,

Recalling that the Treaty on Principles Governing the Activities of States in the Exploration and Use of Outer Space, including the Moon and Other Celestial Bodies of 27 January 1967 affirms that States shall bear international responsibility for their national activities in outer space and refers to the State on whose registry an object launched into outer space is carried,

Recalling also that the Agreement on the Rescue of Astronauts, the Return of Astronauts and the Return of Objects Launched into Outer Space of 22 April 1968 provides that a launching authority shall, upon request, furnish identifying data prior to the return of an object it has launched into outer space found beyond the territorial limits of the launching authority,

Recalling further that the Convention on International Liability for Damage Caused by Space Objects of 29 March 1972 establishes international rules and procedures concerning the liability of launching States for damage caused by their space objects,

Desiring, in the light of the Treaty on Principles Governing the Activities of States in the Exploration and Use of Outer Space, including the Moon and Other Celestial Bodies, to make provision for the national registration by launching States of space objects launched into outer space,

Desiring further that a central register of objects launched into outer space be established and maintained, on a mandatory basis, by the Secretary-General of the United Nations,

Desiring also to provide for States Parties additional means and procedures to assist in the identification of space objects,

Believing that a mandatory system of registering objects launched into outer space would, in particular, assist in their identification and would contribute to the application and development of international law governing the exploration and use of outer space,

Have agreed on the following:

Article I

For the purposes of this Convention:

(a) The term "launching State" means:

  (i) A State which launches or procures the launching of a space object;

  (ii) A State from whose territory or facility a space object is launched;

(b) The term "space object" includes component parts of a space object as well as its launch vehicle and parts thereof;

(c) The term "State of registry" means a launching State on whose registry a space object is carried in accordance with article II.

Article II

1. When a space object is launched into earth orbit or beyond, the launching State shall register the space object by means of an entry in an appropriate registry which it shall maintain. Each launching State shall inform the Secretary-General of the United Nations of the establishment of such a registry.

2. Where there are two or more launching States in respect of any such space object, they shall jointly determine which one of them shall register the object in accordance with paragraph 1 of this article, bearing in mind the provisions of article VIII of the Treaty on Principles Governing the Activities of States in the Exploration and Use of Outer Space, including the Moon and Other Celestial Bodies, and without prejudice to appropriate agreements concluded or to be concluded among the launching States on jurisdiction and control over the space object and over any personnel thereof.

3. The contents of each registry and the conditions under which it is maintained shall be determined by the State of registry concerned.

Article III

1. The Secretary-General of the United Nations shall maintain a Register in which the information furnished in accordance with article V shall be recorded.

2. There shall be full and open access to the information in this Register.

Article IV

1. Each State of registry shall furnish to the Secretary-General of the United Nations, as soon as practicable, the following information concerning each space object carried on its registry:

(a) Name of launching State or States;
(b) An appropriate designator of the space object or its registration number;
(c) Date and territory or location of launch;
(d) Basic orbital parameters, including:
  (i) Nodal period,
  (ii) Inclination,
  (iii) Apogee,
  (iv) Perigee;
(e) General function of the space object.

2. Each State of registry may, from time to time, provide the Secretary-General of the United Nations with additional information concerning a space object carried on its registry.

3. Each State of registry shall notify the Secretary-General of the United Nations, to the greatest extent feasible and as soon as practicable, of space objects concerning which it has previously transmitted information, and which have been but no longer are in earth orbit.

Article V

Whenever a space object launched into earth orbit or beyond is marked with the designator or registration number referred to in article IV, paragraph 1 (b), or both, the State of registry shall notify the Secretary-General of this fact when submitting the information regarding the space object in accordance with article IV. In such case, the Secretary-General of the United Nations shall record this notification in the Register.

Article VI

Where the application of the provisions of this Convention has not enabled a State Party to identify a space object which has caused damage to it or to any of its natural or juridical persons, or which may be of a hazardous or deleterious nature, other States Parties, including in particular States possessing space monitoring and tracking facilities, shall respond to the greatest extent feasible to a request by that State Party, or transmitted through the Secretary-General on its behalf, for assistance under equitable and reasonable conditions in the identification of the object. A State Party making such a request shall, to the greatest extent feasible, submit information as to the time, nature and circumstances of the events giving rise to the request. Arrangements under which such assistance shall be rendered shall be the subject of agreement between the parties concerned.

Article VII

1. In this Convention, with the exception of articles VIII to XII inclusive, references to States shall be deemed to apply to any international intergovernmental organization which conducts space activities if the organization declares its acceptance of the rights and obligations provided for in this Convention and if a majority of the States members of the organization are States Parties to this Convention and to the Treaty on Principles Governing the Activities of States in the Exploration and Use of Outer Space, including the Moon and Other Celestial Bodies.

2. States members of any such organization which are States Parties to this Convention shall take all appropriate steps to ensure that the organization makes a declaration in accordance with paragraph 1 of this article.

Article VIII

1. This Convention shall be open for signature by all States at United Nations Headquarters in New York. Any State which does not sign this Convention before its entry into force in accordance with paragraph 3 of this article may accede to it at any time.

2. This Convention shall be subject to ratification by signatory States. Instruments of ratification and instruments of accession shall be deposited with the Secretary-General of the United Nations.

3. This Convention shall enter into force among the States which have deposited instruments of ratification on the deposit of the fifth such instrument with the Secretary-General of the United Nations.

4. For States whose instruments of ratification or accession are deposited subsequent to the entry into force of this Convention, it shall enter into force on the date of the deposit of their instruments of ratification or accession.

5. The Secretary-General shall promptly inform all signatory and acceding States of the date of each signature, the date of deposit of each instrument of ratification of and accession to this Convention, the date of its entry into force and other notices.

Article IX

Any State Party to this Convention may propose amendments to the Convention. Amendments shall enter into force for each State Party to the Convention accepting the amendments upon their acceptance by a majority of the States Parties to the Convention and thereafter for each remaining State Party to the Convention on the date of acceptance by it.

Article X

Ten years after the entry into force of this Convention, the question of the review of the Convention shall be included in the provisional agenda of the United Nations General Assembly in order to consider, in the light of past application of the Convention, whether it requires revision. However, at any time after the Convention has been in force for five years, at the request of one third of the States Parties to the Convention and with the concurrence of the majority of the States Parties, a conference of the States Parties shall be convened to review this Convention. Such review shall take into account in particular any relevant technological developments, including those relating to the identification of space objects.

Article XI

Any State Party to this Convention may give notice of its withdrawal from the Convention one year after its entry into force by written notification to the Secretary-General of the United Nations. Such withdrawal shall take effect one year from the date of receipt of this notification.

Article XII

The original of this Convention, of which the Arabic, Chinese, English, French, Russian and Spanish texts are equally authentic, shall be deposited with the Secretary-General of the United Nations, who shall send certified copies thereof to all signatory and acceding States.

IN WITNESS WHEREOF the undersigned, being duly authorized thereto by their respective Governments, have signed this Convention, opened for signature at New York on 14 January, 1975.

APPENDIX V

AGREEMENT GOVERNING THE ACTIVITIES OF STATES ON THE MOON AND OTHER CELESTIAL BODIES OF 18 DECEMBER 1979

The States Parties to this Agreement,

Noting the achievements of States in the exploration and use of the moon and other celestial bodies,

Recognizing that the moon, as a natural satellite of the earth, has an important role to play in the exploration of outer space,

Determined to promote on the basis of equality the further development of co-operation among States in the exploration and use of the moon and other celestial bodies,

Desiring to prevent the moon from becoming an area of international conflict,

Bearing in mind the benefits which may be derived from the exploitation of the natural resources of the moon and other celestial bodies,

Recalling the Treaty on Principles Governing the Activities of States in the Exploration and Use of Outer Space, including the Moon and other Celestial Bodies, the Agreement on the Rescue of Astronauts, the Return of Astronauts and the Return of Objects Launched into Outer Space, the Convention on International Liability for Damage Caused by Space Objects, and the Convention on Registration of Objects Launched into Outer Space,

Taking into account the need to define and develop the provisions of these international instruments in relation to the moon and other celestial bodies, having regard to further progress in the exploration and use of outer space,

Have agreed on the following:

Article 1

1. The provisions of this Agreement relating to the moon shall also apply to other celestial bodies within the solar system, other than the earth, except in so far as specific legal norms enter into force with respect to any of these celestial bodies.

2. For the purposes of this Agreement reference to the moon shall include orbits around or other trajectories to or around it.

3. This Agreement does not apply to extraterrestrial materials which reach the surface of the earth by natural means.

Article 2

All activities on the moon, including its exploration and use, shall be carried out in accordance with international law, in particular the Charter of the United Nations, and taking into account the Declaration on Principles of International Law concerning Friendly Relations and Co-operation among States in accordance with the Charter of the United Nations, adopted by the General Assembly on 24 October 1970, in the interest of maintaining international peace and security and promoting international co-operation and mutual understanding, and with due regard to the corresponding interests of all other States Parties.

Article 3

1. The moon shall be used by all States Parties exclusively for peaceful purposes.

2. Any threat or use of force or any other hostile act or threat of hostile act on the moon is prohibited. It is likewise prohibited to use the moon in order to commit any such act or to engage in any such threat in relation to the earth, the moon, spacecraft, the personnel of spacecraft or man-made space objects.

3. States Parties shall not place in orbit around or other trajectory to or around the moon objects carrying nuclear weapons or any other kinds of weapons of mass destruction or place or use such weapons on or in the moon.

4. The establishment of military bases, installations and fortifications, the testing of any type of weapons and the conduct of military manoeuvres on the moon shall be forbidden. The use of military personnel for scientific research or for any other peaceful purposes shall not be prohibited. The use of any equipment or facility necessary for peaceful exploration and use of the moon shall also not be prohibited.

Article 4

1. The exploration and use of the moon shall be the province of all mankind and shall be carried out for the benefit and in the interests of all countries, irrespective of their degree of economic or scientific development. Due regard shall be paid to the interests of present and future generations as well as to the need to promote higher standards of living and conditions of economic and social progress and development in accordance with the Charter of the United Nations.

2. States Parties shall be guided by the principle of co-operation and mutual assistance in all their activities concerning the exploration and use of the moon. International co-operation in pursuance of this Agreement should be as wide as possible and may take place on a multilateral basis, on a bilateral basis or through international intergovernmental organizations.

Article 5

1. States Parties shall inform the Secretary-General of the United Nations as well as the public and the international scientific community, to the greatest extent feasible and practicable, of their activities concerned with the exploration and use of the moon. Information on the time, purposes, locations, orbital parameters and duration shall be given in respect of each mission to the moon as soon as possible after launching, while information on the results of each mission, including scientific results, shall be furnished upon completion of the mission. In the case of a mission lasting more than sixty days, information on conduct of the mission, including any scientific results, shall be given periodically, at thirty-day intervals. For missions lasting more than six months, only significant additions to such information need be reported thereafter.

2. If a State Party becomes aware that another State Party plans to operate simultaneously in the same area of or in the same orbit around or trajectory to or around the moon, it shall promptly inform the other State of the timing of and plans for its own operations.

3. In carrying out activities under this Agreement, States Parties shall promptly inform the Secretary-General, as well as the public and the international scientific community, of any phenomena they discover in outer space, including the moon, which could endanger human life or health, as well as of any indication of organic life.

Article 6

1. There shall be freedom of scientific investigation on the moon by all States Parties without discrimination of any kind, on the basis of equality and in accordance with international law.

2. In carrying out scientific investigations and in furtherance of the provisions of this Agreement, the States Parties shall have the right to collect on and remove from the moon samples of its mineral and other substances. Such samples shall remain at the disposal of those States Parties which caused them to be collected and may be used by them for scientific purposes. States Parties shall have regard to the desirability of making a portion of such samples available to other interested States Parties and the international scientific community for scientific investigation. States Parties may in the course of scientific

investigations also use mineral and other substances of the moon in quantities appropriate for the support of their missions.

3. States Parties agree on the desirability of exchanging scientific and other personnel on expeditions to or installations on the moon to the greatest extent feasible and practicable.

Article 7

1. In exploring and using the moon, States Parties shall take measures to prevent the disruption of the existing balance of its environment whether by introducing adverse changes in that environment, by its harmful contamination through the introduction of extra-environmental matter or otherwise. States Parties shall also take measures to avoid harmfully affecting the environment of the earth through the introduction of extraterrestrial matter or otherwise.

2. States Parties shall inform the Secretary-General of the United Nations of the measures being adopted by them in accordance with paragraph 1 of this article and shall also, to the maximum extent feasible, notify him in advance of all placements by them of radio-active materials on the moon and of the purposes of such placements.

3. States Parties shall report to other States Parties and to the Secretary-General concerning areas of the moon having special scientific interest in order that, without prejudice to the rights of other States Parties, consideration may be given to the designation of such areas as international scientific preserves for which special protective arrangements are to be agreed upon in consultation with the competent bodies of the United Nations.

Article 8

1. States Parties may pursue their activities in the exploration and use of the moon anywhere on or below its surface, subject to the provisions of this Agreement.

2. For these purposes States Parties may, in particular:

a) Land their space objects on the moon and launch them from the moon;
b) Place their personnel, space vehicles, equipment, facilities, stations and installations anywhere on or below the surface of the moon.

Personnel, space vehicles, equipment, facilities, stations and installations may move or be moved freely over or below the surface of the moon.

3. Activities of States Parties in accordance with paragraphs 1 and 2 of this article shall not interfere with the activities of other States Parties on the moon. Where such interference may occur, the States Parties concerned shall undertake consultations in accordance with article 15, paragraphs 2 and 3 of this Agreement.

Article 9

1. States Parties may establish manned and unmanned stations on the moon. A State Party establishing a station shall use only that area which is required for the needs of the station and shall immediately inform the Secretary-General of the United Nations of the location and purposes of that station. Subsequently, at annual intervals that State shall likewise inform the Secretary-General whether the station continues in use and whether its purposes have changed.

2. Stations shall be installed in such a manner that they do not impede the free access to all areas of the moon of personnel, vehicles and equipment of other States Parties conducting activities on the moon in accordance with the provisions of this Agreement or of article I of the Treaty on Principles Governing the Activities of States in the Exploration and Use of Outer Space, including the Moon and other Celestial Bodies.

Article 10

1. States Parties shall adopt all practicable measures to safeguard the life and health of persons on the moon. For this purpose they shall regard any person on the moon as an astronaut within the meaning of article V of the Treaty on Principles Governing the Activities of States in the Exploration and Use of Outer Space, including the Moon and other Celestial Bodies and as part of the personnel of a spacecraft within the meaning of the Agreement on the Rescue of Astronauts, the Return of Astronauts and the Return of Objects Launched into Outer Space.

2. States Parties shall offer shelter in their stations, installations, vehicles and other facilities to persons in distress on the moon.

Article 11

1. The moon and its natural resources are the common heritage of mankind, which finds its expression in the provisions of this Agreement, in particular in paragraph 5 of this article.

2. The moon is not subject to national appropriation by any claim of sovereignty, by means of use or occupation, or by any other means.

3. Neither the surface nor the subsurface of the moon, nor any part thereof or natural resources in place, shall become property of any State, international intergovernmental or non-governmental organization, national organization or non-governmental entity or of any natural person. The placement of personnel, space vehicles, equipment, facilities, stations and installations on or below the surface of the moon, including structures connected with its surface or subsurface, shall not create a right of ownership over the surface or

subsurface of the moon or any areas thereof. The foregoing provisions are without prejudice to the international regime referred to in paragraph 5 of this article.

4. States Parties have the right to exploration and use of the moon without discrimination of any kind, on the basis of equality and in accordance with international law and the provisions of this Agreement.

5. States Parties to this Agreement hereby undertake to establish an international regime, including appropriate procedures, to govern the exploitation of the natural resources of the moon as such exploitation is about to become feasible. This provision shall be implemented in accordance with Article 18 of this Agreement.

6. In order to facilitate the establishment of the international regime referred to in paragraph 5 of this article, States Parties shall inform the Secretary-General of the United Nations as well as the public and the international scientific community, to the greatest extent feasible and practicable, of any natural resources they may discover on the moon.

7. The main purposes of the international regime to be established shall include:
(a) The orderly and safe development of the natural resources of the moon;
(b) The rational management of those resources;
(c) The expansion of opportunities in the use of those resources ;
(d) An equitable sharing by all States Parties in the benefits derived from those resources, whereby the interests and needs of the developing countries, as well as the efforts of those countries, which have contributed either directly or indirectly to the exploration of the moon, shall be given special consideration.

8. All the activities with respect to the natural resources of the moon shall be carried out in a manner compatible with the purposes specified in paragraph 7 of this article and the provisions of article 6, paragraph 2 of this Agreement.

Article 12

1. States Parties shall retain jurisdiction and control over their personnel, space vehicles, equipment, facilities, stations and installations on the moon. The ownership of space vehicles, equipment, facilities, stations and installations shall not be affected by their presence on the moon.

2. Vehicles, installations and equipment or their component parts found in places other than their intended location shall be dealt with in accordance with article 5 of the Agreement on the Rescue of Astronauts, the Return of Astronauts and the Return of Objects Launched into Outer Space.

3. In the event of an emergency involving a threat to human life, States Parties may use the equipment, vehicles, installations, facilities or supplies of other States Parties on the moon. Prompt notification of such use shall be made to the Secretary-General of the United Nations or the State Party concerned.

Article 13

A State Party which learns of the crash landing, forced landing or other unintended landing on the moon of a space object, or its component parts, that were not launched by it, shall promptly inform the launching State Party and the Secretary-General of the United Nations.

Article 14

1. States Parties to this Agreement shall bear international responsibility for national activities on the moon, whether such activities are carried out by governmental agencies or by non-governmental entities, and for assuring that national activities are carried out in conformity with the provisions of this Agreement. States Parties shall ensure that non-governmental entities under their jurisdiction shall engage in activities on the moon only under the authority and continuing supervision of the appropriate State Party.

2. States Parties recognize that detailed arrangements concerning liability for damage caused on the moon, in addition to the provisions of the Treaty on Principles Governing the Activities of States in the Exploration and Use of Outer Space, including the Moon and other Celestial Bodies and the Convention on International Liability for Damage Caused by Space Objects, may become necessary as a result of more extensive activities on the moon. Any such arrangements shall be elaborated in accordance with the procedure provided for in article 18 of this Agreement.

Article 15

1. Each State Party may assure itself that the activities of other States Parties in the exploration and use of the moon are compatible with the provisions of this Agreement. To this end, all space vehicles, equipment, facilities, stations and installations on the moon shall be open to other States Parties. Such States Parties shall give reasonable advance notice of a projected visit, in order that appropriate consultations may be held and that maximum precautions may be taken to assure safety and to avoid interference with normal operations in the facility to be visited. In pursuance of this article any State Party may act on its own behalf or with the full or partial assistance of any other State Party or through appropriate international procedures within the framework of the United Nations and in accordance with the Charter.

2. A State Party which has reason to believe that another State Party is not fulfilling the obligations incumbent upon it pursuant to this Agreement or that another State Party is interfering with the rights which the former State has under this Agreement may request consultations with that State Party . A State Party receiving such a request shall enter into such consultations without delay. Any other State Party which requests to do so shall be entitled to take part in the consultations. Each State Party participating in such consultations shall seek a mutually acceptable resolution of any controversy and shall bear in mind the rights and interests of all States Parties. The Secretary-General of the United Nations shall be informed of the results of the consultations and shall transmit the information received to all States Parties concerned.

3. If the consultations do not lead to a mutually acceptable settlement which has due regard for the rights and interests of all States Parties, the parties concerned shall take all measures to settle the dispute by other peaceful means of their choice appropriate to the circumstances and the nature of the dispute. If difficulties arise in connexion with the opening of consultations or if consultations do not lead to a mutually acceptable settlement, any State Party may seek the assistance of the Secretary-General, without seeking the consent of any other State Party concerned, in order to resolve the controversy. A State Party which does not maintain diplomatic relations with another State Party concerned shall participate in such consultations at its choice, either itself or through another State Party or the Secretary-General as intermediary.

Article 16

With the exception of articles 17 to 21, references in this Agreement to States shall be deemed to apply to any international intergovernmental organization which conducts space activities if the organization declares its acceptance of the rights and obligations provided for in this Agreement and if a majority of the States members of the organization are States Parties to this Agreement and to the Treaty on Principles Governing the Activities of States in the Exploration and Use of Outer Space, including the Moon and other Celestial Bodies. States members of any such organization which are States Parties to this Agreement shall take all appropriate steps to ensure that the organization makes a declaration in accordance with the provisions of this article.

Article 17

Any State Party to this Agreement may propose amendments to the Agreement. Amendments shall enter into force for each State Party to the Agreement accepting the amendments upon their acceptance by a majority of the States Parties to the Agreement and thereafter for each remaining State Party to the Agreement on the date of acceptance by it.

Article 18

Ten years after the entry into force of this Agreement, the question of the review of the Agreement shall be included in the provisional agenda of the General Assembly of the United Nations in order to consider, in the light of past application of the Agreement, whether it requires revision. However, at any time after the Agreement has been in force for five years, the Secretary-General of the United Nations, as depository, shall, at the request of one third of the States Parties to the Agreement and with the concurrence of the majority of the States Parties, convene a conference of the States Parties to review this Agreement. A review conference shall also consider the question of the implementation of the provisions of article 11, paragraph 5, on the basis of the principle referred to in paragraph 1 of that article and taking into account in particular any relevant technological developments.

Article 19

1. This Agreement shall be open for signature by all States at United Nations Headquarters in New York.

2. This Agreement shall be subject to ratification by signatory States. Any State which does not sign this Agreement before its entry into force in accordance with paragraph 3 of this article may accede to it at any time. Instruments of ratification or accession shall be deposited with the Secretary-General of the United Nations.

3. This Agreement shall enter into force on the thirtieth day following the date of deposit of the fifth instrument of ratification.

4. For each State depositing its instrument of ratification or accession after the entry into force of this Agreement, it shall enter into force on the thirtieth day following the date of deposit of such instrument.

5. The Secretary-General shall promptly inform all signatory and acceding States of the date of each signature, the date of deposit of each instrument of ratification or accession to this Agreement, the date of its entry into force and other notices.

Article 20

Any State Party to this Agreement may give notice of its withdrawal from the Agreement one year after its entry into force by written notification to the Secretary-General of the United Nations. Such withdrawal shall take effect one year from the date of receipt of this notification.

Article 21

The original of this Agreement, of which the Arabic, Chinese, English, French, Russian and Spanish texts are equally authentic, shall be deposited with the Secretary-General of the United Nations, who shall send certified copies thereof to all signatory and acceding States. IN WITNESS WHEREOF the undersigned, being duly authorized thereto by their respective Governments, have signed this Agreement, opened for signature at New York on this eighteenth day of December, one thousand nine hundred and seventy-nine.

INDEX

ABM, *92, 93*
  Treaty, *82, 83, 87, 88, 92, 109, 136*
    Article II, *92*
    Article III, *93*
    Article V, *70, 80, 83*
    Article VI, *70*
    Article XI, *83*
    Statement "D", *80, 83, 93*
      Broad interpretation, *70*
Aerospace plane, *9, 14*
Air law, *15*
  IATA, *63, 64*
    Bermuda I, *63*
  ICAO, *2, 40, 65*
Airspace, *39, 40, 59*
Air transport, *132*
Antarctic Treaty, *138*
Anticipation, *see* Legal Process
Apollo II, *113*
(non-) Appropriation, *121, 143*
  of celestial bodies, *13, 46 ff.*
  of outer space, *13, 25-26, 46 ff.*
Arianespace, *57, 62, 63, 126, 133*
Arms race, *69 ff., 110, 114, 119, 136, 137*
ASAT, *11, 70, 80, 90, 91, 92, 94, 114, 119, 136*
Athens Convention 1974, *132*
Bogotà Declaration , *26, 101, 144*
  (*see also* GSO, sovereignty over)
Cable and Broadcasting Act 1984 (UK), *129*
Columbus
  Christopher, *55*
Commercial Space Launch Act 1984, *128*
Commercial enterprise, *36, 37, 132*
Commercialisation, *29, 37, 101, 128, 143, 144*
  of space transport, *57 ff.*
Committee on Disarmament, *119*
Common Heritage of Mankind, *46, 48, 50-55, 101, 143*
Communication Satellites Act 1962, *125*
Concepts of law, *16 ff., 21 ff.*
  Analytical Conceptualism, *21 ff.*
  General Concept of Law, *22*
  Normative Concept of Law, *22 ff.*
Conference on Disarmament, *94, 137*
COPUOS *see* UNCOPUOS
Cosmos 954, *113, 122*
COSPAR, *116*
Counterforce strategy, *87, 88*
Countervalue strategy, *87, 88*
Criminal law *130, 134*
DBS, *30, 39, 40, 113, 118, 129, 144*
Decision-making process, *7 ff.*
Delimitation of outer space, *26, 143*
  functionalist school, *9*
  spatialist school, *9*
Détente, *88 ff.*
Developing countries, *2, 18, 26, 35, 47, 50, 51, 55, 95, 100, 101, 103, 113 ff.*
Disarmament, *86*
Domestic law, *see* municipal law
ELV's, *57, 62, 128*
Environmental aspects, *113, 135 ff.*
  contamination, *15, 128, 137*
  debris, *15, 136, 140*
  Environmental Modification Convention, *136*
  pollution, *136, 141*
EOSAT, *14*
Equilibrium, *62, 84 ff.*
Equitable, *115*
  access, *100, 101, 103*
  allocation, *62, 110*
  distribution, *100, 101, 103*
  space order, *99-105*
  sharing, *12, 20, 52, 54, 103*
ESA, *2, 57, 60, 62*
Exegesis, *84 ff.*
Exploitation of outer space, *143*
  commercial, *45 ff., 101*
  minerals, *45 ff.*

FOBS, *80, 90*
Genesis, *84 ff.*
GSO, *13, 20, 51, 61, 103, 108, 114, 119, 120, 141, 143*
  a priori planning, *18*
  first come, first serve, *18, 120*
  equitable sharing of, *18*
  sovereignty over, *26*
Harmful interference, *46*
IAF, *116*
ICBM, *10, 11, 80, 85, 86, 89, 90, 91, 92, 94, 96*
IFRB, *121*
INMARSAT, *54, 83, 114*
INTELSAT, *54, 83, 114, 120, 144*
International cooperation, *28, 36, 70, 73, 92, 97, 105, 106, 107, 116, 122, 124, 126, 138*
International Court of Justice, *19*
International law, 16, *17, 21, 26, 27, 51, 69, 76, 77, 82, 83, 99, 115, 116, 117, 125, 126, 133, 135, 139, 143, 145*
  acquiescence, *40*
  customary international law, *7, 8, 40, 70, 139*
  erga omnes, *27*
  general principles of, *28, 138*
  usufruct, *45*
  usufructory claim, *48, 49*
INTERSPUTNIK, *114*
ITU, *2, 38, 83, 114, 116, 136, 141*
  International Telecommunication Convention, *55, 72*
    Article 10, *121*
    Article 33, *18, 103, 119, 121*
Jurisdiction, *15, 126, 130, 131, 133*
  and control, *27, 39, 59, 141*
Laissez faire, *57, 61, 64, 65*
Land Remote Sensing Commercialisation Act 1984, *14, 128*
Launching
  state, *39, 139, 143*
  site, *35*
  contract, *122, 123, 126, 133*
Law of the sea, *105, 106*
  Law of the Sea Convention, *2, 3, 48, 53*
Law-making process, *36, 37, 69 ff., 143*
Legal Process, *22, 23-24, 37*
  anticipation, *34, 37-38, 41, 99, 102*
  anticipatory treaty-making, *37-40*
  specification, *38-40, 41*
Liability, *37, 116,121, 123, 126, 129, 132, 141, 144*
Liability Convention, *14, 28, 34, 72, 82, 83, 117, 121, 122, 123, 127, 141*
  Article I, *122, 140*
  Article II, *138*
  Article III, *138*
  Article V, *123*
  Article VI, *139*
  Article VII, *139*
Liner Conference, *57, 60*
Long March, *57*
MAD, *77, 87, 88*
Method of Genetic Effectiveness, *79 ff.*
Method *lato sensu*, *24 ff.*
Method *stricto sensu*, *24 ff.*
Moon Agreement, 2, *12, 46, 47, 48, 50-54, 72, 82, 83, 95, 97, 101, 104, 105, 106, 109, 117, 118*
  Article 3, *83, 136*
  Article 4, *35*
  Article 7, *138*
  Article 11, *3, 50*
Municipal law, *30, 125 ff.*
NASA, *60, 122, 126, 133*
  Cargo Launch Agreement, *122, 123*
    Article V, *122*
  Shared Shuttle Launch Agreement
    Article V, *123*
  NASAct 1958, *125*
NIEO, *55, 100, 101, 102*
Non-aggressive *vs.* non-military, *11, 71 ff., 80, 91-94, 118, 119*
Non-governmental entities, *see* Private entities
NTBT, *see* PTBT

Nuclear Power Sources, *38, 113, 118, 140*

Outer Space Act 1986 (UK), *128, 130*

Outer Space Treaty, *8, 9-16, 21, 23 ff., 46-50, 69, 71, 72, 73, 76-77, 82, 83, 87, 88, 89, 91, 92, 100, 104, 105, 108, 114, 117, 118*
- Preamble, *10, 71, 83*
- Article I, *12, 26, 46, 47, 73, 83, 141, 143*
- Article II, *13, 25, 47, 83, 130, 143*
- Article III, *10, 83, 126, 138*
- Article IV, *10, 11, 28, 35, 71 ff., 80, 83, 90, 136*
- Article VI, *14, 121, 129, 141, 143*
- Article VII, *14, 121, 138*
- Article VIII, *14, 39, 83, 129, 130*
- Article IX, *137, 138, 139*
- Article XII, *59*
- Article XV, *83*
- "Magna Charta", *29, 46, 118, 140*

Palapa B-2, *122, 123*

Patent law, *127, 131, 144*

Peaceful purposes, *9, 28, 35, 69 ff., 89, 99, 110, 116, 143*

Power *69 ff.*
- interests, *74*

Private entities, *19, 47-48*

Private enterprise, *13, 36, 115, 122, 123, 144*
- activities of, *3*

Private international law, 1*3, 39, 129, 133, 134*

Property rights, *38, 51, 127, 132, 144*

Province of all mankind, *12, 18, 28, 35, 46, 92, 143*

PTBT, *82, 83, 85, 87, 88, 89, 136*

Regime
- Civilian Regime of Outer Space, *80*
- definition of, *80*
- legal regime, *26-27, 39, 41, 45, 46, 50, 54, 71, 101, 143*
- Military Regime of Outer Space, *79 ff.*
- Space Regime, *79 ff.*

Registration Convention, *14, 72, 82, 83, 117, 129*
- Article 4, *138*

Remote sensing, *14, 35, 39, 40, 47, 70, 82,83, 96, 97, 100, 113, 118, 128, 136, 144*
- Principles of, *36*

Rescue Agreement, *29, 72, 82, 83, 117*
- Article 5, *138*

Responsibility, *37, 47*
- international, *28, 141*

Right of overflight, *see* Transit and traffic rights

SALT II, *80, 87, 88, 94, 136*
- Article XV, *83*

SDI, *11, 13, 28, 30, 70, 94, 95, 108, 109, 110, 136*

Self-defence, *69, 76*
- (*see also* Art. 51 UN Charter)

Self-reliance, *120*

SLBM, *10*

Sovereignty, *9, 145*

Space object, *35, 39, 122, 129, 130, 132*
- space structure, *113*
  - jurisdiction over, *62*
- Space Station, *15, 36, 38, 39, 58-60, 95, 131, 132, 143, 144*
  - jurisdiction over, *59*

Space transport, *57 ff., 122, 123, 132*
- pricing, *62-64*
- space carriers
  - cooperation among, *64-65*
- spacecraft, *113, 122*
  - and crew, *38, 39*
- Space Shuttle, *57, 62, 113, 122, 123, 127*
- STS, *63, 123*

Specification, *see* Legal Process

SPOT, *14*

Sputnik, *33, 85, 113, 115*

Star Wars, *see* SDI

System theoretical approach, *74-77*

Technological developments, *19, 29-30, 35-36, 37, 72-73, 79, 96, 110, 113, 114, 124, 132, 135, 137, 143*

Telecommunication Act 1984 (UK), *129*

Telecommunications, *39, 113, 114*
- satellite, *40, 47*

Third world, *see* Developing countries
Transit and traffic rights, *40, 58-60, 64*
UN, *34, 38, 54, 55, 69, 76, 96, 125*
  Charter of the UN, *12, 26, 73, 82, 83, 116, 126, 143*
    Article 2, *12*
    Article 51, *73*
    Article 33, *139*
UNGA, *9, 23, 27*
UN Outer Space Organization, *see* World Space Organization
UN Resolutions
  Res. 1962, *21, 23, 72, 82, 85, 116, 137*
  Res. 1884, *72, 82, 83, 85, 116*
  Res. 1472, *82*
  Res. 222, *72*
  Res. 1148, *79, 89, 115*
  Res. 1721, *116*
  Res. 1802, *116*
UNCOPUOS, *18, 23, 34,36, 38, 116, 118, 119, 145*
  consensus, 2, *34, 36*
  COPUOS/LSC, *140*
UNISPACE 2, *107, 114, 119, 120*
Verification, *70, 109*
  national technical means of, *10*
Vienna Convention, *73*
  Article 31 & 32, *80*
Warsaw System, *122, 132*
Wireless Telegraphy Act 1949 (UK), *129*
WMO, *116*
World Space Organization, *106, 107, 109, 140, 141*